The Study Skills Handbook

Stella Cottrell

This edition is published for students of the
University of East London
by Macmillan Press Ltd

UNIVERSITY of EAST LONDON

D0418253

© Stella Cottrell 1999

Illustrations © Stella Cottrell & Macmillan Press Ltd 1999

All rights reserved. No reproduction, copy or transmission of this publication may be made without written permission, except as stated below.

No paragraph of this publication may be reproduced, copied or transmitted save with written permission or in accordance with the provisions of the Copyright, Designs and Patents Act 1988, or under the terms of any licence permitting limited copying issued by the Copyright Licensing Agency, 90 Tottenham Court Road, London W1P 9HE.

Any person who does any unauthorised act in relations to this publication may be liable to criminal prosecution and civil claims for damages.

The author has asserted her right to be identified as the author of this work in accordance with the Copyright, Designs and Patents Act 1988.

First published 1999 by
MACMILLAN PRESS LTD
Houndmills, Basingstoke, Hampshire RG21 6XS
and London
Companies and representatives
throughout the world.

University of East London
Student Edition

ISBN 0–333–77481–7

Not for sale

A catalogue record for this book is available from the British Library.

This book is printed on paper suitable for recycling and made from fully managed and sustained forest sources.

10 9 8 7 6 5 4 3 2 1
08 07 06 05 04 03 02 01 00 99

Edited by Andrew Nash
Designed by
Claire Brodmann Book Designs, Burton-upon-Trent

Printed in Great Britain by
Antony Rowe Ltd
Chippenham, Wiltshire

Purchasers and students are licensed to copy, for educational and individual purposes only, all material on pages containing self-evaluations, checklists, planners and record sheets.

Study skills titles from Macmillan

JOHN PECK and **MARTIN COYLE**,
The Student's Guide to Writing

PATRICK DUNLEAVY,
University Study Skills, Arts and Humanities

Acknowledgements

The author would like to thank the following:

TMP Worldwide Research, 32 Aybrook Street, London W1M 3JL (tel. 0171 872 1500), for permission to reproduce their data on 'soft skills' and employment.

Lynn Chiswick, for her full encouragement and support for *Skills for Success* when all I had to show her were a few pencil-and-paper sketches and a lot of enthusiasm.

Robert Simpson, Pam Dixon and David Gosling in the Learning Development Unit at UEL, for helpful comments and suggestions.

The many lecturers at UEL who used *Skills for Success* and the other materials which have been incorporated into this *Handbook*, including the dyslexia support tutors who piloted some of the new material with dyslexic students at the university – the feedback of all these staff on what to include, and on how to adapt some of the early material, has been invaluable.

Kate Williams, for reading through the original text and for her many useful suggestions on how to improve it, and the kindness, encouragement and sensitivity with which she offered these.

Margaret, Isobel, Andrew, Claire, Felicity, Gabriella, Pat, Ros, Jean, Joan, Jackie and Daniele, whose work behind the scenes made this book possible.

The hundreds of students who were open to discussing their difficulties with me and willing to elaborate new and individual ways of approaching their study – to them, and to all future students who may struggle for even a day, this book is dedicated.

Contents

Introducing

The Study Skills Handbook

The study skills needed for Higher Education are ultimately gained only through studying at that level. Study skills don't hatch fully formed, any more than a grown hen pops from an egg. They evolve and mature through practice, trial and error, feedback from others, and reflection as you move through the different stages of your course. You will be surprised at how your thinking and language skills develop simply through continued study.

However, there are some basic approaches which can start you off on a good footing, help you cut corners, and accelerate the learning process. This *Handbook* developed out of practical work undertaken with hundreds of students over ten years. The core of the book – which in a former life was known as the *Skills for Success Guide* – has now been used by over 30,000 students and hundreds of lecturers, whose varied comments have contributed to this *Handbook*.

Quick tips and deeper learning

A reflective, active, self-evaluating approach to learning develops deeper understanding in the long term. However, quick tips are also invaluable to students, especially in emergencies. This *Handbook* offers both approaches. To meet your immediate and long-term study needs, move flexibly between the two approaches.

LEARNING OUTCOMES

The Study Skills Handbook aims to help you to manage your own success as a student. It does this by:

- preparing you for what to expect from Higher Education (university or college)
- encouraging you to think about the skills you have already, which you will need both as a student and in your working life
- providing resources to help you evaluate, reflect upon and manage your own learning
- making suggestions on how to develop positive approaches and good study habits
- offering guidance on how to tackle activities that many students find difficult
- helping you to understand more about how learning, intelligence and memory work, and how to develop critical and analytical thinking styles
- encouraging you to understand that success as a student is about more than being 'clever' – good marks, as well as other kinds of successful outcome, are possibilities for any student.

How to use *The Study Skills Handbook*

This is a guide that you can dip into as you need – or use by working through the chapters related to a particular aspect of study. You can do as little or as much as you find helpful. Of necessity, the *Handbook* focuses on a different aspect of study in each chapter. However, as your study progresses, you will notice that these skills are interconnected. Developing one area of your study will also help with other aspects.

Finding what you need

- Each chapter begins with an outline of the learning outcomes for that chapter. Browsing through this list may help you decide whether or not you need to read the chapter.
- Each chapter deals with several topics, and each topic is introduced by a heading like the one at the top of this page. These headings make it easier to browse through to find what you need.
- The index (at the back) gives page references for specific topics.

Keeping a journal

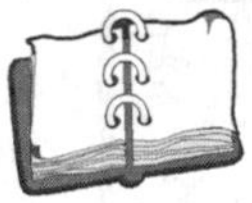

This symbol reminds you to note down your reflections in your study journal. For details, see page 57.

Photocopiable pages

Pages containing self-evaluations, checklists, planners and record sheets may be photocopied for reuse. (You may like to enlarge some of them onto A3 paper.) When you have used the photocopies, keep them with your journal for future reference.

Cartoons and page layout

The cartoons and different layouts act primarily as visual memory-joggers. Even if you cannot draw well, you can use visual prompts like these in your own notes. (This will also help you to find things more quickly.) The variety will encourage learning through different senses, too – see Chapter 10 for more details.

The self-evaluation questionnaires

The self-evaluation questionnaires will help you in two ways:

- by breaking down major study skills into their component sub-skills
- by enabling you to pinpoint which components make the study skill difficult for you, and to notice steps or activities that you missed out in the past.

Sometimes just going through the questionnaire will be all you need to do if this helps you identify the missing link. Use the questionnaires to monitor your progress and identify your strengths.

The 'challenging' chapters

Don't be put off by chapters that look difficult, or by words you don't know. You may need to read some chapters several times – but that's typical of advanced learning. When you have lived with them for a few weeks and thought about them, the ideas and vocabulary will become everyday words to you.

Knowledge of specialised terms and of underlying theories empowers you as a student. It sharpens your thinking, allows you to describe things more accurately, and improves your overall performance.

Where to begin

- Read through the 'Seven approaches to learning' used by *The Study Skills Handbook* (page 4). The *Handbook* will then make more sense to you.
- Complete the ***What do I want from university?*** questionnaire (page 6). This will help you to orientate yourself as a student.
- Browse through the *Handbook* so you know roughly what is in it. You may not know what to use until you start assignments.
- Use the ***Study skills: priorities*** planner (page 27) to focus your thinking.
- If you are unsure where to begin with a study skill, do the ***Self-evaluation*** questionnaire in the appropriate chapter to clarify your thinking.
- Chapters 2–4 cover groundwork and approaches basic to the rest of the *Handbook*. You will probably find it helpful to work through these early on.

If you are thinking of applying to university or know little about university life ...

Start with Chapter 1, 'Preparing for university'. This gives you an idea of what to expect from university, helps you decide whether you are ready for university yet, and gives advice on how to prepare yourself for your first term. Chapter 4 is also likely to be useful.

You may also find it helpful if you:

- identify your current skills and qualities (see pages 23–6)
- look at your motivation (***What do I want from university?***, pages 6 and 81–2)
- develop confidence in your reading (pages 109–15) and writing (pages 132–7).

If you have done BTEC or A-levels ...

You may find that you can browse through the early sections of each chapter quite quickly. Chapters 4, 5, 8, 9 and 10 may be the most useful for you. If you feel uncomfortable about a book that uses images as learning tools, read page 43 and Chapter 10 on 'Memory' and the methods may make more sense.

Dyslexic students

There are now thousands of dyslexic students in Higher Education. Many aspects of this book were designed with dyslexic students in mind, including:

- the contents
- the use of visual images
- the book's layout
- the emphasis on structure
- the use of varied and multi-sensory approaches to learning.

Pace yourself

If you have been away from study for a while, or if you are finding study difficult, be kind to yourself. It takes time and practice to orientate yourself to the Higher Education environment and to develop study habits, especially academic writing skills. Your first-year marks may not count towards the final grade, which means you have time to practise and improve.

Everybody learns in their own way

There are many avenues to successful study. Experiment. Explore. Be creative. Find what suits *you* best.

Chapters 2–4 encourage you to look for your own learning patterns, and make suggestions on how to experiment with your learning.

Seven approaches to learning

The Study Skills Handbook uses seven approaches to learning.

1 Learning can be an adventure

It is difficult to learn if you are stressed or bored. This *Handbook* encourages you to be effective rather than virtuous, and to seek out ways of making your learning more fun. Degree courses take several years, so you need to find ways of making your learning enjoyable.

Small children learn extraordinary amounts without trying particularly hard – simply through being relaxed, observing, playing, role-playing, trying things out, making mistakes, and being interested in what they are doing. They don't regard setbacks as failures; they don't worry about what others think; and they don't tell themselves they might not be able to learn. When a child falls over, she or he just gets up and moves again, and eventually walking becomes easy. Adults can learn in this way too – if they allow themselves.

2 Use many senses

The more we use our senses of sight, hearing and touch, and the more we use fine muscle movements in looking, speaking, writing, typing, drawing, or moving the body, the more opportunities we give the brain to take in information using our preferred sense.

The use of several senses also gives the brain more connections and associations, making it easier to find information later, which assists memory and learning. This book encourages you to use your senses to the full and to incorporate movement into your study. This will make learning easier – and more interesting.

3 Identify what attracts you

It is easier to learn by keeping desirable outcomes in mind than by forcing ourselves to study out of duty. Some aspects of study may be less attractive to you, such as writing essays, meeting deadlines or sitting exams, and yet these also tend to bring the greatest satisfaction and rewards.

It is within your power to find in any aspect of study the gold that attracts you. For example, visualise yourself on a large cinema screen enjoying your study – or your later rewards. Hear your own voice telling you what you are

achieving now. Your imagination will catch hold of these incentives and find ways of making them happen.

4 Use active learning

We learn with a deeper understanding when we are both actively and personally engaged:

- juggling information
- struggling to make sense
- playing with different options
- making decisions
- linking information.

For this reason, most pages of this book require you to *do* something, however small, to increase your active engagement with the topic.

5 Take responsibility for your own learning

As you will see from Chapter 1, universities generally expect you to be ready to study on your own, with minimum assistance, especially for basics such as spelling or grammar. As a college student, you are expected to be largely responsible for your own learning.

One way in which you can act responsibly towards yourself is to ensure that you *are* ready for the stage of study that you are entering. Many students enter college without adequate preparation. This can make study more stressful and difficult than it need be, and undermine confidence. Make sure *you* are ready.

6 Trust in your own intelligence

Many students worry in case they are not intelligent enough for their course. Some did not do well at school, and worry that being a good student is 'not in their genes'. Panic about this can, in itself, make it hard to learn. That is why this book considers ideas about intelligence (in Chapter 3) and stress (in Chapter 11). Many students who were not ideal pupils at school do extremely well at college, following thorough preparation.

7 Recognise your own learning preferences

Each of us learns in an individual way – though we also have a lot in common.

Some theorists divide people into 'types' such as *visual*, *auditory* and *kinaesthetic*, or *introverted* and *extroverted* – there are lots of ways of dividing people up. The important thing, however, is not to discover which 'type' you are but rather to recognise the many different elements that contribute to how you yourself learn best.

If you regard yourself as a 'type' you may over-identify yourself with that type. You may then get stuck with that image of yourself – and always consider yourself a 'visual introverted' type, or a 'chaotic extrovert'. This may leave you with rigid views about the one way you learn. What you *need* to do is experiment with strategies and skills you currently under-use. The human brain is highly adaptable: able learners move easily between different strategies and learning styles, depending on the task in hand.

The good thing about being aware of how *you* learn best is that you can adapt new learning to fit where you are now. You may also be able to see more clearly why you did well or badly at school, depending on whether the teaching matched your personal learning preferences.

What do I want from university?

Our imaginations are extremely powerful. Just try *not* to think about something, such as whether you left the cooker on, and you quickly discover how easy it is for your imagination to see your home burnt to the ground! If you give your imagination any leads, it will act on them.

You can use this capacity of the imagination in many ways to help your study. Try using the following questionnaire to consider what, in five years' time, you would like to be saying to yourself about what you achieved at college. You may then find that your orientation towards your work and to different activities on campus starts to change, as your imagination goes to work.

You may also like to come back to this at different times in the future, to see whether your thinking about what really counts for you has changed.

Imagine yourself five years from now, thinking back on what you achieved at university. From your chair in the future, rate the following desirable outcomes (1, 2, 3, etc.) in their order of importance to you then.

- ☐ I made good friends
- ☐ I got a good degree
- ☐ I made full use of college facilities
- ☐ I developed new interests
- ☐ I developed skills which helped me find a good job
- ☐ I learnt to work better with other people
- ☐ I learnt to express myself better
- ☐ I really enjoyed myself
- ☐ I found out more about who I was as a person
- ☐ I learnt to think and reason better
- ☐ I developed my creativity
- ☐ I took care of my health and well-being
- ☐ I took on positions of responsibility
- ☐ I learnt to manage myself as an effective adult
- ☐ I stretched myself intellectually
- ☐ I learnt to manage stressful situations with calm
- ☐ I learnt how to balance work, friendship and family

What do these priorities suggest to you now about how you could best use your time at university?

Enjoy the book

Enjoy the rest of
The Study Skills Handbook –
and enjoy your time at university!

© Stella Cottrell 1999, *The Study Skills Handbook*, Macmillan Press Ltd

Chapter 1

Preparing for university

> **LEARNING OUTCOMES**
>
> This chapter offers you opportunities to:
>
> - find out the basics of applying to university
> - evaluate whether you are ready for university yet
> - discover what to expect from a Higher Education environment, and what is expected from you as a student
> - explore your anxieties and resources
> - prepare for university so that you are ready for all it has to offer.

This chapter looks at ways to prepare yourself practically and mentally for your first term at college. If you already know what to expect from Higher Education, you may wish to skip quite quickly over this chapter. If you are a student in Further Education or at school, you may like to leave this chapter until later in your course. On the other hand, you may know little about university. You may wonder what it is like, whether you could cope, and whether you are ready yet. This is especially true if you have been out of education for a few years, or if you are the first member of your family to attend university.

Some aspects of studying at university are very different from school or college. The following pages will give you a general idea of what to expect. On page 9 there is an exercise you can use as a guide, ***Am I ready for Higher Education?*** If you are almost ready, there are some suggestions of things to do to ease the transition into university study.

Preparation courses

It pays to be well prepared before you start your course. In general, universities do not provide much help at more basic levels to help you 'catch up' – they expect you to be ready. Look at the list on page 9: before you start college, you will be wise to bring yourself to a position where you can say 'yes' to most of these items.

Don't rush into study for which you are not ready – it can be very expensive, in money, stress, health and relationships. Your local Further Education college may offer 'access' and other courses leading to university level, or the university itself might offer a 'foundation year'. The Open University offers foundation courses by correspondence.

Applying to university

Choosing your subject

Find a logical progression

It is advisable to choose a degree course that follows logically from your A-levels, BTEC, HNC or access course. This ensures that you have the appropriate knowledge base, the right specialist language, and other skills needed in managing the course.

You may be offered a place on a course for which you don't have an appropriate foundation. If so, find out from the course admissions tutor exactly what you need to do to catch up, and don't underestimate the extra work involved.

Examine the course content

Read course outlines carefully. Find out exactly what you will be required to do – course titles can be very misleading. Some courses, for example, appear to be creative or practical but are far more theoretical than they sound. Almost all courses involve a great deal of reading and writing.

Form a coherent programme

Some universities allow you to combine very different subjects. This can make study interesting, but will add considerably to the overall workload. Interlinked subjects feed into one another, so the workload is less and you gain a much deeper understanding of the subject.

Consider career opportunities

If you have a particular career in mind, check that the options you choose count towards it. Not all education or psychology modules, for example, are recognised by professional bodies. If you are in any doubt, speak to a careers adviser or the university admissions tutor.

Some colleges have advice centres which offer guidance to mature students about which subjects to study, preparatory courses they need to take, and whether previous study can count towards the degree.

Choosing a university

Each university has its own character and ways of doing things, so find out about the ones that interest you.

Look at the prospectus

Your school library, local library or careers office will have copies and contact addresses.

Attend an open day

Speak to the admissions tutor. Find out what the courses really involve. How many will be in your seminar and tutor groups? What teaching methods are used?

Visit the university campus

Look around the department, and especially the library. Do they seem well organised? Are staff friendly? Would you like to study there?

Some colleges have sites some way from the main campus. Where would you be studying?

Where would you be living?

Check accommodation. Think about transport – how would you get from where you lived to where you studied?

Consider everyday life

Would you feel comfortable there? Would you fit in? Choose a university where you are likely to be happy for the three or four years of the course.

Application forms (UCAS forms)

To make an application you will need a form from UCAS, the Universities and Colleges Admissions Service. The form needs to be submitted almost a year before the course begins, although late entry is also possible. Forms are available from: UCAS, Fulton House, Jessop Avenue, Cheltenham GL50 3SH. Telephone: 01242 222444.

Am I ready for Higher Education?

The more items in the following list that apply to you, the more likely it is that you are ready for Higher Education. Put a tick ☑ against those that are true of you.

- ☐ Successful course completion at an advanced level (A-level, BTEC National, HNC, access course, or a foundation course) in a subject similar to the one you intend to study
- ☐ *and* if advanced study was not a great struggle for you
- ☐ *or* the course is related to your current profession and level of work (e.g. a BA in Nursing if you are a nurse)
- ☐ *and* you have GCSE English (plus maths for many courses)
- ☐ *and/or* you regularly read advanced text, such as a quality newspaper weekly and several books a year, whether by eye or using taped books
- ☐ *and/or* you have had recent practice at writing essays, reports, projects or a similar level of writing
- ☐ *and* you are reasonably confident about being able to work on your own, without help, for most of the time (though the college may offer specific help for students from overseas or with disabilities, including dyslexia)
- ☐ *and* you feel you are ready to study in the environment described on pages 10–11
- ☐ *and* you can cope with the anxieties explored on page 14
- ☐ *and/or* you can translate your personal skills into academic skills (see page 26)
- ☐ *and* you can type or word-process reasonably well
- ☐ *and* you are comfortable using a library.

If you ticked few items, it may mean that:

- you underestimate yourself, or
- you need more preparation.

Speak to a careers officer or a teacher at your school or local college, or to a mature-student adviser or admissions officer at the university. Discuss with them the points from the list above where you feel that you are weak.

However, what is most important is that you feel ready – intellectually, emotionally and financially – before you begin. Don't be rushed into university study.

© Stella Cottrell 1999, *The Study Skills Handbook*, Macmillan Press Ltd

What to expect in Higher Education

Teaching methods

Teaching methods differ but you can expect at least some of the following.

Lectures

These vary according to course and subject but in general, expect:

- size: 50–300 people
- length: 1–3 hours
- weekly: 5–20 hours
- no individual attention.

See also pages 126–7.

There is usually a set of lectures for each unit or option. You are likely to be with different students for each unit. Lectures are used to give an overview of the topic. Usually, students listen and take notes whilst lecturers speak or read from notes, write on a board, or project information onto an overhead screen. Some lecturers encourage questions and include activities; others do not. Occasionally, lectures are delivered on video or transmitted from another campus.

Tutorials

These are usually used to give feedback on your work and discuss your general progress. It may be the only time that a lecturer is able to help you with study problems, so it is important to prepare your questions in advance.

- size: in small groups or on an individual basis
- length: usually an hour at most
- frequency: possibly one or two per term.

Seminars

These usually involve group discussion of material presented either in a lecture or in set reading.

Often, a student (or a group of students) is asked to begin the discussion by making a presentation. It is important to prepare for seminars by reading through lecture notes and background reading, even if you are not asked to make the presentation yourself.

- size: 12–30 people
- length: 1–3 hours
- weekly: varies – perhaps 1–3 each week.

See also Chapter 5.

Other teaching styles used at university

Colleges are becoming more flexible in the ways they teach, so you may experience a wide range of teaching styles, including some or all of the following.

Groupwork

This could be for discussion or mutual support, or to undertake a joint project. Students are often expected to form their own support groups. (See Chapter 5.)

Work placements

Many vocational courses require students to spend some time on work placement. While there, they may be supervised by a lecturer from the college or by somebody at the workplace – or a mixture of the two.

Laboratory work, studio work and practicals

Science students may spend most of their time doing practical work in laboratories; fine arts students may work predominantly in studio space they are allocated at the university. The amount of practical work of this kind will depend on the course. (See page 129.)

Distance learning

Students on some courses work mostly at home. Materials are either sent by post or over the Internet. Contact with tutors may be by letter, by e-mail, by video conferencing at a local centre, or in local meetings.

Private study

This is the most common and possibly most challenging feature of university study. Apart from timetabled elements such as lectures, almost all courses expect students to work on their own for the rest of the week.

Seeing your lecturers

University lecturers are likely to be much less available than your teachers at school or college. Teaching is only one of their responsibilities. They are expected to undertake research and to examine or to lecture at other universities. They may also be consultants outside the university. Some are contracted for only a few hours a week.

A tutor may have a great many students to see. For all of these reasons, you may need to book an appointment well in advance.

Lecturers' varied approaches

University subject areas or departments have their own traditions, and even individual

Now let me get this straight. Mr Jiff wants work on both sides of the paper, Dr Lank on one. Ms Snape wants everything word-processed. Mr Kip wants essays sent by e-mail. Ms Snape wants sub-headings ...

lecturers may have strong personal tastes in how things should be done. You need to be alert to this and notice your lecturers' preferences. (See page 164.)

The university week

Most full-time college courses are considered to be the equivalent of an average working week in employment. This means that you are expected to study for 35–40 hours a week, in a mixture of private study, at home or in a library, and scheduled classes on campus.

The way that time is divided up varies greatly. Some courses require students to attend 15 hours of lectures a week, and research around the subject, read, think, and write assignments for the rest of the week. A practical course may involve only 2 hours of lectures a week, with very few written assignments in the year and most of the time spent on placement or in the studio.

> **Will this suit you?**
>
> If you have strong preferences about how you spend your time, investigate how the course breaks up the study week and the kinds of teaching methods used.

The student's year

Induction week

The academic year usually begins late in September or early October, with an induction week for first-year students. Some universities start in January. Although you may be able to enrol earlier, many students enrol then.

During induction week you receive a student number and pass card, you meet lecturers, you are given handouts for the term, you find out essential information about services, and you are told when and how to hand in work. The week includes a 'Fresher's Fair' where you can find out about student clubs and activities.

Terms and semesters

Traditionally the academic year has three terms, from September to Christmas, New Year to Easter, and Easter to the Summer. Some universities have two longer 'terms', known as 'semesters', the second semester starting in February.

Choosing options

When the year begins, you may be asked to select individual units, modules or options at different levels of study, which combine to make your degree.

A 'pathway' is a given set of modules leading to a particular qualification such as a degree in architecture or social work. Even within a pathway you may have 'electives' – modules about which you have some choice.

Teaching staff for the year

You are likely to have the same teaching staff for one term or semester, and sometimes for the whole year. Most academic staff are lecturers, although they are often referred to as tutors.

Personal tutors

You will probably have a year tutor or a personal tutor, who will be concerned with your study overall. Talk to this person if you experience life or study difficulties that could prevent you from completing your course.

Assessment

Courses vary in how they assess your work. Some assess by coursework only, some by exams, and others by a mixture of coursework and exams. Exams typically take place at the end of each term or semester, although some courses leave exams until the end of the year.

If you are marked by coursework, you could be asked to hand in essays, reports, case studies or project work, or to make an oral presentation to your seminar group.

Deadlines and extensions

It is important that you keep to deadlines, although extensions may be given if you ask in advance and for a good reason. If something unforeseen happens, you may be able to ask for extenuating circumstances to be taken into consideration when your work is being considered by the examination board.

Always speak to your tutors as soon as there is any possibility of a deadline being missed or in special circumstances such as illness or family or health problems. The longer you leave it, the less likely it is that tutors will be able to take your circumstances into consideration.

Tutors have little flexibility in granting additional time for work. Usually the work has to be marked by two lecturers, sent to an external examiner for inspection, and then returned and presented to an exam board by a set date at the end of the term.

The college or course regulations should detail what to expect, and how to apply for extensions.

The summer vacation

Between July and September there is time to catch up on missed study, to resit failed exams, to prepare for the next term, to rest – and, for many students, to earn some money.

What is expected from you?

It's not like at school where you were stuck in a classroom from 9 till 4
and teachers told you what you needed to do.

Ade, first-year student

As a university student you are expected to have the following characteristics.

Independence

You must be able to 'stand on your own two feet'. However, there is help available. The Student Union and Student Services will have details.

Self-motivation

You have to be able to work on your own a lot.

Openness to working with others

You will need to organise study sessions with friends.

Ability to work out things out for yourself

'How successful was the 1944 Education Act?'
It's terrible! The lecturers expect us to tell them all the answers!

To cope with a university environment, you need to be reasonably good at:

- adapting to new people and environments
- surviving in potentially very large groups
- being flexible in your learning style.

Ability to set goals to improve your work

Whoopee!! B+! Next time I want an A!

Ability to organise your time

You need to keep track of time. You must:

- know when and where you should be for scheduled classes, events and exams
- know when work has to be handed in
- keep to deadlines for handing in work.

	MONDAY	TUESDAY	WEDNESDAY
9-10	put notes in order	Ecology lecture Rm G10	prepare for botany seminar
10-11	lecture Dr Shah Rm X22		
11-12	do plan (Science Report)		Botany Seminar Rm R21

(See Chapter 4.)

Ability to work out when, how and where you learn best

On second thoughts maybe I do work better indoors, in the daytime.

Anxieties and resources

It is quite natural to feel some anxiety when you start something new, and many students have concerns about starting at university.

It is easier to work out strategies for handling potential challenges and to manage your anxieties if you have:

- sorted out in your own mind what your worries are
- considered how serious they really are
- realised that many other people feel the same way.

On the right are listed some anxieties which are common amongst new students. Tick the box beside any that apply to you, or add in others in the empty spaces.

Study and learning

- [ ] Keeping up with other people
- [x] Finding the time to do everything
- [x] Understanding academic language
- [ ] Having the confidence to speak
- [x] Developing confidence in myself
- [ ] Writing essays
- [ ] Getting used to university life
- [ ] Meeting deadlines
- [ ] ....
- [ ] ....

Personal, family, work commitments

- [ ] Making friends with other students
- [ ] Coping with travel
- [ ] Organising childcare
- [ ] People treating me differently
- [ ] Coping with job requirements
- [ ] Family responsibilities
- [ ] ....
- [ ] ....

Look again at the items you have ticked. Beside each, write the number of the statement below that most closely corresponds with your feeling. Then read the comments on the next page.

1 I expect this to be a minor difficulty: I will get round it easily or in time.

2 I expect this to be quite a serious difficulty: I will have to work at it.

3 I expect this to be a great difficulty: I will have to work very hard at it.

4 I expect this to be a major difficulty: I may need to ask for help.

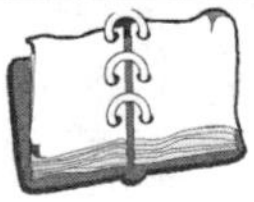

- What initial ideas do you have about how you could manage some of these anxieties?
- What strategies have you used in the past to deal with a new or difficult situation? Which of these strategies could be helpful now?

© Stella Cottrell 1999, *The Study Skills Handbook*, Macmillan Press Ltd

Managing anxieties

Study and learning anxieties

It is important to give yourself time to settle in and see what is required. Many universities pace the first year more slowly, to give you time to find your feet.

Focus on planning your own activities rather than worrying about how well other students are doing. Some people play psychological games, claiming that they do no work and can write essays overnight. Very few people can really do this; it is certainly not expected of you, and it is not a sensible way to study.

Find support. Many students will be anxious about some aspect of their study and it helps to share concerns. Make time to meet other students in your classes. Once you have formed a bond with other students, you will have more confidence about joining in.

The following chapters make practical suggestions on ways of handling aspects of study such as speaking, essay writing, meeting deadlines, managing stress, and generally setting yourself up to succeed. Focus on your motivation for study, and be determined to enjoy your course. Think of yourself as being on an adventure – not on trial!

Managing other anxieties

There is pressure on students to juggle family and work commitments in ways that were not expected in the past. Students have to be more creative in problem-solving, and very organised in their time management.

In many universities and colleges, Student Services and the Student Union offer advice on managing finance, finding work, grants, childcare, health-care, counselling, disability, and many other issues that arise for students.

Make an action plan

Look back to the items you ticked on page 14.

Set priorities

- What needs to be done immediately?
- Which things can wait?
- In which order do you need to deal with these anxieties?
- Use the ***Priority organiser*** (page 72).

Resources

- What sources of help are available? Contact the university and ask.
- Fill out ***What are my personal resources?*** (page 17).
- Talk to other students who may have the same worries. See if you can form a study or discussion or support group including other students with whom you feel comfortable.

Reflection

It helps if you write down and explore your anxieties.

- Note down your feelings.
- Write down your options and decide between them (see pages 83–5).
- Record how you dealt with each problem so you that can evaluate your progress later.

How do other students manage?

The short passages on the next page were written by students about their first term. You may notice that their time seemed very pressurised; being organised is an important theme in these writings. However, these students made space for themselves to relax, meet others, and use university facilities such as sports or drama clubs, which are also important to the overall university experience.

My first term

After the terrible time I had in school, I was very worried about what I might be putting myself through coming back to study as an adult. I was sure I wouldn't be able to keep up. When I got my first few pieces of work back, the marks were not very good, and I felt I ought to leave.

Luckily, I was talked out of leaving. I made an effort to meet other mature students and found many of them were having similar experiences to me. One of them encouraged me to ask my tutors for more detailed feedback on my work. I had not wanted to ask for any help in case the lecturers thought I was not good enough for the course. Bit by bit my marks started to get better, and some were very good. This boosted my confidence.

I had expected study to be difficult. What I had not expected was that other aspects of being a student could be just as hard. It took me ages to build up the confidence to eat in the canteen – it seemed so enormous and bustling. I used to rush away after lectures rather than talking to strangers. My train service is very erratic and I kept arriving late. My sister, who was going to look after my children, moved house. Sorting out all these things has made me very skilled at problem-solving!

I have to say that there are many positive things about being a student. Now that I have got to know other people here, I look forward to coming in to study. I feel like I am escaping into time which is just for me. I like having the library to work in – and not being disturbed while I just get on with it.

I would recommend to new students that they give themselves a chance to settle in, and not panic if anything seems to be going wrong. If they have children, I cannot emphasise how important it has been to me to have plans to cover every eventuality. I wish I had had reserve plans for childcare right from the beginning because that, more than anything else, had an effect on my studies. I also recommend that new students find other people who have similar experiences to themselves – talking to each other you can come up with good ideas about how to tackle problems, and boost each other's morale.

You are bound to find you think differently about many things by the time you finish your course – for me, discussing things with other people has become a very exciting activity. Above all, I think students have to think, 'I might never get this chance again – how am I going to get the most out of it?' There are many facilities available and it is a very good opportunity to try things you might never have imagined yourself doing – starting your own group, karate, or going on an expedition. It is a wonderful opportunity – but you have to make it work for yourself.

Sasha

A typical day

On Tuesdays I have a lecture from 10 a.m. to 12 noon. This lecturer does not just talk at us: she breaks the time up into short tasks, discussions, videos, etc. When all 90 of us are discussing something in groups, it can be rather noisy, but you get used to it. The rest of the day is 'free' but as I am already on the site, I go to the library and prepare for the next day's lectures, or do some reading for the seminars I have on every second Wednesday. Some Tuesday afternoons, I go to the gym, and study in the evening instead.

Krishna

My Thursday as a student

Dash the kids to the nursery. Dash into the labs for 10. Suddenly time changes. I am caught up in what I am doing – the project I am working on with two other people. I am working on with two other people. I can spend hours mixing and measuring, comparing my findings with others'. We talk a lot about what we are doing, and why, and make suggestions on why our results are different. I always ask my lecturers if I am unsure – some are very helpful, but some are not. In the afternoon, I have one lecture. Recently, I have arranged it so I can go to drama club on Thursday nights.

Charlie

What are my personal resources?

Have you considered all the resources that might be available to you? Try brainstorming (adding in your own ideas) around key words on the pattern notes below. If you feel you have few resources, if may help to speak to a student counsellor.

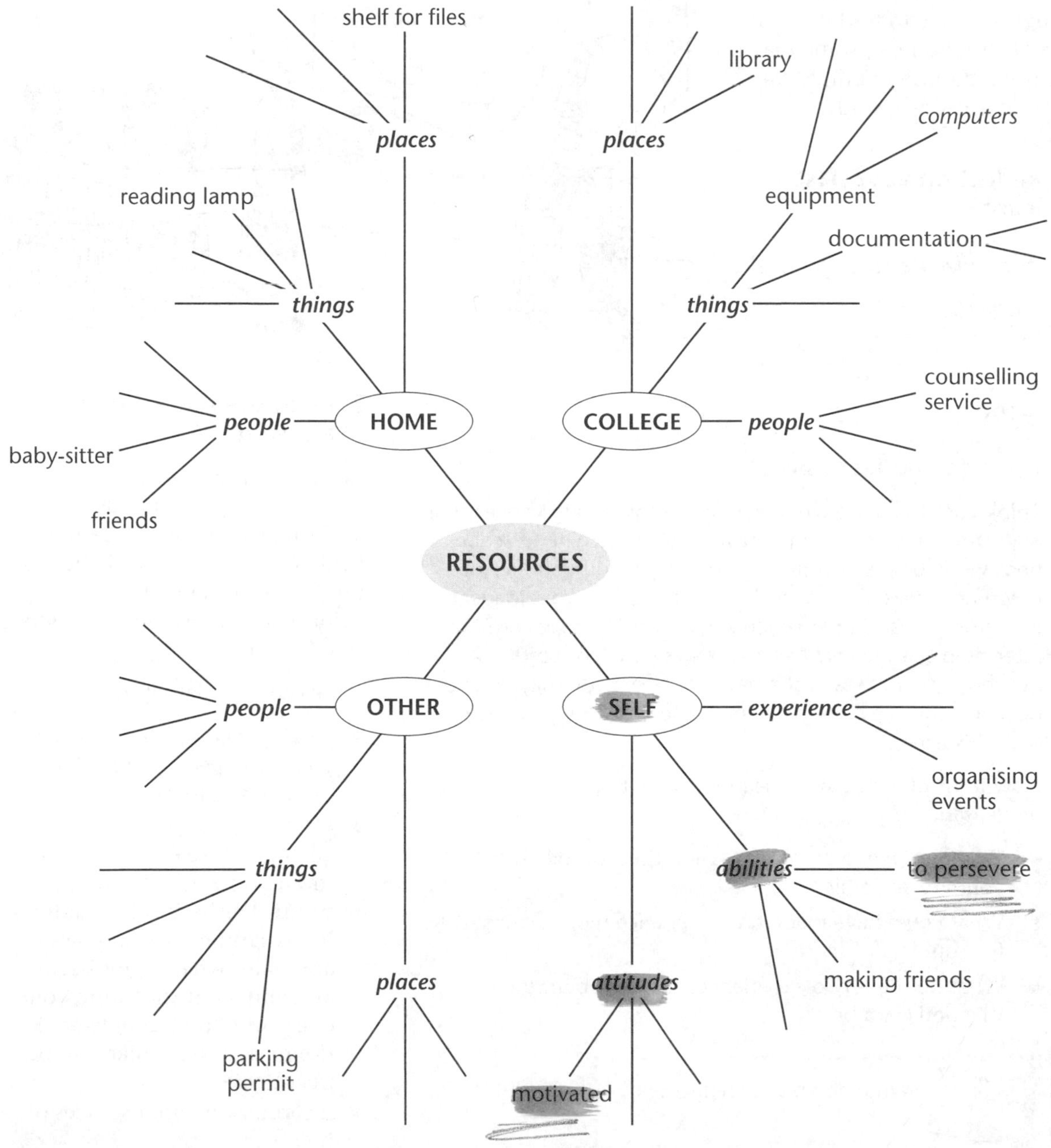

Eight things you can do before starting at university

1 Familiarise yourself with this book

Browse through the book so that you know what it contains, and roughly where to find it. Some may be useful now; some may not be needed until you undertake certain aspects of study.

2 Reflect on your past learning

Start a reflective study journal

See pages 55–7.

Activity

How do you learn best?

Think back to a time when you found something very easy or enjoyable to learn. It might have been something at school, or at work, or even putting up shelves. In your journal, jot down any ideas about *why* this was the case. What made it into a good learning experience for you? The teaching? Your interest in the subject? Because it was visual, or used numbers? Or because each step was clear? You may find your notes for the exercises in Chapter 2 (pages 23–4) can help with this exercise.

Now think of a time when learning something was difficult or unpleasant.

- What happened on that occasion that was different from your first example?
- What could have made the experience more manageable for you?
- What do these two experiences tell you about the way that you learn best?

Write down your reflections.

3 Read the literature you are sent

Read anything the university sends you, such as handbooks and subject guides. When term begins, you will probably be too busy to read these, but the information they contain might be essential.

Look out especially for:

- details of course texts which you are expected to read for early in the term
- essential dates, such as for enrolment, selecting options, induction week, meeting your tutors, Fresher's Fair, deadlines for assignments, exam dates, and dates when terms begin and end – put these into your diary and don't double-book them: they are unlikely to be negotiable
- information about sources of help.

4 Set up a 'general information' file

Put together in a separate file all the general information you are sent on matters such as college regulations, sources of help, appeals and grievance procedures, and student clubs and facilities. You never know when you might need them.

5 Familiarise yourself with libraries

If you are not a regular library user, spend time in your local library or a local college library. Many students are fearful of appearing foolish in libraries, especially when using library technology such as catalogues on CD-ROM or microfiche, or working out the numbering system.

It is best to get over these fears before term begins. Librarians are used to people not being able to use libraries: if you need help, ask for it.

6 Know your bookshops

Wander round bookshops that stock academic books. Find out where the relevant books for your subject are shelved, and browse the authors and titles for your subject area. Find out where new books are displayed and how long it takes to order books. Check bookshops regularly for new titles: this will give you a rough idea of what is topical in your course subject.

7 Start to develop your study skills

If you have been out of education for a while, use some of the suggestions below to get you into the study habit. There are also ideas listed at the beginning of the relevant chapters in this handbook.

Writing

- Write in your journal (page 57) every day.
- Practise writing short passages from notes you make when reading.
- See Chapter 7.

Keyboard skills

If you don't have keyboard skills and cannot use a word-processor, see if you can enrol on a short course at a local college or find out if they have an Open Learning Centre computer you can use. Most courses require typed work, and it is a great benefit if you can type at a reasonable speed before you start at university.

Reading

- If you don't do so already, start to read the quality newspapers. Jot down the key points for one thing you read. Practise writing only a few key *words*, rather than writing in sentences or copying.
- Read books that are a little more challenging than those you read now. Choose subjects that really interest you.
- Read texts faster than you usually would, even if you feel you are losing some of the meaning. See if you can still grasp the gist of what is written. Being able to find the general meaning at speed is very useful to academic study.
- Do background reading for your course. Find something very general or basic to read for each subject area. This will give you an overview of the subject – leave details for later. (See pages 109–15.)

Get used to sitting and studying

- Set some time aside at least once or twice a week for both reading and writing.
- Keep a pen and paper nearby when you read, and jot down any ideas that come to you.
- Write a few lines about some of the more interesting things you read.
- A few days later, look back over what you wrote. Add further ideas, thoughts or details. Rewrite your notes, trying to make the text flow better.

8 Be prepared

- See Chapter 4, 'The C·R·E·A·M strategy for learning', on organising time and space.
- Organise childcare before term begins. Have back-up plans for emergencies.
- Contact the university if you are in doubt about enrolment or start dates.

Review

In this chapter you have looked at a number of ways in which you can prepare yourself for the start of your first term.

To begin with, you looked at the basics of choosing an appropriate subject and university. You will benefit from researching the different options open to you – talk to as many students, admission tutors and careers staff as you can. A number of very personal considerations will go into your eventual choice, but think carefully about the implications of your choices before you fill in the UCAS form. You might also find it useful to read about 'Motivation' (pages 80–5).

Your chances of getting a degree once at university depend crucially on whether you are *ready* for the course before you begin. This is a completely different question from whether you have the *ability*. In some countries almost the whole population studies at a higher level, so it seems that with sufficient preparation most people have the ability. If you are not ready yet, go to your local College of Further Education or the library to see what preparatory courses you can take.

You now have an idea of what the Higher Education environment is like, and what you can expect in terms of teaching methods, the university week and year, the way time is broken up, and some of the terminology used. A visit to a university campus and talking to students who are already there will give you a clearer picture of what is involved.

As an undergraduate, you will be expected to take a lot more responsibility for your own learning than you may be used to from school or college. This makes the study more exciting, but you do need to develop good study and coping strategies.

Am I ready?

- ☐ *If* you ticked several items on the ***Am I ready for Higher Education?*** questionnaire (page 9)
- ☐ *if* you are able to find resources to meet your anxieties
- ☐ *if* you are able to give yourself reasonable scores for skills that match those needed for academic study (***Turning personal skills into academic skills***, page 26)
- ☐ *and if* you feel ready and excited at the thought,

then you should be able to start university with confidence.

Finally, it can take time to orientate yourself at the beginning of the first term, especially as there are so many new people to meet and so many interesting things to do on a college campus. The better prepared you are for the term, the easier it will be to settle into a study routine, and the more time you will have to enjoy other aspects of undergraduate life.

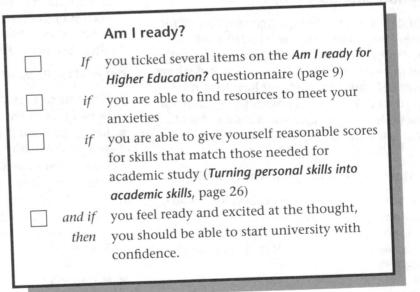

Chapter 2

Identifying your skills

LEARNING OUTCOMES

This chapter offers you opportunities to:

- reflect on what is meant by a 'skill'
- consider the five main study skills components
- develop your awareness of skills and qualities you bring with you to university
- identify areas of strength in your current study skills and areas to be developed
- set priorities for developing your study skills
- consider the wider range of skills you can develop at university
- discover how to map out a profile of your own abilities, and develop a portfolio so that you are prepared for job applications.

Skill

To be skilled is to be able to perform a learned activity well and at will.

A skill is a learned activity – something you can develop through practice and reflection. You can fine-tune skills, just as runners perfect their movement, breathing and pacing.

Fine-tuning a skill involves developing personal qualities as well, such as:

- awareness
- commitment
- determination
- perseverance.
- self-motivation
- time management
- positive thinking

These qualities are also of key importance to successful study: the more obvious study skills, such as knowing how to write essays and use techniques to pass exams, are only part of the story.

Most undergraduates hope that their degree will lead to a good career. Many employers are more interested in your wider range of skills than in which degree you studied or your marks. This chapter looks at how academic study can be an opportunity to develop skills that are 'transferable' to employment.

Sub-skills

Each skill consists of *sub-skills* – the component skills that make up the overall skill. A weakness in one sub-skill can affect what would otherwise be a good performance. For example, you might have the potential to be an excellent essay writer but have weaknesses in structuring your ideas or using paragraphs. This *Handbook* focuses on sub-skills to enable you to develop the wider study skills.

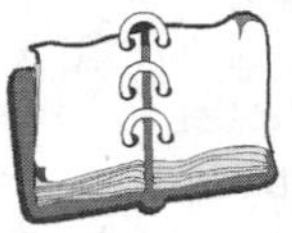

What are your own ideas about what a 'skill' is and how skills are developed?

Five study-skills components

1 Self-awareness and self-evaluation

To develop a skill you need first to know where you are starting from. What are your current strengths and weaknesses? What do you want to achieve? Where do you need to improve? How are you going to improve? What are your resources? What could obstruct your goals?

Ways of developing this awareness include self-evaluation questionnaires, reflective journals, group discussion, and using tutor feedback on your work.

2 Awareness of what is required

To score a goal you need to know where the goalposts are. In an academic context, you need to know what is expected of you and what your lecturers are looking for.

Essential information on this is usually provided in course handbooks and handouts. For each subject, find out about:

- the curriculum – the course content
- the outcomes or objectives – what you must know or be able to do by end of the course
- how marks are allocated – what gets good marks? what loses marks?
- the special preferences of each lecturer – if in doubt, ask!

3 Methods, organisation, strategies

It is easier to study and saves you time if you have a method for working and are well organised. A skilled student uses strategies – and with practice these strategies become nearly automatic.

4 Confidence and permission

To succeed well and without undue stress, you need to feel that you are entitled to learn and achieve, Many students, however, feel that academic success is for other people. This may be because of their experiences at school, or because nobody from their family has a degree. Often, it is because they hold particular ideas about intelligence – and especially their own intelligence – so Chapter 3 focuses on what we mean by intelligence and learning.

If you are to succeed as a student, it is very important that you believe that success is possible.

5 Familiarity: practice and habit

All skills improve through practice, feedback and monitoring. The more you study, the more you are:

- adept at finding shortcuts
- aware of sub-skills you need to improve
- able to see patterns in what you do
- able to focus on study for longer
- able to perform sub-skills automatically.

The way to study well and easily becomes a habit. It is important to develop regular study habits in the first year, especially if you have been away from study or are not used to managing so much unscheduled time.

You don't have to be 'clever'!

When you consider these study-skills components, it is clear that good study skills have little to do with being 'naturally clever'. They owe much more to awareness, strategies, confidence and practice, leading to an overall development in your learning. Each of these aspects is covered in the various chapters of the *Handbook*.

Skills and qualities you have now

This section offers you the chance to undertake a skills audit. It looks at how your current sub-skills – such as observation, selection, and concern for others – may be transferable to *academic* skills, and how academic skills may later be transferable to *employment* skills. In the process you can identify your current study priorities, and map out your skills and qualities within a personal profile or portfolio so that you can monitor your own progress. This record will also be useful when applying for work.

Skills audits

The most important aspects of making a skills audit are these:

- you can become used to self-evaluation, rather than depending on the estimation of others
- you can become aware of your strengths, so that you can present yourself well to others
- you can develop the confidence and insight to identify areas of potential weakness
- you can learn to set your own priorities for developing new skills.

Identifying your current skills

Think about something you do well, a difficulty you overcame, or a personal achievement, no matter how small. It might be success in your A-levels, skill in a particular sport, making a good cake, or being accepted at college.

What did you do to create the conditions that led to success? Which skills, attitudes and qualities did you exhibit? Did you practise? Did you urge yourself on in a particular way? Did you find people to help? Or did you just believe you could do it? Look at the example below for some ideas.

Example: The beautiful garden

Supposing one year your garden or a window box was absolutely beautiful. How did that happen?

Many small things may have brought about a perfect outcome. For example, maybe you watered the plants very carefully, depending on the weather. If so, you used powers of *observation* and *deduction*. You may have weeded and pruned in the rain, when you wanted to stay indoors. Here you *kept in mind your long-term goal* for the garden, showing *dedication* and *perseverance*.

You may have *selected* some new plants from a wide range of options, to match your garden conditions. You *followed specific instructions* on how to grow them. You probably did *research* by reading gardeners' books and seed packets, talking to other gardeners or watching television programmes. You may have purchased special fertiliser and pots, or prepared the ground in a certain way or pruned at particular times: such care requires *attention to detail, time management* and *task management*.

All these skills are relevant to study. Whether your experience is in cooking, riding a bicycle, sport or bringing up children, you are likely to have developed a range of strengths such as those described in the example above. The important thing is to recognise which qualities and abilities you already have so that you can draw on them when you need them.

Activity

Skills from experience

Write down all the elements that go into something you have done well, as in the example of the garden. Note the skills, qualities and attitudes you identify in yourself.

Were you surprised to discover how many skills you have already? Do you tend to under-estimate or over-estimate your skills?

By doing the 'Skills from experience' exercise, you probably discovered you have more skills than you thought. If not, go through the exercise with someone who knows you, or use the list opposite as a prompt. Most people already have qualities and skills which they can adapt to study in Higher Education.

- Students who enter university from school have the benefit of recent study experience and established study habits.
- Mature students often have practice in managing time and responsibility, show perseverance, and can evaluate other people's views. These are valuable assets when studying.

Keep your notes to the 'Skills from experience' exercise near you for use in the following exercise.

Activity

Current skills

1 Photocopy the list *Current skills and qualities* on page 25 so that you can use it again.
2 On your photocopy, tick all the items at which you are reasonably good.
3 Put a star by items at which you excel.
4 For each of the skills and qualities you have ticked from the list, starting with the starred items, think of one example of an occasion when you demonstrated that skill or quality. Write down your examples. If you find it hard to remember, the 'prompt box' on the right lists some situations in which you might have developed these skills.
5 Hang the list where you can see it. Congratulate yourself!

Where did I develop the skills and qualities that I have now?

School or college	Saturday jobs
Employment	Unemployment
Applying for jobs	Voluntary work
✓ Family life	Making a home ✓
✓ Domestic responsibility	Friendships
✓ Caring for others	Travel/holidays
Interests and hobbies	Clubs/societies
Independent study	Personal setbacks
Emergency events	Ill-health ?
✓ Personal development	Sport

If you did not tick many items, you may need to search through your past experiences again for examples – or go through the list with a friend. You may be being too modest!

File your answers for use later in the chapter.

Evaluating your skills and setting priorities

The next pages offer a series of resource sheets to help you to evaluate your current profile of strengths and weaknesses, to relate academic skills to life and employment skills, and to set priorities for skills development. This helps both study and applying for work.

Update your profile

Awareness of your current skills increases your confidence, which in turn increases your chances of success.

As you progress with the course, your skills profile and self-evaluation will change. Take time to update your skills profile or portfolio, at least once every six months.

SELF-EVALUATION

Current skills and qualities

People

- [ ] Ability to get on with people from different backgrounds
- [ ] Ability to see and understand other people's points of view
- [ ] Dealing with the general public
- [ ] Teamwork
- [ ] Managing other people
- [ ] Teaching or training others
- [ ] Negotiating
- [ ] Helping others to arrive at decisions
- [ ] Being sensitive to others' feelings
- [x] Caring for others
- [ ] Ability to read other people's body language
- [ ] Dealing with others by phone
- [ ] Ability to cope with 'difficult' people
- [ ] Speaking clearly and to the point
- [ ] Being able to take direction from others
- [x] Courage to speak out against injustice

Activities

- [ ] Creativity, design and layout
- [ ] Ability to see the 'whole picture'
- [ ] Classifying and organising information (e.g. filing)
- [ ] Being good at argument and debate
- [ ] Making decisions
- [ ] Managing change and transition
- [ ] Setting priorities
- [ ] Working out agendas
- [ ] Organising work to meet deadlines
- [ ] Staying calm in a crisis
- [ ] Facilitating meetings
- [ ] Reading complex texts
- [ ] Word-processing
- [ ] Computer literacy
- [ ] Working with numbers
- [x] Selling
- [ ] Problem-solving
- [ ] Practical things
- [ ] Seeing how things work
- [ ] Writing reports or official letters

Personal qualities

- [ ] Ability to recognise my own needs and ask for help
- [ ] Ability to learn from mistakes
- [ ] Stress management
- [ ] Willingness to take risks and experiment
- [ ] Assertiveness
- [ ] Determination and perseverance
- [ ] Ability to set my own goals
- [ ] Maintaining a high level of motivation
- [ ] Ability to take responsibility for my own actions
- [x] Trust in my own abilities

© Stella Cottrell 1999, *The Study Skills Handbook*, Macmillan Press Ltd

Turning personal skills into academic skills

The ***Current skills and qualities*** exercise (page 25) includes specific skills which have more relevance in some courses than in others. For example, 'selling' is more relevant to marketing than to history.

The following exercise is an opportunity to map out your current skills in terms of the general (or 'generic') skills required for most academic courses, and to rate how well you already perform them. This will give you a better idea of how well you may cope with academic study.

Academic skills (skills used in everyday life which relate to academic skills)	**Self-rating** 5 = good; 1 = very weak	**Examples: Where or when you developed this skill**
e.g. Managing deadlines	4	*Get children to school on time* *Got UCAS form in despite illness*
1 Managing deadlines		
2 Being self-motivated and able to persevere with difficult tasks		
3 Having the confidence to 'have a go' and to express my own ideas		
4 Finding out information from different sources (research)		
5 Reading complicated texts or forms to find the gist of what they are saying		
6 Being able to select what is relevant from what is irrelevant		
7 Comparing different opinions and deciding what are the best grounds for deciding who is right		
8 Being able to weigh up the 'pros' and 'cons', the good points versus the bad		
9 Writing things in my own words		
10 Being able to argue my point of view, giving good reasons		

© Stella Cottrell 1999, *The Study Skills Handbook*, Macmillan Press Ltd

Study skills: priorities, stage 1

Column A Tick if the statement is generally true of you.
Column B Rate how important it is to acquire this skill: 6 = unimportant; 10 = essential.
Column C Rate how good you are at this skill now: 1 = very weak; 5 = excellent.
Column D Subtract the score in column C from column B (B–C). Items with the highest scores in column D are likely to be priorities. Then turn to page 28.

Later in the term, do this exercise again. Compare your ratings, then and now.

Study-skills statements	**A** This is true (✓)	**B** Skill needed? (scale 6–10)	**C** Current ability? (scale 1–5)	**D** Priority (B–C)
I am aware of how I learn best, and how to reflect upon and evaluate my own work				
I am well motivated and know how to set myself manageable goals				
I have good time and space management skills, and am able to organise my workload				
I have strategies for getting going with a new task or assignment				
I am confident of my research skills				
I am aware of which strategies suit me best for reading under different conditions				
I am able to make, organise, store, find and use my notes effectively (checklist, page 116)				
I am able to use lecture time effectively and get the best out of lectures				
I know how to prepare for and deliver oral presentations, playing to my strengths (page 102)				
I know how to make the most of groupwork and seminars (sub-skills list, page 98)				
I am able to manage a range of writing tasks appropriately (sub-skills list, page 132)				
I know how to use IT to help in academic study				
I am able to think critically and analytically, and evaluate my own and other people's arguments				
I have good memory strategies				
I have good revision strategies and exam techniques (sub-skills list, pages 220 and 226)				

© Stella Cottrell 1999, *The Study Skills Handbook*, Macmillan Press Ltd

Study skills: priorities, stage 2

Column A Using the scoring from stage 1, decide whether each item really is a priority, whether it could wait, who else could do it, or any other options you have.

Column B Number your priorities in order. Highlight in yellow the one you are going to work on next. Highlight it in red once you have worked on it.

Column C Shows the pages of this *Handbook* related to the given study skill.

Study skill	A Priority for action? Tick, or enter 'can wait' or other options	B	C Pages
I am going to find out how I learn best, and how to reflect upon/evaluate my work			55–60, 86
I am going to be better motivated and learn to set myself manageable goals			80–5
I am going to improve my organisational and time-management skills			61–76, 121, 146
I am going to develop strategies for getting started on a new task or assignment			61–2, 136–7
I am going to improve my research skills			Chs. 6, 9
I am going to develop my reading skills			109–15
I am going to improve my note-making and organise and use my notes effectively			115–23
I am going to use lecture time effectively to get the best out of lectures			126–7
I am going to improve my oral presentations			100–2
I am going to make the most of working with others (groupwork, seminars, etc.)			Ch. 5
I am going to develop my writing skills			Chs. 7, 8
I am going to make more use of IT to help my academic study			74–6, 106–8, 156
I am going to develop my critical and analytical thinking skills			Ch. 9
I am going to improve my memory strategies			Ch. 10
I am going to develop good revision strategies and exam techniques			Ch. 11

© Stella Cottrell 1999, *The Study Skills Handbook*, Macmillan Press Ltd

PLANNER

Study skills: action plan

Go back over your answers to the different exercises and the self-evaluations you completed for Chapters 1 and 2. Bring together the different ideas about your current strengths, the areas you wish to develop, and your priorities.

Date:
Summary of my current strengths, skills and qualities: what I have achieved so far
Summary of what I need to work on, develop or improve
My priorities: what I am going to do, when, and how
How will I know that I have improved? (E.g. What changes would I expect in my work, in myself, or in the attitudes of others?)

Personal profiles

What is a profile?

A profile is simply a snapshot of yourself as you are – your skills, qualities, attributes and achievements. It has several uses, of which these are especially important:

- it gives you a sense of where you are now, so that you can work to a personal development plan
- compiling it develops habits of reflection and self-analysis
- experience of evaluating and describing yourself is valuable preparation for job interviews.

In this chapter you have already started to put together your profile of strengths, qualities and priorities. If you photocopied the pages, you can use them again to update your profile as you progress on your course. The profile will help when drawing up a curriculum vitae for job interviews. Add in your achievements and skills from other areas of your life.

'Soft skills' are skills such as oral communication and teamwork, which are less easily quantifiable than academic qualifications. The 'Soft skills' evaluation can be used to develop a skills profile (pages 31–2) for employment.

What are employers looking for?

As you can see from the diagram below, employers want graduates to have 'soft skills'. The lighter bars indicate how desirable each skill is to employers, and the darker bars indicate how few students actually demonstrate those skills.

Soft skills: as desired by employers and actual incidence

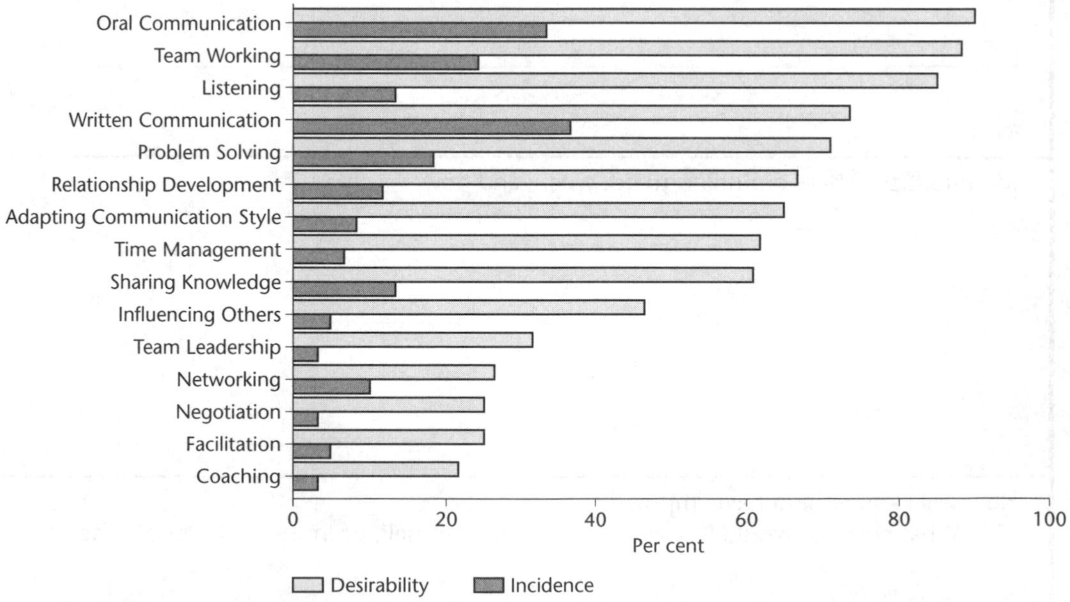

Adapted from TMP Worldwide Research, 1998: *Soft Skills, Hard Facts* (London: TMP Worldwide Research).

Transferable and soft employment skills

Just as you identified how the skills you brought to university could translate into academic skills, so you can see how academic skills translate into the 'transferable' and 'soft' skills required in employment. These skills are needed especially at 'team leader' and other management levels.

On the chart below are some of the soft skills which you could develop as a student – you will be able to think of others. On the next page, map out for yourself the skills you actually develop as a student. This exercise is especially useful in your final year, but if you do it earlier as well you will be better prepared to make use of the various opportunities that college offers.

Area of academic activity	Examples of potential transferable and soft skills which could be developed
Attending lectures, seminars, tutorials, etc.	Time-management; working flexibly
Lectures	Listening skills, identifying and selecting relevant points, written communication, information management
Seminars, group work, team projects	Teamwork, negotiating, oral communication, learning to take directions from others and to give directions, taking responsibility, problem-solving, listening, working with people from a variety of backgrounds, dealing with differences in opinion, relationship development, sharing knowledge
Oral presentation	Speaking in public, persuading and influencing others, making a case, time-management, presentation skills, using audiovisual aids, planning, sharing knowledge, adapting communication style
Writing essays and other forms of academic writing	Written communication skills, developing an argument or putting a strong case, working to word limits, working to deadlines, task analysis, sharing knowledge, breaking tasks into component parts, attention to detail
Maths and statistics	Problem-solving, presenting information, interpreting data, sharing knowledge
Observation	Listening skills, working with people from a variety of backgrounds, information management, attention to detail
Research	Time management, managing large amounts of information, working to deadlines
Exams and revision	Working to deadlines, managing stress and crisis, planning

SELF-EVALUATION

Turning academic skills into transferable and soft employment skills

Use the exercises you completed in Chapter 2 to complete the profile below, showing soft and transferable skills developed at university and elsewhere. Look especially at page 25, ***Current skills and qualities***.

The first four items from the employer's list are already written in. Add in others at which you are particularly good.

Skills, qualities, attributes and achievements	**Specific examples**
Oral communication	
Team working	
Listening	
Written communication	
Other transferable skills I can offer	
☐ Current driving licence ☐ Computer literacy ☐ Languages:	

© Stella Cottrell 1999, *The Study Skills Handbook*, Macmillan Press Ltd

Developing a portfolio

What is a portfolio?

A portfolio is simply a file where you keep together relevant information about yourself.

What is the purpose of a portfolio?

A portfolio has several uses:

- it keeps related documents together
- it helps the process of reflection
- it gives the process of self-evaluation and personal development a higher focus in your life
- in some vocations, you can take it to job interviews
- it can hold relevant examples and information for when you need them, such as when applying for work placements, work or other courses.

Do you have to keep a portfolio?

This depends on your course. It may be compulsory for your course; if not, then it is a matter of personal choice. However, even if you don't *have* to keep a portfolio, you will probably find if helpful to do so – to organise your thinking about what you need to do, and to monitor your progress.

Checking and updating your portfolio

Update your portfolios regularly – at least once or twice a year, and whenever you achieve something new. Re-reading or rewording what you have written may refocus your energies.

What to put in your portfolio

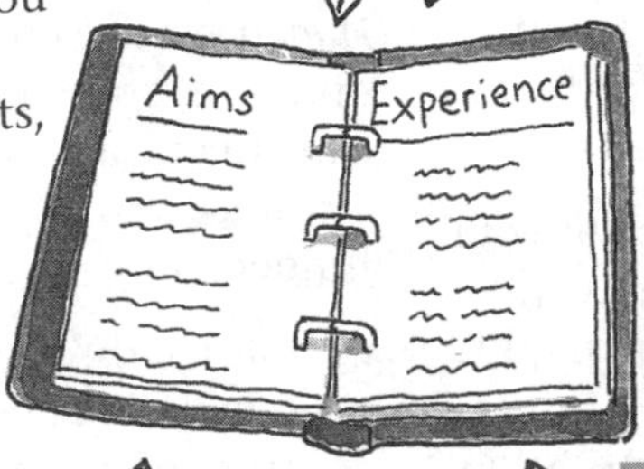

1 Self-evaluation and profile sheets from Chapter 2, and other self-evaluation sheets you find helpful (such as motivation and priority sheets from Chapter 4).

2 A profile of vocational and technical skills you have developed.

3 An up-to-date list of courses and training.

4 Certificates (exams, a copy of your driving licence, etc.).

5 An up-to-date list of your work experience, with the dates, addresses of employers, brief job descriptions, your main responsibilities, skills or qualities you demonstrated, and what you learned from doing that work.

6 Your curriculum vitae (CV). (A careers adviser can help you to compile this.)

7 Your ideas about where you would like to be in seven years' time, and what you need to do to achieve this goal.

8 Examples of your work and interests, if relevant – but without breaching anyone else's confidentiality. For example, you might include a copy of a report or assessment you made of a client during a work placement, slides of your artwork, or a copy of an article you wrote for a student magazine.

9 **Personal statement** Write about 300–500 words, drawing all this information together. Summarise your progress, your immediate priorities, and your long-term aspirations.

Review

The term 'study skills' is often used in a loose way. There is a temptation to look at the end product, the finished essay or the good exam mark, and to imagine that knowing a few tips is all that is needed to achieve these. Alternatively, people may think that high marks are something they can never achieve.

This chapter and Chapters 3 and 4 emphasise that real progress in study skills occurs when skills development is treated as part of a wider, general process of learning. At its best, this is a process in which you learn about yourself and how you perform to your potential under *any* circumstances, not just academically. It involves developing an understanding about how personal opinions, attitudes and states of mind influence your success. Fundamental to that process is self-awareness, based on reflection and self-evaluation, so that you know what you do well and why, and what needs to be improved and how.

This chapter has encouraged you to look at your current qualities and skills in a different way. The process of self-evaluation can begin in quite mechanistic ways, such as filling in questionnaires, rating yourself, setting priorities, and assembling information about yourself. In time, however, this can develop into a deeper process of self-reflection and self-development that benefits any aspect of your life, including your study.

Some students feel as if they have no academic skills. Others, especially those who entered university straight from school, can be anxious about having the right skills to find employment when they leave. For this reason it is important to see the parallels between skills used in academic study, and those used elsewhere. Everybody brings to college experiences and skills which contain sub-skills that are transferable to academic study. In turn, academic study develops skills and ways of thinking that can be of great benefit in employment. However, skills cannot usually be transferred from one situation to another unless the person concerned can *see* similarities in the two situations. This takes creative reflection, and may require help from others, but it is worth the effort. Graduates who do well in the job market are not necessarily more skilled than others, but they have learnt to *identify* their skills and can therefore talk about them confidently and with examples of their application.

Students may also feel that they do not know where to begin to develop their study skills. The ideas of mapping or profiling skills, identifying weak points for improvement, setting priorities, and drawing up action plans, are themes that run throughout this book. However, the *Handbook* also encourages you to look at opinions, states of mind or belief systems that can affect learning. Chapters 3 and 4 focus on attitudes and approaches which can help or hinder study.

Chapter 3, on 'Intelligence and learning', has been included because so many students consulted during the writing of this book expressed secret doubts about their ability to study or about their intelligence. Most of these students have had their confidence undermined in the past, sometimes by a chance comment. Earlier anxieties about failure can remain for years, eating away at self-esteem and preventing positive outcomes. Looking at underlying myths about intelligence and the realities about learning can enable some students to re-evaluate their learning, and go on to perform extremely well. If you feel this applies to you, you may find it helpful to read Chapter 3 now; if not, you may prefer to come back to the chapter later in the year.

Chapter 3

Intelligence and learning

LEARNING OUTCOMES

This chapter offers you opportunities to:

- develop awareness of your own views about intelligence and learning
- evaluate how these views, or the views of others, may have affected your previous learning
- consider different theories about intelligence
- reflect on varieties of learning, and the conditions that facilitate learning
- put together a plan to optimise your learning
- reflect on how study skills fit more generally into your overall learning development.

When to read this chapter

This chapter is more theoretical than the others and requires you to reflect on your beliefs about learning. If you are in a mood to be more active, you may prefer to leave this chapter until another day.

The learning process

Study skills are important as an aspect of learning, and make the learning process easier. *Learning* is about more than just study skills, however. This chapter focuses on the learning process itself, looking at how intelligence develops through learning, and the conditions that are necessary for learning to occur.

It is often taken for granted that 'success' is the result of 'being clever', and that this is something you are either blessed with at birth or not. For mature students especially, this was part of the educational doctrine with which they grew up.

Nevertheless, the world is full of successful people who did *not* do well at school – and so are universities, and sometimes even university teaching departments! Each of us has to discover for ourselves that the early opinions of others were not necessarily accurate – what they thought of us does not define our real potential nor determine what we can become. None of us really knows what we are capable of achieving: but usually this is a great deal more than we suppose.

Self-belief and the right conditions for learning are both vital in developing as a learner. To develop confidence in yourself as a learner, it is important to understand your own learning history, and become aware of any beliefs and practices arising from it that might constrict you in the present.

'Am I intelligent enough for university?'

This 'ghost' question haunts many undergraduates, even if their marks are excellent. They worry that 'secretly' or 'deep down' they are not clever enough to succeed.

'So far I've been lucky ...'

Your marks were OK last time – but that was a fluke. This time you might fail, and you'll be so embarrassed because now everyone expects you to do well.
64%

One reason for this anxiety is that students are rarely taught to evaluate their own work. They have no criteria to let them assess their own performance. Instead, they feel prey to the whims of chance: good or bad marks 'just happen', or depend on luck (such as which lecturer they have), or reflect their level of 'natural cleverness'.

This can leave students feeling disempowered or adrift, even if their marks are good. Students can feel very vulnerable, and may worry about suddenly being exposed as stupid. Anxiety may create a vicious cycle: such students can't settle down to study, can't focus attention, can't take in what they read, or can't remember what they learnt, and this reinforces their suspicion that 'really' they lack intelligence. This is very common, so it is important to look at what we mean by intelligence.

What is intelligence?

Tick any response that you feel is true.

- ☐ **1** Intelligence is an underlying, general cleverness which, because it depends on genetics, is fixed for life.
- ☐ **2** There are many kinds of intelligence.
- ☐ **3** Intelligence can be developed.
- ☐ **4** Intelligence depends on your life opportunities.
- ☐ **5** What is regarded as intelligence depends on the environment and the culture.
- ☐ **6** Intelligence is about applying what you know easily to new contexts.
- ☐ **7** Intelligence is a question of how much you know.
- ☐ **8** Intelligence is easy to measure.
- ☐ **9** Intelligence is a question of habit and practice.

Note down how your own views – and other people's views – of your intelligence might have affected your previous performance. Then read the following opinions about intelligence.

Afterwards, return to the notes you have made and note down whether your opinions about yourself or your intelligence have changed because of your reading and reflection.

Nine different views of intelligence

1 *Intelligence is a general, underlying 'cleverness' which is fixed for life*

Early psychologists such as Spearman (1927) and Terman (1975) believed that each individual has a general level of intelligence, known as the *intelligence quotient* or IQ. They regarded intelligence as a single, fixed, underlying capacity: a person who did well on one test would do well on all or most intelligence tests; and no matter what happened in life, those born 'very intelligent' would remain generally more intelligent than those born 'less intelligent'. More recently, psychologists have used studies of identical twins to support this idea, arguing that some traits, including intelligence, are up to 80 per cent dependent on genetic inheritance.

However, other psychologists, using the same data, argue that genetic influence is as little as 20 per cent or even zero (Gardner 1993). Pairs of twins used in twin studies are often brought up in similar environments and, as they look the same, they may evoke similar responses in other people so that their experiences may be unusually alike.

There is also strong evidence to suggest that environment plays a great part in intellectual performance. For example, the *Raven's Progessive Matrices* – an intelligence test used to measure abstract reasoning ability – were designed for use with people of any language, age or culture. The person being tested has to choose a visual pattern from a selection of options, in order to complete a larger visual sequence. Scores are graded, according to age, to give an IQ score. Scores for Raven's correlated very well with those of other IQ tests, including language-based tests. So far, this supports the notion that intelligence is 'general'.

However, although Raven's is supposed to be culture-free and language-free, it was found that Asian children's scores, scaled according to age, went up by 15–20 points after they had lived in Britain for five years – a very significant change (Mackintosh and Mascie-Taylor 1985). This suggests that what is measured by an intelligence test is at best only a snapshot of a person's experiences and learning up to that moment. It is not an indication of the person's underlying intelligence or potential.

We feel she has infinite potential for future improvement

A snap-shot of current performance

A Ravens-style question

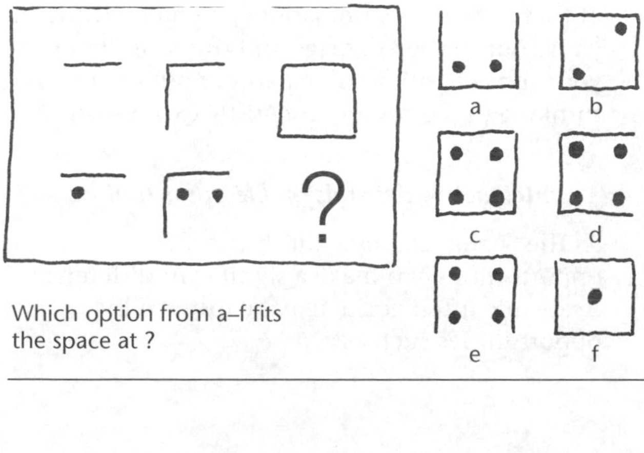

Which option from a–f fits the space at ?

2 *There are multiple intelligences, not one general intelligence*

Thurstone (1960), after experiments involving hundreds of college students, concluded that there was no evidence of any *general* form of intelligence. Similarly, Gardner (1993), argues that intelligence consists of many separate, independent systems, which interact with each other. For Gardner, there are at least seven main 'intelligences'; each consists of abilities to

Gardner's multiple intelligences

1 **Linguistic**
   – such as reading, writing, talking, listening, or poetry

2 **Logical, mathematical**
   – such as ability with numbers, or legal or scientific thinking

3 **Spatial**
   – such as navigating a boat or plane, driving, or architecture

4 **Musical**
   – such as singing, composing, playing an instrument, or appreciating music

5 **Bodily-kinaesthetic**
   – such as sports, drama, dance, or making things

6 **Interpersonal**
   – such as counselling and teaching skills, or understanding others

7 **Intrapersonal**
   – such as self-understanding, self-management, or reflection

solve the problems or produce the objects that are relevant within the person's culture and environment.

Current research in neuropsychology suggests that different cognitive abilities, such as speech, may be semi-separate 'domains' of ability, controlled by different circuits within the brain (Karmiloff-Smith 1992). Some people show a weakness in one area, such as a complete inability to recognise faces. Other people show poor development for most skills, but have an outstanding ability in one area, such as drawing or mathematical calculation. This supports Gardner's view that intelligence is 'multiple' rather than 'general'.

It is obvious that most of the intelligences on Gardner's list can be developed. For example, people can attend workshops to develop interpersonal skills, and counselling or meditation to develop intrapersonal awareness. A scientific way of thinking is formed through practice, training and exposure to the language and conventions of scientific research (see pages 169-70). Skill in writing poetry or essays can also be developed through practice.

For which of Gardner's multiple intelligences do you show most aptitude? What reasons might there be for your having developed those intelligences rather than others?

3 *Intelligence can be developed*

In Japan, the Suzuki Violin Talent Education Programme has trained many children to play the violin to virtuoso level. The programme begins with exposure to music from soon after birth, and involves daily practice from an early age. Even the less remarkable students perform to a level that in other cultures would be considered that of a child prodigy (Gardner 1993).

Similarly, children exposed to several languages from an early age tend to become multilingual quite naturally. People who start later in life can also develop into good violinists or linguists. The Suzuki Programme suggests the importance of the belief that *anyone* can learn to a high standard, as well showing the role of environment and practice in developing skills. Excellence need not be the preserve of the few.

Just as we would not, in general, expect excellent violin playing from somebody who rarely played the instrument, we would not expect outstanding intellectual performances from people whose minds are not regularly challenged by ideas and problems. University provides part of that necessary stimulation. As you go through your course, the language and thinking styles of your subject will become part of your own thinking processes and linguistic expression.

4 *Intelligence depends on life opportunities*

As the Suzuki example illustrates, life opportunities can make a significant difference. Academic intelligence may be fostered by opportunities such as:

- easy access to books, equipment, and appropriate teaching
- sufficient time to study, think or practise
- stimulating conversations that require active engagement and reflection
- validation by people who are important to you of your specific learning interests, whether for geometry, philosophy or *cordon bleu* cookery
- being part of a culture that values academic intelligence.

There are ways in which you can increase these opportunities, such as making use of local libraries, doing courses at a local college or university, and even through your choice of newspaper and radio or TV programmes. If you did not have ideal opportunities for learning when you were younger, or if you were not then ready for them, it may take some time to catch up. But it can be done – and it *is* done, every year, by thousands of adult students.

> In what ways could you make more of the opportunities currently available to you?

5 *Intelligence depends on what is needed and relevant within a culture*

According to this view, intelligence is not just something that individuals carry around in their heads, but includes the equipment and tools available to them – their filing systems, the amount of memory on their computers, the sophistication of the tools they can use, the lines of communication within their society, the people they meet. Intelligence is not cut off and measured in relation to individuals, but regarded as a *social* phenomenon (Vygotsky 1978; Resnick, Levine and Teasley 1991).

For example, the intelligence needed in industrial settings may be very different from that required for a rural economy or for life in the mountains. Similarly, the education valued for girls, or for the youngest child within a family, may be different from that sought for boys or for older children. Children are skilled at adapting to what is expected of them.

Sternberg (1985) described intelligence as being, in part, a sensitivity to the environmental context. This can apply to learning contexts also. One learning environment may match what a person is used to, making learning easy. For another person, the same teaching methods may not work. Some people learn best in quiet stillness; others find that sitting quietly is a torture. Some find it difficult to learn from books and learn better by ear. Some learn best when the curriculum is very structured; others when it is flexible and open.

If you did not do as well at school as you might have done, it may be worth reflecting on how *you* learn best – then compare this to the way you were taught. You might also consider what you were good at when you were a child, and what you valued as important. Were your interests shared and valued by the people around you – your teachers, parents and friends? If not, this may have made learning more difficult for you.

Are the things you value *today* shared by the people around you? Do they understand and support your desire to study? If not, as an adult, you can now take responsibility for setting up the right environment for yourself as a student. You may need to find a table you like in the library, or set up a space to study that nobody else can use.

Similarly, you can organise information in a way that suits your learning preferences. For example, you could record your materials onto tape or convert information to images – whatever works for you.

On the whole, your lecturers will not be able to create the ideal environment *for* you, as each person's needs will be different. So it's up to you to look after your own needs.

> How could you change your total learning environment so that you don't repeat earlier learning experiences? Do you need to surround yourself with more people who support your study ambitions? (Chapters 1, 4, 10 and 11 may give you some ideas.)

6 *Intelligence is about applying what you know to new contexts*

Sternberg (1984) emphasised that any skill is made up of underlying processes and sub-skills; he saw intelligence as the ability to transfer those skills easily when confronted with a new task. What is important is not just that you are able to perform a given task, such as making a pancake or writing an essay, but that you are able to apply what you know to new situations, such as making a cake or writing a report.

However, it is not necessarily an easy matter to transfer a skill from one learning situation to another. Research into mathematical problem-solving suggests that for skills to be transferred from one problem to another, the student has first to be helped to identify their common features and the underlying principles in solving that kind of problem. If students can recognise that two problems have similar underlying structures, they can apply the principles for solving one problem in solving the other. Unless the teacher makes the link between the old and the new learning explicit, the student may not realise that two problems are connected. Further, the new learning needs to be at around the same level of complexity as that already covered (Reed, Dempster and Ettinger 1985).

If teaching has not followed these lines, the student may feel lost and give up. Further, the student may think that the fault lies with her or his intelligence, rather than in the way the problem was presented. A good teacher will help students to see what they already know, and to use this as the basis for the next step in their learning.

Applying multiple intelligences to study contexts

Gardner suggests that different intelligences interact. Students who work in a multi-sensory or a multi-disciplinary way often find that learning in one area enhances learning in other areas. If you develop a sense of rhythm, this can improve not only music and dance, but maths and spelling. Similarly, students who are sensitive to shades of colour can use these to structure and organise information visually and spatially, which in turn can help memory and understanding.

It is important to look for connections between the intelligences you have already developed, and those in which you feel you are weak. You don't need to be a genius in music or art to harness music, colour, shape, and movement as learning tools. Croaky singing of chemical formulae, imagining your relatives as courtroom personalities for law revision, or using the rainbow to sequence paragraphs from pattern notes, are ways of using multiple intelligences to make studying easier – and more interesting.

> Look back to your answer to viewpoint 2 on multiple intelligences (pages 37–8). How could you transfer abilities from your area of strength to help your learning?

7 *Intelligence is a question of how much you know*

The popular view of intelligence is that it is an ability to answer the type of closed questions set on *Mastermind*. This does not take into consideration aspects of intelligence such as creativity or coping in real-life situations. Another view is that intelligence is a capacity for abstract reasoning, such as formulating general hypotheses, and that you don't need to *know* much at all to reason well.

Donaldson (1978) argued that the way we reason depends upon the particular context we are in and on what we already know. For example, she demonstrated that both children and adults interpret what they hear by attending not just to the meaning of words, but also to their understanding of those words based on their own thoughts and previous knowledge. It follows that the amount and kinds of background knowledge you bring to academic study will affect the ease with which you can process new information and reason with it.

Our ability to think in abstract ways about something may depend on having already had real-life experience of problems of a similar nature. Butterfield (1992) describes how abstract notions such as 'generosity' are actually concrete social realities. The real-life, concrete experience allows us to develop a mental model, and this model later provides the basis for abstract thinking. If we have gaps in concrete experience – for example with manipulating numbers – we are likely to find it harder to move on to more abstract examples until we have filled the gaps.

Butterfield suggests that when presented with a familiar problem in an unfamiliar context, we may be unable to recognise that the two are the same. This can make us look like complete beginners when we are not. We may need somebody to point out the similarity between what we already know and the new learning. When we see the link, we can do the problem.

Plastic brains

The brain has 'plasticity': it is capable of change and development. When a person takes up a new skill, millions of fresh connections are set up between different neurons in the brain to deal with the new information – rather like a set of telephone wires relaying information. The more you develop an ability, the more elaborate the neural networks or wiring system, and the faster your brain can process information related to that skill.

When you begin to study a new subject, the speed at which you will be able to take things in and make sense of them will depend on how far your brain can use past learning experiences. If you have studied something very similar in the past, you may experience the new learning as quite easy.

If a subject is very new, however, there is little foundation for you to build upon. Your brain has fewer connections it can use to make sense of the new information. If the language used is also unfamiliar to you, the brain will need to build connections for this too. You may *experience* this as finding it harder to listen or harder to read: you may get tired more quickly, or you may feel that your brain is 'dead', or that nothing makes sense. As you go over the same material from different angles, though, the new connections will get stronger and learning will become easier.

8 *Intelligence can be measured*

IQ tests only measure things that can be measured! Many areas of human excellence, however, cannot easily be measured – such as artistic and musical creativity, emotional maturity, intuition, sensitivity to the needs of others, keeping a cool head in emergencies, being able to impersonate other people, and inventiveness. Some people may excel in these areas and yet perform poorly in tests that are language-based. Students who have failed in language- or number-based GCSEs often do very well on university courses in the arts. Similarly, some people who are poor at languages are excellent at computer sciences.

Einstein's schoolwork was not very good – yet IQ tests are supposed to correlate well with school performance. Einstein claimed that his initial ideas on the relativity of time and space struck him in a moment of inspiration while he was daydreaming that he was riding on a sunbeam. This kind of imaginative thinking is difficult to measure using IQ tests.

9 *Intelligence depends on study habits and study skills which can be learnt*

This book is based on the premise that what we regard as intelligence is often a question of good study habits, strategies and skills that you can develop. For example, research shows that students who do best at problem-solving spend longer than other students in working out exactly what the problem is before trying to solve it. Other students look at the surface of the problem and do not see the underlying structure which connects it to problems they already know how to solve. Some students fail because they don't spend enough time considering the examples and information they are given; others copy out examples without reflecting on the underlying purpose of the activity (Keane, Kahney and Brayshaw 1989). Successful students use strategies that can be learnt.

Although the research mentioned above referred to a particular *kind* of problem-solving, its findings apply to university study in general. Some students skim across the surface of their learning, copying a bit from one book and a line from another, without really looking at why the work was set, what the information means, or its relevance to themselves. With most university assignments you will benefit from taking time to reflect, clarifying what is really being asked, the issues within the title, the reasons for that piece of work being set, and the best strategy to use. Over time, this way of working becomes a habit.

With which of these nine views of intelligence are you most familiar? Which make most sense to you? Which best encourage learning?

What is 'learning'?

We have looked at how intelligence can be fostered though a learning process. At each new stage of study it is important to reflect on *how* to learn at that level. Many people have never 'learnt how to learn', and some universities now offer 'learning to learn' courses.

So what is 'learning'? It's clearly more than just study skills. In fact it is a multi-faceted process, involving each individual learner and her or his learning history, the current learning environment, and the interaction between these. We can say that learning has taken place when we both understand something and can explain, teach or demonstrate it to others.

The ways in which we can learn are very varied. Below are listed five dimensions along which learning activity can vary.

Five learning dimensions

1 *Conscious or unconscious*

Conscious learning

Learning is conscious when we are *aware* that we are learning, as when we set out to memorise a poem or a phone number, or when we recognise that we have understood new material. Typical methods of learning consciously are:

- repeating something
- writing it out
- checking that we have remembered it
- telling someone else what we know.

Unconscious learning

We are aware of a small part only of the information taken in by the senses, which the brain processes. Learning is unconscious when we are unaware of it happening. Occasionally, unconscious learning may emerge into consciousness later, as when we feel we 'just know' something we didn't realise we had learnt.

You may have experienced suddenly recognising which way to go on an unfamiliar car journey, or surprising yourself by answering a question without thinking and then wondering, 'How did I know that?'

2 *With different levels of attention*

Our level of attention may vary, depending on:

- our mental or physical state for learning
- the way information is presented to us
- whether the material is completely new.

As we saw from the example of Einstein and the sunbeam (page 41), learning can take place in a relaxed, aware state – it does not always require effort and great concentration. You will be able to recall many occasions when you tried hard to remember something but forgot it quickly, such as a telephone number, while remembering easily something to which you had paid little attention, such as an advertisement on a hoarding or a line from a song.

3 *Via different sense sequences*

Each of us has our own preferred order for seeing, hearing, speaking, writing and using information in order to learn it.

Experiment with your own preferences. Make a list of words that you have difficulty spelling (or some other information you need to learn). Try learning them using different sense sequences. For example:

- Look at it; say it aloud; write it; check what you've written.
- Say it aloud; look at it; write it; check what you've written.
- Draw it; look at it; say it aloud; write it; check what you've written.
- Tape-record it; listen to it; repeat it; write it; look at what you've written; check it.

Which sequence works best for you?

(For other visual, auditory and kinaesthetic activities, see pages 209–11.)

4 *By detail or by the whole picture*

Some people learn best when they see the overall picture first; they are confused or overwhelmed by too much detail early on. Others learn best through building up details, allowing the whole picture to emerge. This whole picture may be meaningless to them until they have a flavour of the specific details.

5 *By fast track or by the scenic route*

Some people find efficient 'motorway routes', learning exactly what they need and only that. Others take scenic routes, gathering material which may not be essential but which makes the learning more interesting. The scenic route can lead to deeper processing, and can be a richer experience. However, it can also generate a lot of information that is not essential to the task in hand. Which way is appropriate depends on what you have to learn, why you are learning it, and how long you have in which to learn it.

Combined methods

Most of the time we change places along each of these five dimensions, depending on information from the environment and according to our needs and focus. It is easier to develop good study strategies when you are conscious of these dimensions and of your own individual approach to learning.

Some conditions are essential to learning, while others are desirable. Awareness of these allows you to create optimal learning conditions.

Six conditions for learning

For learning to occur at all, and for us then to know that the learning is complete, we need:

1 New experiences
2 Foundations
3 Rehearsal
4 Processing
5 Understanding
6 Demonstration

1 New experiences

In order to learn, we need to be exposed to novelty: to new ideas, new information, new situations, new challenges, new emotions.

Imagine, for example, discovering that when Hannah put her hand in a flame, she did not feel pain. This discovery might challenge your previous learning: that fire burns and is likely to cause pain. It might stimulate a series of questions about why and how this might *not* happen.

A new experience is an opportunity to learn – based on curiosity, a desire to know, a wish to see how everything fits together. Our brains try to fit new information into what we already know: to assimilate it. If that is not possible, the brain adapts previous knowledge to accommodate the new data.

2 Learning foundations

Learning is easier if it builds on earlier learning – if it can use similar or related experiences as a foundation to 'make sense' of new information. Thus, if we look at the object in the diagram and are asked what we know about it, we can only describe what we see.

However, if we are told it is a *fruit*, we know how to react to it, what to expect from it: it can be eaten, it will probably be sweet; it is unlikely to move, make a noise, attack us, or want to go for a walk. If on the other hand we are told it is an *animal* or a musical *instrument*, we will automatically call upon different sets of knowledge. Our knowledge provides models (or schemata) to help us to make sense of the world.

The same is true of academic learning. For example, it is easier to read when we have a good vocabulary. If we need to keep looking up words in the dictionary, our attention to what we are reading is continually interrupted – we lose the flow, which affects our comprehension. We also have to try to make sense of what we are reading, whilst simultaneously remembering the meaning of the new words and fitting it all together. This leads to overload, and is often the point where people feel they 'can't learn'. In reality, they are learning a great deal – but too much at once.

Your brain will take time to assimilate new information, and may need to see how it all fits together, as well as what all the parts are individually, before it feels it 'knows' what it is taking in. People who seem to learn things very quickly may simply have good foundations of information, and practice in similar problems.

3 Rehearsal

Academic learning is similar to learning physical activities, such as dance or football. We generally need to repeat the action or the new information several times to take it in, and we need to come back to it or practise. Otherwise, we become 'rusty' and forget. This is just as true of writing essays or reading academic books as it is of football, drawing, playing a violin or making a soufflé.

If you think back to what you learnt at school, you will probably be aware of a vague overall knowledge of some subjects even though the details may seem hazy. You would learn these subjects more quickly a second time around. Just glancing again at some old schoolbooks may bring whole areas of knowledge flooding back.

4 Processing new information

Superficial or 'surface' processing

We may process new information at a superficial level. For example, we may just note and remember that Hannah (page 44) does not feel pain, and then think no further about this. We may learn it by heart as a fact, like learning maths tables, or record it as an entry in our notebooks.

Memory and recording are only part of learning, however. If we use only surface methods, we don't develop a sense of the underlying structure or the significance of what we learn. This makes it more difficult to apply the new knowledge in other situations.

Deep processing – making sense of what you learn

Alternatively, we may try to make sense of Hannah's experience, looking for explanations. We may ask ourselves questions to stimulate our thinking, exploring the problem from many angles. Perhaps Hannah is very good at exercising mind over matter? Maybe she has a neurological condition that prevents her from feeling pain? Maybe she *does* feel pain, but hides this?

We may also start to wonder what pain really is. How does it work – is it regulated by the brain? Or chemicals in the body? Or our attitude? Or maybe the flame was different from the flames we are used to? Maybe the answer is not in Hannah but in chemistry?

As you analyse the experience from different angles, raising new questions and experimenting with possible answers, you process at a deeper level.

'No, I don't need to practise – I have a natural gift!'

5 Moving to another level of understanding

In order to understand a new phenomenon, such as what happens when Hannah's hand is in the fire, we may have to change our previous views of the world. We may have thought that everybody would feel pain from fire.

- When we realise that there are situations in which people don't feel pain in quite the same way as others, we move to a different level of knowledge.
- When we know *why* this occurs, we move to a deeper level of understanding.
- When we appreciate how we came to hold our previous set of beliefs, and why we now hold a different set, we are learning at an even deeper level – understanding how knowledge is constructed, and how we come to know and understand at all.

When we learn in this way we have to be prepared to open our minds to new ways of seeing and doing things, even to new ways of thinking about ourselves, looking at how we came to believe what we believe. This makes study exciting, and is one reason why so many students return to postgraduate study.

6 Demonstrating learning

We are not really sure of our knowledge until we have put it to the test – demonstrating to ourselves and others that we really do *know* it.

One way of testing our understanding of new material is to put it to use. In some cases there may be a practical use, such as fixing a piece of machinery or producing a new design. In other cases, such as understanding how pain works, we can demonstrate learning by explaining it to other people. If we can do this

- in writing, speech or a diagram, or by practical demonstration
- without checking the details during the presentation
- and in a way that is clear and makes sense to our audience

then our thinking is also likely to be clear, and a stage in our learning is complete.

If we *cannot* demonstrate what we feel we know, then our thinking may be rather confused and our understanding incomplete. We may need to check back over what we have learnt. It may help:

- to take a different angle on the issue
- to use a different book
- to see whether we missed a step earlier.

The section on encoding information in 'Memory' (Chapter 10) and 'The C·R·E·A·M strategy' (Chapter 4) may also help.

Learning at university

Some people think that memorising 'facts' is all there is to learning. Certainly it *is* always useful to have information readily available in your head for when you need it. For most college courses, however, what counts is not how many facts you can fit into your answers, but how you *use* information. You will be expected to demonstrate:

- that you can evaluate and select what is relevant and important, and what can be omitted
- that you know how ideas are linked and interconnected
- that you have made sense of your course
- that you can structure your ideas and knowledge to make a convincing argument.

Optimal learning

A number of factors determine whether or not you can learn effectively. Learning is easier when circumstances are favourable in the following ways.

Learning is easier when ...

When you are in a physical state to learn

- You can't learn easily if you are tired, stressed, hungry, dehydrated or on a high-sugar diet.

- A glass of plain water several times a day helps neural activity in the brain, and gives the body energy. Other drinks do not have the same effect. If you tire easily when studying, or if your thinking is muddled, drink some water.

- Foods such as cereal-based products (rice, oats and wheat), which release natural sugars slowly, help balance your energies.

- Stress may put you into 'survival mode', diverting your energies away from your brain to your muscles (see page 206). We learn best when relaxed, interested and motivated.

When you *believe* you can learn

- Believe in your intelligence (Ch. 3).
- Believe you have the right to learn.
- Create a positive state of mind for learning.

When the medium suits you

- Rewrite, draw, act, tape or sculpt new information so that it is easier to absorb – whatever suits you best.
- Experiment with different layouts, colours, fonts, page sizes.
- Personalise information to make it your own.

When information is organised

Organise information so that your brain can structure it (see page 211).

When you use C·R·E·A·M strategies

Be creative, reflective, effectively organised, active and highly motivated (see Chapter 4).

When you use your whole brain

Take full advantage of your brain. Use:

- both the left and right sides of your brain
- the triune brain (page 206)
- all your senses to encode information (see page 209).

When the five study-skills components are in place

You need:

- self-awareness
- awareness of what is required of you
- methods and strategies
- confidence and permission
- familiarity, practice and habit.

See page 22.

When you enjoy what you learn

Make the learning fun. Make sure:

- that it has meaning for you
- that you really care about the outcome, attracted to success like a bee to honey
- that you are fully engaged in what you are learning.

When you work with others

See Chapter 5.

Look over the notes you made for each section about intelligence. In your journal, note your thoughts now in response to these questions.

- Have your ideas changed or been reinforced as you read through this chapter?
- What is your own learning history? As a child, were you encouraged or discouraged in learning? What effect did that have?
- Is your current learning affected by patterns from the past? If so, do you need to make any changes to improve your learning?
- What is necessary for you to achieve optimal learning? Based on what you have read in this chapter, list three things you could do now to enhance your own learning.
- How do your study skills needs fit with your other learning development needs?

Review

This chapter has provided an opportunity to reflect upon your attitude to intelligence and learning, and how your attitude could be affecting your ability to learn. It has considered the idea of study skills in a broad sense, looking at the relationship between intelligence, life experiences and learning.

There are many different views about intelligence. Some traditional attitudes have been limiting. They reduced people's self-esteem, making it more difficult for them to learn and overlooking their potential to develop new areas of ability.

Different cultures and different environments require, appreciate and develop different aspects of intelligence. How much early support individuals have for their own learning preferences and subject choices may have long-term effects on their performance and indeed their self-esteem. As an adult learner, you have much more control over your learning than you did as a child at school. You can now decide to alter aspects of your environment, your social networks, your attitudes and your study habits, as well as personalising your study materials to support your own learning preferences. You can give yourself permission to succeed.

The chapter has also looked at how concrete experience and previous learning affects our performance in new areas of learning – including coping with academic information or writing essays. If these skills are under-developed through lack of adequate prior experience, study may seem difficult and we may feel less intelligent. On the other hand, as explained in Chapter 2, the sub-skills required for academic study are often similar to those used in other areas of life. No student begins from scratch.

Finally, the chapter has encouraged you to think that there are different ways to approach learning. As you become more used to study at a higher level you will find that being flexible in your approaches to learning can make study both more efficient and more interesting. This idea is developed further in Chapter 4, 'The C·R·E·A·M strategy for learning'.

Chapter 4

The C·R·E·A·M strategy for learning

LEARNING OUTCOMES

This chapter offers you opportunities to:

- become aware of the contribution of each aspect of the C·R·E·A·M strategy to the learning process – and know how to apply it to your own study
- develop ideas on how to take more creative and active approaches to your study
- understand the difference between being a *virtuous* student and being an *effective* student
- develop tools for organising your space and time more effectively
- learn how to organise yourself when using IT for more effective study
- explore and clarify your motives for study, and learn how to set yourself clear and achievable goals
- build upon the reflective work started in Chapters 2 and 3.

C·R·E·A·M

C·R·E·A·M stands for:

C – Creative

Have the confidence to use your individual strategies and styles, applying imagination to your learning.

R – Reflective

Be able to sit with your experience, analyse and evaluate your own performance, and draw lessons from it.

E – Effective

Organise your space, time, priorities, state of mind and resources (including information technology, IT), to the maximum benefit.

A – Active

Be personally involved and doing things, physically and mentally, to help you to make sense of what you learn.

M – Motivated

Be aware of your own desired outcomes; keep yourself on track using short- and long-term 'goals'.

Developing each of these aspects strengthens all the others. For example, being motivated involves reflection about what you really want. Active learning and creativity require motivation, and also help you stay motivated. Good organisational strategies benefit from imagination and reflection – and so on.

Finding your creative streak

Creativity is especially important for generating ideas in the early stages of new assignments. You can use more logical approaches later, to evaluate which creative ideas to use.

Attitudes that prevent creativity

- 'It's a waste of time.'
- 'It's childish.'
- 'There's a time for work and a time for play.'
- 'There's a right way of doing things.'
- 'It's not logical.'
- 'I'm not creative.'
- 'I can't.'

Do you express any of the above attitudes? Were you given any messages when you were younger which stifle your creativity now?

Approaches that foster creativity

Playtime: lateral thinking

Choose any two random objects, such as a cup and a plant. Think of as many ways as possible that they could be considered connected (e.g. by size, colour, the way they break, whether they are opposites, how they spin, when they were bought). How can you apply this type of play to your coursework?

You find what you are looking for

- Find three round things in the room.
- Find three things that 'open'.

You will probably find that the room is suddenly filled with these things. If you look for new ways of doing things, or for answers, you will find them too.

There's more than one right answer

Once you have come up with an answer, look for another one. It may be better – or give you a way of fine-tuning the first idea.

Combine things

Take the front half of one animal and the rear of another. What new animal have you invented? The essence of invention is mixing two different ideas or contexts to create a new variety. This helps in academic thinking too – such as comparing viewpoints.

Metaphor

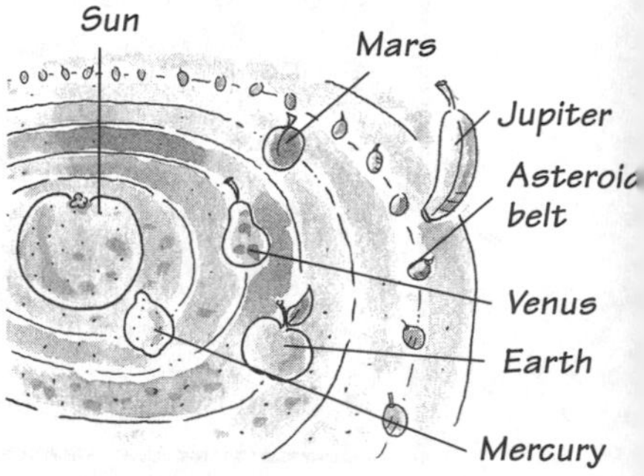

'Suppose this apple is the earth, this orange is the sun, and these other fruit are the rest of the solar system....'

Let one thing stand for, or represent, another: this is using metaphor or analogy. Play at seeing an object, or a study problem, from different perspectives. Make problems visual or concrete. Take an issue out of the academic context and see what it looks like in the world of oranges and apples, or knives, forks, salt and pepper.

If something doesn't make sense, map it out with objects on a table – just as generals mapped out different strategies using 'toy' soldiers.

Activity

Search for connections

See how many ideas you can generate by completing the sentences below.

- Writing an essay is like making cakes because ....
- Study is like a game of football because ....
- Being a student is like being a sandwich because ....

What other metaphors can you think of to describe what study or learning is like?

Be a professor – and other ideas

Give yourself a new sub-personality

In our minds and even in our bodies, we carry various sub-personalities – an internal *critic* who tells us off, a *playful child* who sees the funny side of things, a *hero* who wades in to save the situation, and many others.

Listen to yourself think and you will gradually become aware of those different characters within.

Add to your dramatic cast and find a professor within you

Go through the ideas later to see which you can use. Many may lead nowhere – that's part of the creative process – but sometimes one will be just what you need.

Be curious about what you don't know

Creative people are curious. They want to know everything – just in case it fits together with something else one day.

It is difficult to be creative if you are frightened of what you don't know. Be open to the curious child in you who wants to have a go at everything.

Activity

You are the world's leading expert

When you cannot think of a way of doing a piece of work, imagine you are a professor or inventor, dealing with a world-important problem. Experts don't find problems easy, but they are more open to dealing with the seemingly impossible.

Those working at the forefront of research cannot look up the answer in a book – it isn't there yet! Like Einstein daydreaming on a sunbeam (page 41) they may play with ideas, juggle with options that seem crazy, and go on flights of fancy, imagining 'what if ...?', generating lots of possible answers, and then examining them more closely to see whether any could actually work.

You can do that too. What does your internal professor look like? Sound like? How do you move your hands and head when you are in 'professor' mode? Let your professor come alive, and talk to you about possible approaches to study problems.

Keep an ideas notebook

Value each passing idea, as writers and artists do. Jot ideas down at once in a notebook or on Post-it® labels. Keep a notebook and pen by your bed.

Create opportunities to break a routine

When you take a different route, even if it is not the quickest way, you discover new things of interest.

Examine your routines. Ask:

- Why am I doing it this way?
- Have the original reasons now changed?
- How else could I do things?

Imagine alternatives

Ask 'what if ...?' questions

What if the weekend were three days long? What if this essay had to be in tomorrow? What if I were only allowed 100 words to write up my research – what would I include?

How would others do it?

Consider: how might Pablo Picasso approach this study problem? Or Nelson Mandela? Mahatma Gandhi? Agatha Christie? Mozart? Whoopi Goldberg? A politician? A choreographer? Your mother? Your internal professor? Whose approach would most help and inspire you?

Creative learning

People devise many different strategies to help them to learn. Here are a few. Tick the box beside any *you* could use. What other methods can you think of?

☐ 1
We like to argue with each other.
No – we discuss things, really.
It's a sort of argument, though.
☐ 2
I make a big chart out of wallpaper – and link up all I learn on one subject.
☐ 3
I sort my ideas out while I vacuum – then no-one can hear me talking my ideas through.
☐ 4
I talk my ideas into a cassette recorder.
testing testing
☐ 5
I have a notebook to jot down ideas as they come to me – I take it with me everywhere.
☐ 6
We talk a lot …
… Share ideas …
… Work things out together.
☐ 7
I like a method:
a I work out the main ideas;
b think of headings;
c summarise notes;
d summarise onto one page.
☐ 8
'I write lots of skeleton essay plans. I fit new information into one of the plans.'
☐ 9
I try to imagine I am a lawyer – I always have to argue the other side of what I think.
"It is therefore clear, my Lord that …"
☐ 10
Swahili
Ibo
Esperanto
Farsee
Chinese
I imagine crazy pictures to help me to remember things.
☐ 11
I use "look and cover": I read or try to learn something; then I cover the page. I write down what I can remember. Then I check back to see what I got right. Then I try again.
☐ 12
I scribble my ideas down as fast as I can and see where my mind takes me. I sort them out later to see which bits I can use.

 © Stella Cottrell 1999, *The Study Skills Handbook*, Macmillan Press Ltd

What is my learning style?

Below are a range of approaches to learning. Identify which, if any, most aptly describes you. Note your learning strengths, and things you could develop to broaden your study strengths.

The diver

Characteristics

- ☐ You tend to jump in and have a go.
- ☐ You like to get things over with.
- ☐ You like to see if things work.
- ☐ You like to get onto the next thing quickly.
- ☐ You work well with short bursts of activity.

Learning strengths

- ☐ You don't waste time worrying.
- ☐ You start tasks early.
- ☐ You can motivate others.
- ☐ You are good in role-play activities, problem-solving, and crises.

Areas to develop

- Reflection and planning.
- Creative thinking.
- Considering alternatives.
- Listening to and working with others.
- Increasing your personal interest, so that you can work for longer periods.

The dreamer

Characteristics

- ☐ You think a lot about the subject.
- ☐ You like to research things thoroughly.
- ☐ You put off practical aspects such as writing.
- ☐ You have no idea where time goes.
- ☐ You continually rewrite your time-planner.

Learning strengths

- ☐ You reflect and evaluate well.
- ☐ You are creative, with lots of ideas.
- ☐ You get to the root of things.
- ☐ You listen well and sensitively to others.

Areas to develop

- Effective learning strategies.
- Timekeeping and organisational skills.
- Taking responsibility for self and others.
- Participating.
- Setting priorities and taking decisions.
- Assertiveness and risk-taking.

The logician

Characteristics

- ☐ You like things to make sense.
- ☐ You like to know the reasons behind things.
- ☐ You are organised in your approach to study.
- ☐ You enjoy tackling complex problems.
- ☐ You are a perfectionist.

Learning strengths

- ☐ You are good at analytical and critical thinking.
- ☐ You have organisational skills.
- ☐ You are good at science, maths, law, problem-solving.
- ☐ You have a questioning approach.

Areas to develop

- Creative and imaginative thinking.
- Sensitivity to the differences in others.
- Personal reflection.
- Working with others.
- Stress management.

© Stella Cottrell 1999, *The Study Skills Handbook*, Macmillan Press Ltd

The searchlight

Characteristics

- ☐ You find everything interesting.
- ☐ You like to see the big picture.
- ☐ You have bits of information on lots of things.
- ☐ You are fascinated by details but don't remember them.
- ☐ You find it hard to select what is relevant.

Learning strengths

- ☐ You have high motivation and interest.
- ☐ You have broad general knowledge.
- ☐ You can see connections between things.
- ☐ You are creative and inventive.

Areas to develop

- Setting goals and priorities.
- Analytical and critical thinking.
- Categorising and selecting.
- Editing skills.
- Developing memory for detail.

Personalise your learning style

She says she's experimenting with her learning style.

You probably found that using general categories like these excluded some of your individual learning attributes. Invent a style that sums up just *you*.

- Consider whether you prefer to
  - see, hear, speak or sing information
  - work alone or with others
  - have support or be independent
  - receive encouragement and feedback
  - involve physical movement of some kind
  - be at home or on campus
  - have guidance or work things out yourself.
- List your learning strengths.
- List areas you need to develop.
- Then choose a word, phrase, animal or object that best sums up how *you* learn.

You may use one set of learning styles for subjects you like, and another set for those that bore you. If you are open, flexible and creative in trying new approaches, you will develop into a more rounded personality and a more effective learner, and you will have more options and more strategies available to you in the long term.

Adapting your course to suit you

If your course is structured in a way that does not already match your learning preferences, you can 'adapt' it through the way you choose to study.

Example 1

If you prefer to work with others, organise a study group, or arrange to work with a friend. Work in libraries and get involved in student activities.

Example 2

If you like to work to your own agenda, focus on time management so that your time feels like your own. Look for articles that nobody else is likely to use. Find examples that others may not think of.

Example 3

If you prefer to work by ear, tape lectures and read extracts from books onto tape, listen to them on the bus, record your own ideas onto tape, form a support group so that you can learn through discussion.

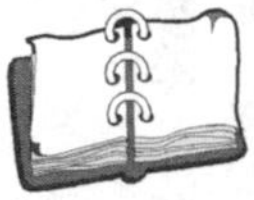

In your journal, note ways you could organise your approach to the course, to suit your own learning style better. Try this exercise later in the year, and compare your results and comments.

© Stella Cottrell 1999, *The Study Skills Handbook*, Macmillan Press Ltd

Reflective learning

As a student in Higher Education, you are responsible for your own progress – for your development as an autonomous learner. Although you will receive formal assessment (marks, grades and comments) from lecturers, it is important not to be dependent upon the assessment and views of other people. You benefit from being able work out for yourself, through a process of analysis and reflection, what you do well, what you need to improve, and your priorities. You started work on this process in Chapter 2.

Developing the habit of reflection

Your performance as a student is likely to improve if you develop a habit of putting time aside to reflect on how you learn. You will find that you study more effectively if you consider such things as:

- your motivation
- changes in your attitude and ideas
- the appropriateness of your current study strategies to the tasks you are undertaking
- which skills you need for different kinds of assignment
- what is blocking your learning
- any gaps there are in your knowledge or your skills audit.

Five methods of developing reflection

1. Keep a learning journal (page 57).
2. Use the self-evaluation questionnaires.
3. Keep an updated profile or portfolio (page 33).
4. Make constructive use of feedback from tutors (page 182).
5. Fill in progress sheets regularly (page 56).

Evaluating your own progress

Questionnaires and checklists

- Use these as starting points to focus your thinking about your learning.
- Select a few points from each questionnaire to consider in your journal.

Be fair to yourself

When you decide that you are 'good' or 'bad' at something, consider your *reasons* for thinking that. What criteria are you using to assess yourself? Work out what is involved in the task, breaking it into smaller tasks or sub-skills. Are you better at some parts than others? What makes some parts more difficult than others?

People may easily underestimate themselves when:

- they have been out of formal education for a few years
- they learn more about a subject (the more we know, the more we are aware of what we don't know).

Monitor your performance

- Photocopy the empty questionnaires and fill them in again later in the term. Compare answers, looking for progress.
- Read through your journal regularly. Comment on your progress.

SELF-EVALUATION

How well am I doing?

Course, unit or module:	Date:
Level:	Year of study:
1a Generally, how well am I doing in this unit?	**1b** On what am I basing this self-evaluation? (my marks? feedback from tutors? self-monitoring? other ways?)
2a In this unit, I am best at: What makes me better at these aspects?	**2b** On what am I basing this self-evaluation?
3a To do better in this unit, I need to improve: What prevents me from doing as well at present?	**3b** How will I bring about this improvement? My timescale for this improvement is:
4a What have I learnt, or improved, already since starting this unit?	**4b** How do I know this? How do I measure or monitor what I have learnt? (How long it takes? My level of confidence? My understanding? My level of enjoyment?)

© Stella Cottrell 1999, *The Study Skills Handbook*, Macmillan Press Ltd

Reflective learning journals

Find a strong notebook that you like the feel of and start a reflective learning journal.

Start a reflective learning journal now!

Why?

- The act of writing things down helps you to clarify your thoughts and emotions, to work out strategies, and to focus on your development and progress.
- A written record will help you see how you are progressing from week to week and from term to term.

Who is it for?

For yourself – to help you focus on your own development.

What do you write?

Anything which helps *you* to reflect on:

- your feelings about the course, the lecturers, other students, your progress
- things you find difficult: challenges
- changes in your attitude or motivation
- how you tackle tasks – your strategies
- things you find out about yourself
- thoughts about how you learn best
- ideas that arise from your studies
- how different areas of study link up
- how your studies relate to real life.

Use the 'How well am I doing?' sheet (page 56) to prompt ideas. Identify the criteria you are using to assess yourself.

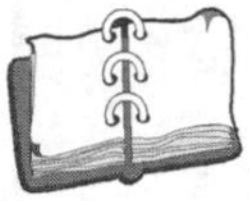

This sign is used in the guide at points where it may be useful to stop, think, and write in your journal.

'... I can't believe the difference between my first essay (very bad!!!) and this one. Keeping an ideas book has helped.'

'I used to read the hardest books first – to be a 'real' student. Now I look for a simple overview first.'

'Why am I always late? I think it's because I always try to get somewhere on time, whereas I should think about getting there 5 minutes early – then I might be on time!'

Other uses of reflective learning journals

As a basis for discussion

You might like to discuss your journal entries with other students on your course. How does their experience of the course compare with your own? Have they worked out strategies which might help you?

Preparing for tutorials

Go through the journal and make a list of issues that you want to discuss in your next tutorial. Put these in order of priority. If you have any problems, think through some possible options, so that the discussion with your tutor will be more focused.

Risky writing

Keeping a journal helps to develop your writing. You can experiment with different styles if you want to. You can take risks. The journal is for *your* benefit – and for your eyes only. This may make a welcome change from writing to the demands of your course or tutors!

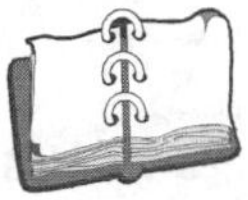

Start now

How do you feel about starting your course? What challenges do you anticipate? How can you use your experiences to help you to meet these challenges? (See Chapter 2.)

Virtue versus effectiveness

Studying hard is not the same as working efficiently. Consider the table below which shows the study strategies of one student, Leila. Leila feels she should get good marks because she works very hard. She studies 50 hours a week, and gets all her work done by the deadline.

Can you see why Leila's marks are getting worse, even though she is working harder? Note your thoughts in your journal.

Leila's study strategies	
Leila feels virtuous ...	**... Yet her study strategy is inefficient**
1 She reads every book on the reading list.	● The same information is repeated in several books. She does not select from one book to another.
2 She reads every book from cover to cover.	● Not all of the book is equally relevant. She does not use a reading strategy (see pages 110–12).
3 She writes very detailed notes.	● She has more information than she needs. ● Her notes are repetitive and take a long time to read. ● She doesn't think much about what she is noting down. ● It takes her a long time to find things in her notes. ● She has to rewrite her notes to revise from them. ● She copies large sections – and copies these into her own work – which loses her marks.
4 She writes her notes neatly, and in full sentences.	● Using abbreviations would save time. ● As long as she can read her notes and find information easily, they do not need to be neat
5 She works long hours with few breaks.	● She gets tired and cannot think as clearly. ● She gets bored and loses interest easily. ● Her mind wanders and she forgets what she has read. ● Sometimes she takes notes without realising she has done so – with no idea what they say.
6 She locks herself away to work solidly.	● She misses out on other people's opinions, suggestions and perspectives.

Virtuous or effective?

Activity

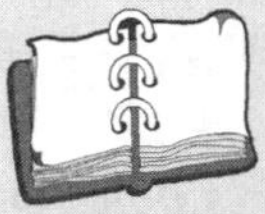

Do you think the following examples are 'virtuous' or 'effective' or neither?

Write V for virtuous
E for effective
N for neither

1. Linking new information to what you already know or have studied.
2. Learning difficult information 'off by heart'.
3. Copying chunks from textbooks – because the writer says it better than you could.
4. Questioning whether what you have heard is really true or representative.
5. Writing fast so that you can take down almost everything the lecturer says.
6. Reading your essays and other writing slowly and out loud before you hand it in.

Start tasks early …

- You only need a piece of paper and a pencil to get started. Don't wait until you have all your books, or tidied your desk (excuses to put off getting started).
- If you don't feel like studying, give yourself permission to study for only ten minutes. Quickly jot down questions to focus your ideas; write a list of things you need to do, etc. Attend to the 'excuses' afterwards – if you still want to. You will probably find you are 'hooked' into the study and want to keep going.
- Get your mind working on a problem as soon as you can. Your mind continues working on the problem even when you go on to do something else. This is why it pays to start looking at new assignments as soon as you receive them.

Answers to activity

1. *Effective* This helps you to understand and remember your subject.
2. *Virtuous* Whether or not it is effective depends on what you are learning and why. You may need to learn formulas, equations, names and dates by heart. For written text, however, this is an ineffective method. (See Chapter 10.)
3. *Neither* You are expected to show that you understand your material and can write it in your own words. Even your notes should be in your own words: this also helps you to avoid plagiarism (see page 122).
4. *Effective* You need to develop your knowledge and understanding by asking questions.
5. *Neither* This is an ineffective strategy. You need to note the main points in your own words. You will also end up with more notes than you need and have to spend time editing them. (See Chapter 6.)
6. *Effective* Reading out loud helps you spot mistakes which you need to correct.

PLANNER

Effective learning

Ineffective approaches

Do you:

- feel guilty if you are not working?
- feel you are cheating if you don't read a book from cover to cover?
- worry if you cannot remember every detail of what you have learnt?
- worry that other people have taken far more notes than you?

Instead, work out a strategy for learning in the most effective way.

Examples of ineffective learning

Your learning is likely to be ineffective if you:

1. work when you are too tired to concentrate
2. listen or read without questioning and challenging what you hear or read
3. sit down to study but let your mind wander to other matters
4. learn things off by heart without really understanding them
5. don't ask for help when you need it
6. don't make connections between what you learn in different subject areas
7. don't relate your studies to real life.

Jot down any other examples you can think of. Which ones apply to you?

Consider this 10-point 'effective learning' checklist

1	☐	Do I need to be more reflective and aware in relation to my study habits?	*See pages 55–7, 86.*
2	☐	Am I in touch with my reasons for study? Do I need more motivation?	*See pages 81–5.*
3	☐	Are there anxieties and concerns I need to sort out first?	*See pages 14–17.*
4	☐	Am I being too virtuous rather than effective?	*See pages 58–9.*
5	☐	Am I working to my preferred learning style?	*See pages 52–4.*
6	☐	Are my time and space organised effectively?	*See pages 61–73.*
7	☐	Am I aware of my priorities for developing my study skills?	*See pages 27–9.*
8	☐	Am I in the best frame of mind for study?	*See page 61.*
9	☐	Is my learning active enough?	*See pages 77–9.*
10	☐	Do I need more support from others?	*See pages 89, 99.*

© Stella Cottrell 1999, *The Study Skills Handbook*, Macmillan Press Ltd

Settling down to study

Effective study depends on having your state of mind, space, time, and materials organised in the ways that best suit your learning.

Creating a state of mind for study

For many people, it is quite difficult to get into a study mood. Everyone has their own particular distracters: endless cups of coffee, chats on the phone, another pint, more laundry, watching TV – anything rather than settling down to study. Many people need to use 'triggers' to start a study session.

Give yourself study triggers

One student clears his desk each time he finishes studying: his study trigger is a clear, inviting surface. Another student has a 'ritual' of switching on the computer, bringing in a glass of water and then opening her books at the appropriate pages before she feels she is ready to begin. Another begins by making a coffee while standing in the kitchen, brainstorming ideas onto paper. He feels he has already started to study before he sits down.

What actions or thoughts could trigger *you* into a study mode? If you don't know, make some up and try them out until you find the ones that suit you.

Create the right environment

What kind of study environment suits you best for different stages of the study process? Make a conscious note of what it is that enables you to begin study: is there quiet or music or background noise? Do you need to be at home or in a library or with friends? Do you need a clear table? What else is needed?

Use your distractions to help you study

Study on the move

If your distractions involve movement (such as going to the shop or housework), spend ten minutes browsing a chapter or going over notes first. Then give in to your distraction task if you still want to – but go over what you have just read as you do it. For example, rehearse information in your head as you walk or cook. See how much you remember. Plan what you will do next, or try to solve a study problem in your head as you move.

This can be especially helpful if your mind goes blank when you sit down to study. Some people learn better 'on the move'.

Deprive yourself of study

Begin by allowing yourself only ten minutes to study – maybe standing. Then do something else, but keep thinking about what you have just studied in that ten minutes. For example, consider whether you agree with what you have read. Has the author or lecturer given enough evidence to prove the case? As your ideas develop, jot them down.

If you come to a standstill or can't remember something, take a brief look – a mere moment or two, to refresh your memory – and then continue with the painting or ironing, and with your mental recall and study. Keep pen and paper nearby.

Use distractions as resources

If you tend to ring your friends as a distraction, ask them to help you focus on your work. Tell them to ask you about the assignment or use them as a sounding board. Set time limits for calls.

Connect to your motivation

See pages 80–5.

When, how and where?

If you are finding it difficult to start a piece of work, it may be because you have not established the right conditions for study.

For each of the five aspects below, work out which conditions suit you best for starting and completing a piece of work. For example, do you know what kind of task you do best early in the morning or late at night? Do you know the best time and place for you to redraft a piece of writing? Or read difficult texts?

Experiment until you find which times and places suit you best for different types of task. Note these down. Whenever you find you cannot settle down to a piece of work, check this page and your own notes.

Organise your time, space and mind for study

For each of the five areas below write at least one suggestion of some change you could make now to improve your studying.

Am I doing this for myself?

- ☑ Am I clear about my motivation for doing this course?
- ☐ Have I thought about how to make this more interesting for myself?
- ☐ Have I thought about how to make this study as enjoyable as possible?

Are my expectations realistic?

- ☐ Am I taking things step by step?
- ☐ Am I setting myself manageable goals?
- ☐ Am I rewarding myself for meeting goals and for other achievements?
- ☐ Am I taking breaks, eating, relaxing and sleeping?
- ☐ Am I selecting particular aspects of my study for improvement today (and leaving others for another time)?

Am I in the right place?

Where do I work well?

- ☐ Do I have a good surface to write on?
- ☐ Do I feel comfortable?
- ☐ Do I have good light and ventilation?
- ☐ Do I have the equipment I need?
- ☐ Am I likely to be uninterrupted?

Am I working at the right time?

- ☐ Do I work productively at this time of day?
- ☐ Is this the best time for this activity?
- ☐ Am I completing tasks in order of priority?

Am I aware of my distractions?

- ☐ Do I know my excuses for putting off getting started ('First, I just need to ...')?
  1 ....
  2 ....
  3 ....
- ☐ Do I know my weak points for getting distracted (e.g. cups of tea, 'quick' phone calls, chatting)?
  1 ....
  2 ....
  3 ....
- ☐ Am I taking steps to prevent such distractions?
- ☐ Do I use distractions creatively?

© Stella Cottrell 1999, *The Study Skills Handbook*, Macmillan Press Ltd

Organising space for study

Dedicated study space

Create a separate space for study where you can leave things and come back to them. If you don't have access to a desk or table, use a shelf or cupboard to keep all your study things together.

Light and comfort

It is good to work near a window, so that you have adequate light. Sitting with the window behind or to one side will cut down on distractions. A reading lamp and natural daylight bulbs are a good investment if you study in the evening.

Make the study area a pleasant one to come back to – preferably with a comfortable chair, so that it encourages you to return to study. As far as possible, keep surfaces clear and papers organised. This not only makes it easier to find things, but is relaxing for study.

Study tools

You will probably need:

- A4 lined, punched paper
- an A4 ringbinder for each subject – use different colours
- lots of file dividers
- plastic 'envelopes' (for files)
- a smaller folder to carry your day's work – use file dividers to separate the contents by subject
- an attractive notebook for your reflective journal
- a diary – preferably with 'a week to view'
- a dictionary and a thesaurus
- an address book in which to note spellings alphabetically
- a calculator, perhaps
- essential books
- large sheets of paper or wallpaper (or backs of posters) for wallcharts
- *lots* of coloured pencils, felt-tips, pens and highlighters, plus a ruler, correction fluid, glue, etc.

Note: make sure you know which of the books on your reading list you are expected to buy.

A computer?

Consider this carefully.

- Do you really need one? Will college facilities do?
- Does it need to be compatible with university software? If so, what specifications are recommended?
- Do you need any special software?

Filing notes

- See page 116.
- Ensure you file notes every few days.
- Cut-out cereal boxes make good holders for spare sheets and articles.
- Label everything!

Managing your time

As only part of your week and year will be formally timetabled, you will be responsible for organising most of your study time. This can be challenging when there are commitments such as work, family, and friends to fit in.

Organise your time

To manage time well, it helps to do the following:

- be aware of your own time management
- be aware of how much time it takes you to complete each type of study task
- be aware that many aspects of study take much longer than expected
- schedule time for unforeseen events
- schedule time for relaxation and leisure
- be very specific in your time-planning.

How well do I manage my time now?

	yes	no
Do I usually turn up on time?	☐	☐
Do I keep most appointments?	☐	☐
Do I manage to fit in most of the things that I need to do?	☐	☐
Do I find I often have to rush things at the last minute?	☐	☐
Do I meet deadlines?	☐	☐
Have I any time for myself and to relax?	☐	☐

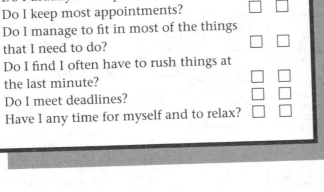

What do your answers to these questions suggest about how well you manage your time now? Do you need to change any of your attitudes to time in order to manage your studies well?

Improving time management

If your time management needs further improvement, you could:

- check the ***Ten time-saving suggestions*** (page 67)
- complete a ***Study time*** record sheet, so that you know exactly how you spend your time (page 68)
- do the ***Where does the time go?*** exercise (page 69)
- use the ***Time management*** sheet (page 71)
- use the ***Priority organiser*** (page 72)
- use the ***Working backwards from deadlines*** planner (page 73).

Set your priorities

You may find that you have more things to do than there is time to complete. If so, it will help you to think through what your priorities are, either for the day, or the week, or the year. The ***Priority organiser*** (page 72) and the following checklist may help you to sort out what to do and when to do it.

Priority-setting checklist

Have you:

- ☐ written a list of everything you have to do?
- ☐ underlined essential tasks in one colour, and items that can wait in another colour?
- ☐ identified the most urgent item on the list?
- ☐ worked out the best order in which to do things?
- ☐ worked out how long you can spend on each?
- ☐ entered each essential task into your timetable and diary?

Effective diary-keeping

A 'week-to view' diary for the academic year is ideal. Fill in all the important dates for the year, such as family holidays, medical appointments, and study activities. Include everything you do.

What to put in about your study

To be effective, your diary needs to be a *complete* record of what you have to do:

- write in all study deadlines, exam dates, field trips, etc.
- write in exactly where, and with whom, each appointment or lecture is.
- add in very specific study tasks, such as 'Read Chapters 2–4 of *Book Title*'.
- schedule some free time to be used in catching up on what got missed.

Map into the diary the times when you will:

- think about the subject
- prepare for lectures and seminars
- prepare for other formal sessions
- plan your work
- organise and refile your notes
- reflect on your learning
- discuss work with others
- research each subject
- write early drafts
- edit and redraft your writing
- check your work.

Allow some time for emergencies and unforeseen events.

How to use the diary

The diary will be effective only if you keep it up to date and *use* it:

- carry your diary with you at all times
- check it several times a day, especially at night and first thing in the morning
- add new appointments straight into it
- write inessential appointments in pencil, so you can make changes easily
- organise entries so you can see at a glance which time is filled – to make sure you cannot double-book yourself
- use the diary's year-planner.

Colour codes and symbols

Use colours and symbols to indicate different activities and subjects in your diary. If you use colour and symbols consistently, you will find after a while that you don't need to 'read' the entries: you will be able to see at a glance what is there. Use a positive or energising symbol for activities you dislike.

Examples of symbols you could devise

Diary entries

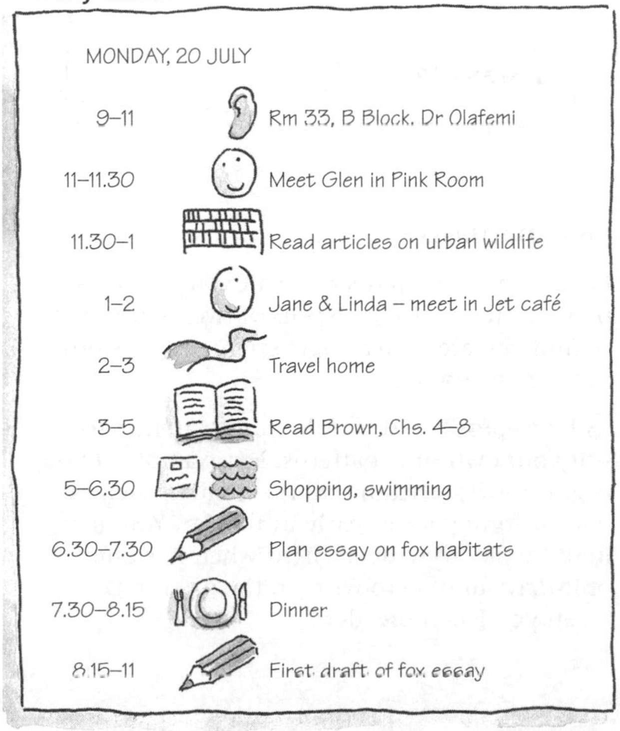

MONDAY, 20 JULY
9–11
Rm 33, B Block, Dr Olafemi
11–11.30
Meet Glen in Pink Room
11.30–1
Read articles on urban wildlife
1–2
Jane & Linda – meet in Jet café
2–3
Travel home
3–5
Read Brown, Chs. 4–8
5–6.30
Shopping, swimming
6.30–7.30
Plan essay on fox habitats
7.30–8.15
Dinner
8.15–11
First draft of fox essay

Diary lists

- Write a fresh list of things to do on a piece of paper or Post-it® label.
- Divide the list into 'Today' and 'Soon' (so you are aware of what you need to do long-term).
- Write items under headings so they are easy to see: 'Study', 'Home', 'Other' (or whatever headings suit you).
- Star or highlight the essential items.
- Attach or paperclip the list to the page opposite the current page of the diary.
- Cross out all completed items so you are clear what is left to do.

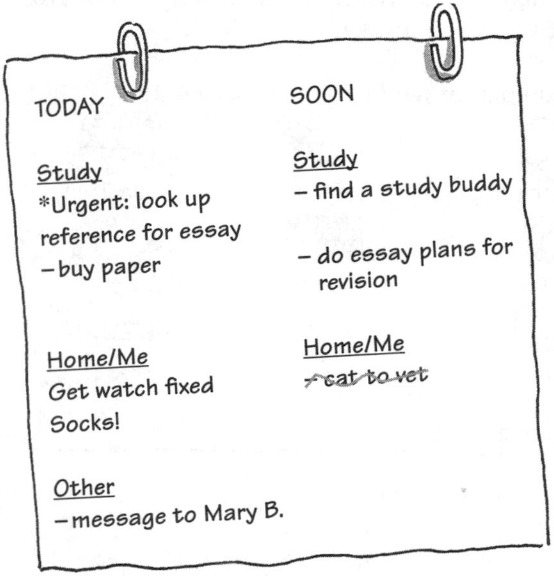

Time patterns

Look for time patterns that suit you. You may prefer to work in short spells of twenty minutes, or find you are increasingly engrossed by study as the day progresses.

As far as possible, schedule study activities to suit your own time patterns. For example, if you begin slowly, schedule short activities, such as brainstorming ideas, early in the day. You may find it easier to write at night when it is quiet – or it may suit you to write in the mornings when you feel more alert.

Give yourself manageable short-term goals

Mini-goals

Set yourself mini-goals, so that you have a sense of achievement.

- Break larger assignments, such as writing a report, into smaller tasks: 'Read course notes', 'Find resource materials', etc.
- Break each of *these* sections into smaller tasks: 'Make notes on pp. 20–40 of *Business Management*'.
- Set a realistic time allowance for each mini-goal: 'Make notes on pages 25–45: 20 mins.'
- Give yourself a start time – and stick to it!
- Set a target end-time. However, if you have not finished, keep going until you have.
- The important thing is not how long you spend studying, but to *complete* each mini-goal.

Mini-goals work best when they are:

- *integrated:* clearly linked to a larger plan, such as your essay, project or your overall motivation for the course
- *manageable and realistic:* set yourself achievable goals
- *specific:* so you know precisely what you are going to tackle
- *measurable:* such as a set number of pages to read, or a report section to write.
- *flexible:* plan 'empty' spaces into your timetable for emergencies, and be prepared to change things round if necessary.

Ten time-saving suggestions

1 Save rewriting notes, and find more quickly what you have written

- Write on ready-punched filepaper. (It can be moved more easily between files, and rearranged as needs arise.) Notebooks are much less convenient.
- When taking notes, write each major point on a different sheet. Then, when you are writing essays or reports, you can shuffle pages as necessary. Make sure each page is adequately headed so that you can put it back in the right file afterwards.

2 Save time writing notes

- Avoid writing notes in full sentences – use headings and keywords.
- Don't rewrite notes 'in neat'.
- Leave lots of space so you can add details later.
- Don't write the same information twice – if two writers make the same point, note in the margin a cross-reference to your earlier notes.

3 Save time looking for notes

- Keep them all in one place.
- File them as you go along.
- Number your pages, and label or colour-code them by subject in the top outer corner, so that you can arrange and find information easily.
- Note where the information came from.
- Keep an (updated) guide to your files.

4 Save time reading

- Use 'smart reading' strategies (***Am I smart reader?***, page 110).
- Read only what is relevant to this essay or assignment.
- If something looks interesting for the future but is not relevant now, fill out an index card recording what looked worth reading.

5 Save time in writing and looking up your references

- In the margin of your notes, write the page reference from the book.
- For every book, article, etc. that you read, complete an index card (page 125).
- Alternatively, keep an updated file of your references on the computer – you will probably use some for more than one assignment. Some word-processing packages have a card-index facility.

6 Use word limits to focus your energies

- You need to research less, read less, note less, and write less for a 1500-word essay than a 3000-word essay. If you don't spend *less* time preparing and writing, you will take *extra* time later, reducing your notes and cutting text to meet the word limit.
- Map out your work to match the word limit (page 150).

7 Save time thinking

- Always carry a small book in which you can record ideas as they occur to you.
- Try 'brainstorming' to get your mind working.

8 Save time organising information

- Use numbers and highlighter pens to group information written on different pages, rather than writing it all out again.
- In the early stages of pattern notes, use small Post-it® labels so that you can shuffle ideas around.

9 Save time writing

- Write assignments directly onto the word-processor.

10 Avoid duplicating effort

- Find a study partner to share research tasks and tactics, and to bounce ideas off.

RECORD SHEET

Study time

Use a photocopy of this sheet for each study period until you are happy with how you use your time.

Column 1 (fill out during study)	Column 2 (fill out after study)
Date: Where: Time I am starting: Study conditions:	Were the conditions, time and place the best possible? Could I improve anything?
How long am I going to study for altogether?	How long did I study for?
How many breaks do I intend to take? Times of breaks (approx.)? Length of breaks?	When did I take breaks? Did I stick to the break time? If not, what do I need to do to get back to study?
Interruptions that occurred Type of interruption Length 1 2 3 4 5 Time finished: Total time worked:	How could I prevent these interruptions? Actual time spent really studying:
Thoughts and observations about my studying	

© Stella Cottrell 1999, *The Study Skills Handbook*, Macmillan Press Ltd

Where does the time go?

If you are not sure where your time goes, for a few days pencil into your diary everything you do – roughly every hour. Be as accurate as you can – nobody will see this except you!

Work out approximately how many hours each day you spend on sleep, exercise, lectures, etc. Make two photocopies of the ***Time circle*** (page 70), which is divided into a 24-hour day.

Circle 1: How I use time now

Using different colours or symbols for each type of activity, mark in where your time usually goes in a day. Treat each segment as roughly one hour.

Which activities are left out or don't receive enough time? Which activities take up too much time?

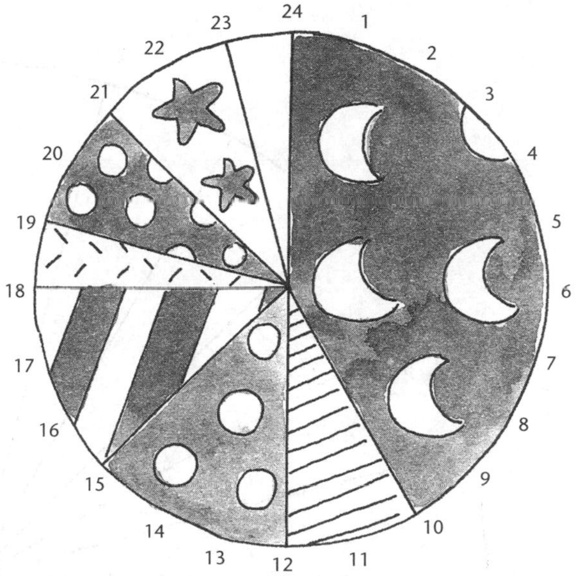

Example

- *sleep – 10 hr*
- *eating – 2 hr*
- *socialising – 3 hr*
- *personal/home – 3 hr*
- *travel – 1 hr*
- *lectures, seminars, tutorials – 2 hr*
- *reading – 2 hr*
- *writing – 1 hr*
- *thinking – 0 hr*
- *exercise/relaxation – 0 hr*

Circle 2: How I want to use my time

On the second circle divide the day into how you would *prefer* to use your time so that your day is balanced between different activities. This is your goal to work towards.

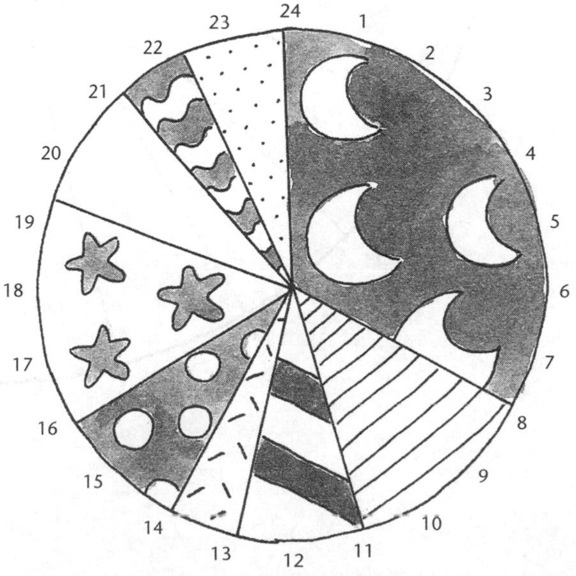

Example

- *sleep – 8 hr*
- *eating and socialising – 3 hr*
- *personal/home – 2 hr*
- *travel – 1 hr*
- *lectures, seminars, tutorials – 2 hr*
- *reading – 3½ hr*
- *writing – 2 hr*
- *thinking – 1 hr*
- *exercise/relaxation – 1½ hr*

Time circle

Date:

Highlight one heading:

How I use time now *or* **How I want to use my time**

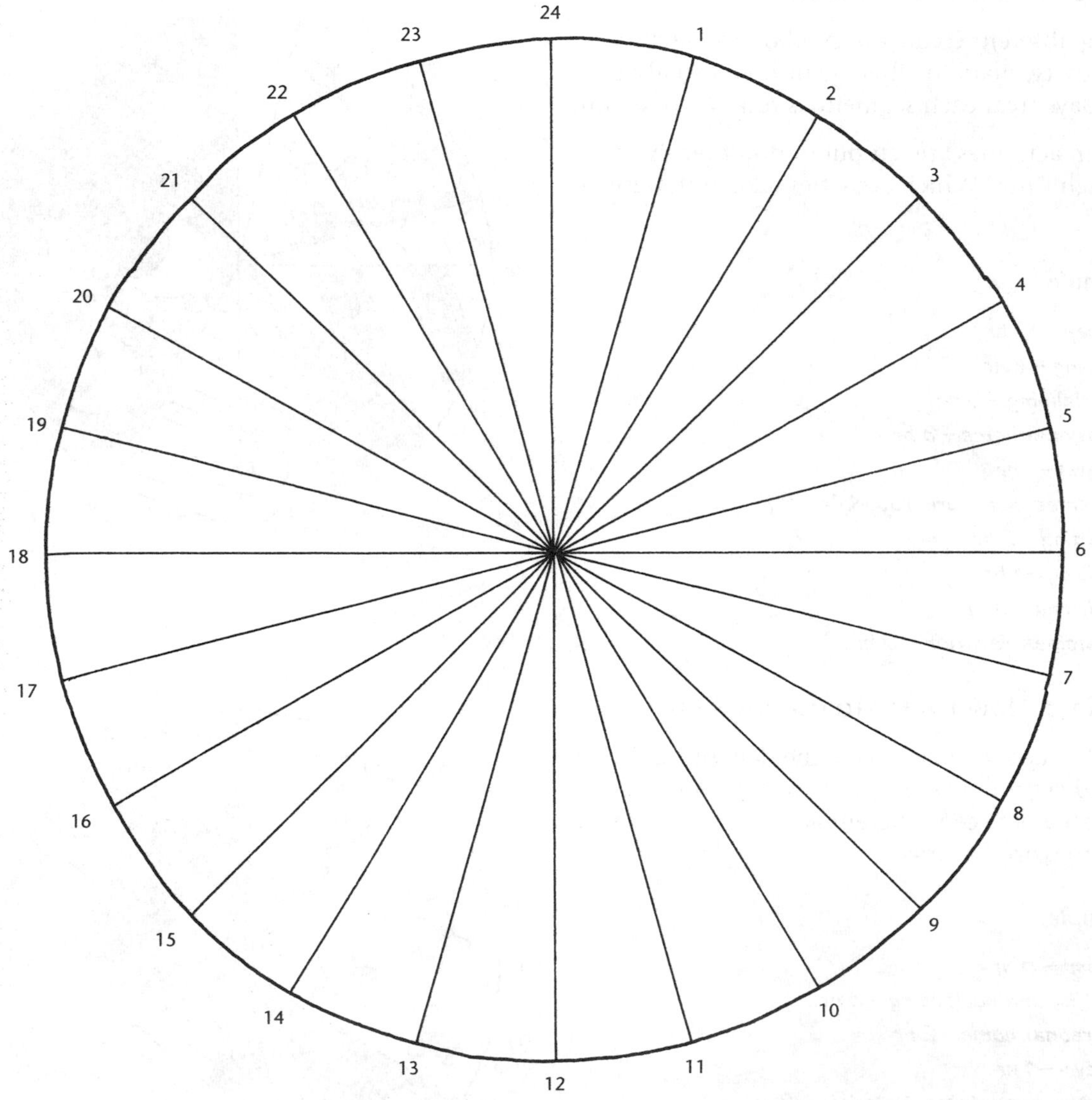

 © Stella Cottrell 1999, *The Study Skills Handbook*, Macmillan Press Ltd

Time management

	Analysis: How well do I spend my time?	Strategy: What I will do to improve?
1 Do I use time efficiently? How do I waste time?		
2 What or who distracts me from study?		
3 Do I need to plan out my time: – for the year? – the term? – the week? – the day? – each piece of work?		
4 Do I waste time getting started?		
5 Do I make the most of spare moments?		
6 Do I find time passes and I don't know what has happened? (See 'Active learning', pages 77–9.)		

© Stella Cottrell 1999, *The Study Skills Handbook*, Macmillan Press Ltd

Priority organiser

If you have difficulties in setting priorities, try using or adapting this sheet.

- *Column A* Rate how important is it to do this at all. (6 = unimportant; 10 = essential.)
- *Column B* If this is to be done at all, how important is it that you do it soon? (1 = must be done at once; 5 = it can wait.)
- *Column C* Subtract the score in column B from column A. The highest scores in column C are the most likely to be priorities.
- *Column D* Number the order for completing the tasks, and the time or date to do each.
- Highlight in yellow the thing you will do next. When it is complete, highlight it in red.

List of things to do	**A** **need to do** **(scale 6–10)**	**B** **do now** **(scale 1–5)**	**C** **(A–B)**	**D** **order of** **priority/when**

© Stella Cottrell 1999, *The Study Skills Handbook*, Macmillan Press Ltd

Working backwards from deadlines

	How long will it take?	When will I do it?	How long it actually took*
Preliminaries			
● Early brainstorming, reflection and discussion with others	______	______	______
● Working out what is required	______	______	______
Research			
● Working out which research methods to use	______	______	______
● Working out what information/data I need	______	______	______
● Assembling information (to read, watch videos, gather data, experiment, etc.)	______	______	______
● Digesting and reflecting on the information collected	______	______	______
Organising the content			
● Grouping and organising information	______	______	______
● Selecting what to include	______	______	______
Writing draft versions			
● Thinking about and improving each draft	______	______	______
● Writing each draft	______	______	______
● Likely number of drafts	__ *expected*		__ *actual*
Completing the task			
● Writing up the references	______	______	______
● Writing the final draft	______	______	______
● Checking through the work	______	______	______
● Final deadline	______	______	______

* *Use this information in planning your next assignment*

© Stella Cottrell 1999, *The Study Skills Handbook*, Macmillan Press Ltd

Using computers for effective study

Why bother with computers?

Presentation

You can present your work to make a better impression, using headings, tables and other tools (page 163). Computers can also spell-check your work, number pages, and count words.

Drafting

You will probably write several drafts of each piece of writing. Computers allow you to edit easily, to move, delete or add text, and to correct errors without having to rewrite the whole text for each draft. This saves time, and allows you to experiment more when writing.

IT skills

Increasingly, IT skills are required by tutors and employers. For example, you may be asked to word-process your work, send your essay by e-mail, or find information on the Internet.

Handling data

You can use databases and spreadsheets to sort information quickly, to calculate long lines of figures, and to do complex statistics quickly.

Storage and mobility

IT enables you to store large files of information on small disks. This makes it easy for you to store information and carry it around.

Almost anybody can use IT

There's no need to be left behind by the IT revolution!

- You don't have to type well.
- You don't need specialist computer knowledge.
- Training and advice is available at most universities or local colleges.
- There are computer adaptations to match most disability requirements.

Information technology can help you

To store information

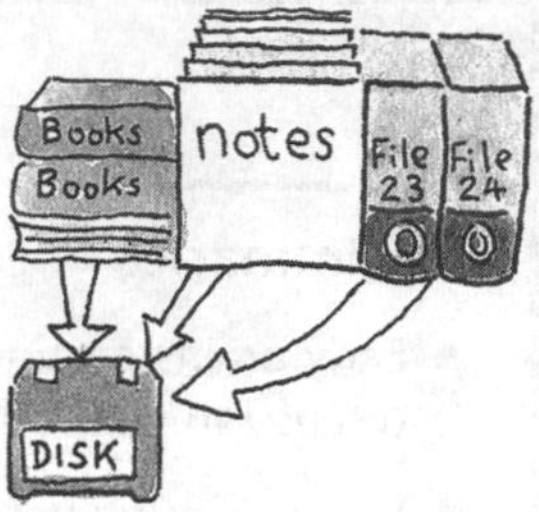

To sort information

a	→	b
Michael		Ade
Aleesha		Aleesha
Siobhan		Joanne
Joanne		Michael
Rashida		Neeta
Ade		Rashida
Neeta		Siobhan

To do other tasks

You can also use IT:

- to move text around
- to edit writing
- to use statistics
- to use tables
- to count words
- to check spellings
- to store references
- to calculate
- to organise data
- to use electronic mail
- to research on the Internet

... and much more.

The chapters that follow include further information about using IT for study.

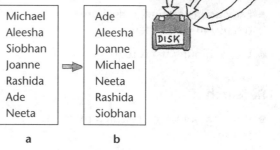

Organisational skills for studying on the computer

The most challenging aspects of working on a computer are:

- keeping track of where information is filed
- losing information, if something goes wrong
- computer faults of one kind or another, which may eat into your time.

The following suggestions can help to organise your work, avoid frustration, and save time in the long term.

Name a new file as soon as you open it

It is not unusual for people to save a piece of writing without giving the file a name. They may then think the computer has gone wrong when they cannot find the document.

Choose filenames carefully

- Use a name that reminds you of the contents of the file.
- Observe the rules for the computer you are using. For example, on many computers you are unwise to put a dot (.) in the filename as the computer may misinterpret following letters and make it hard for you to find the file.

Put the filename in the 'footer' text

As soon as you have named your file, type its name in the running text at the foot of each page, so that it will appear on the document when you print it out. If you need to find a file several months later, you are unlikely to remember which file relates to the paper document unless you have put the filename in the footer. If you make several drafts of a document, make sure you know which is the latest version.

In the footer, record details of where the file is stored. (On many computers the location would include the name of the 'directory', and perhaps a 'sub-directory' too. If you have used a floppy disk, you could include the disk's name as well.)

Example

Suppose that you are using a personal computer (PC) running the DOS operating system. You have saved the third draft of an essay on Piaget for cognitive psychology in a directory called 'cogpsych', on a disk you use for all cognitive psychology essays. The footer might then say:

piaget1c.doc / dir cogpsych / disk cognitive psychology

(On such a computer system '.doc' indicates that the file uses Word, a word-processing package.)

Keep files small

It can take a long time to move up and down a large document on screen, so it may help to divide your material into smaller files. Use filenames that indicate the sequence (for example, 'piaget2.doc' and 'piaget3.doc').

Use a different file for each draft

Add a number or letter to indicate to yourself that this is the second draft. (For example, you could use 'piaget1b.doc' for the second draft of the first part of a long essay on Piaget.)

Save your work every few minutes

If the computer goes wrong for some reason, such as a temporary loss of power, you may lose all the work you have done since the last time you told it to 'save'. To protect your work, save your file frequently. (You may be able to set the computer to save the file automatically, such as every ten minutes.)

From time to time, copy the file to a floppy disk as well. Losing information and having to start all over again is very frustrating.

Organise your disks

- Save files regularly to floppy disk.
- Name your disks.
- Write the names of important files on the disk

label. Keep a list of the files on the disk on an index card with that disk.

- Use a different disk for each subject.
- Keep your disks in a clean, dry box.

Make directories

Most computers have some way of grouping files, so that you can keep files relating to a particular subject together. (In DOS this facility is called the 'file manager', and files are grouped in 'directories'.) This is like keeping related papers in separate files, and organising the files in drawers of a filing cabinet: it keeps things together and enables you to find what you want more quickly. Below is a description of how files are stored on the computer.

Make hard copies

A 'hard copy' is a printout of a document. If there is a problem with the computer or a disk, the hard copy allows you to see what was in the file whilst waiting for the problem to be fixed. Printed text is easier to proof-read than text on the screen.

Keep a list of filenames

Print out a list of files on each disk and keep this near the computer. You may find it helpful to add a few words saying what each file holds, especially if you are limited to a short filename which cannot tell you very much about the file. (Opening files repeatedly to check what they contain wastes time.)

Compatibility

If you are working at home, check whether your software is compatible with the university's.

Other ways of using computers for effective study are included within the following chapters.

How information is stored on computers

Information is stored on computers in a way that is designed to appear to the user like sets of Russian dolls, or drawers inside filing cabinets.

Files

A file typically consists of one essay, or one report, some notes, or a shopping list. One essay or report per file is ideal.

Disks

Files, individually and in groups, may be stored on the 'hard disk' within the computer. They may also be copied onto floppy disks so that they can be transported to a different computer, and to provide back-up in case of computer breakdown.

This diagram shows typical file organisation on three separate disks.

Floppy disk name	Directory (folder)	Sub-directory (folder)	Filename
1 Psychology	Psychology	Cognitive	methods.doc concepts.doc memory.doc *etc.*
	Psychology	Social	early year.doc Piaget.doc *etc.*
2 History	History	Essays	Henry8.doc Elizab1.doc Suliman1.doc *etc.*
3 Family	Family	Letters	mother.doc Gina.doc *etc.*
		Pets	cat vet.doc dog vet.doc *etc.*

Active learning

Why is it important to develop the habit of active learning techniques?

1 Look at the illustrations on page 78.
2 Look at the characteristics of both passive and active learning, summarised in the chart below.

From these, you should be able to see for yourself why active learning methods make success more likely.

> What initial reflections and ideas do you have about whether your study habits are passive or active?

Characteristics of passive learning	Characteristics of active learning
1 You wait for directions and information to be fed to you.	**1** You look for ways of being more involved in what you are learning.
2 Information is delivered to you – you just follow what is said or written, and do as you are told.	**2** You are engaged in the whole learning process (and in a position to see why information has been selected).
3 Different pieces of information are treated as separate units.	**3** You look for links between different things that you discover.
4 You repeat information without understanding.	**4** You make a conscious effort to make sense of, and find meaning in, what you learn. Understanding is usually deeper.
5 You don't reflect upon what you have learnt.	**5** You are involved in reflection and self-evaluation.
6 You may become bored and tired easily.	**6** Your attention span is longer because your mind is more fully engaged.
7 You use surface processing (page 45), in which case you are less likely to understand or remember.	**7** Long-term memory is assisted. If you understand what you learn, and keep relating what you learn to what you already know, you are more likely to remember what you have learnt.
8 You are less likely to be able to use what you learn.	**8** Linking information helps you to see how you can apply it to different situations.
9 What you study may seem irrelevant.	**9** Learning is personalised and interesting.

Emphasis on action!

Consider the illustration below and the ideas on page 79. Jot down any ideas you have about making yourself a more active learner.

Inactive learning strategies

A1

A2

A3

A4

A5

Active learning strategies

B1 Prepare for lectures

B6 Mull things over

B2 Set yourself questions

B7 Organise information

B3 Rework your notes

B8 Draft and redraft work

B4 Link ideas and information

B9 Evaluate your own work

B5 Discuss with others

B10 Use feedback constructively

Active learning strategies

1 Put a tick by any of these active learning strategies you could try.
2 Select *two* to try this week.
3 Select two more to try later this month.

- ☐ Summarise a passage in 8–12 words. This makes you think about what you have read.
- ☐ Make spider diagrams – or other patterned notes. (See page 118.)
- ☐ Think of 3–5 real-life examples of what you have learned. This helps you to apply what you learn.
- ☐ Work out which is the best example, and why. This will help you to prioritise and evaluate.
- ☐ List 50 mini-questions about one aspect of the subject ('what, why, who, where, when, how did *x* happen?'). This helps you to explore the subject.
- ☐ Answer your own mini-questions. This helps you to research in an organised and focused way.
- ☐ Draw a diagram or a cartoon to illustrate a theory or concept.
- ☐ Write action plans – of things to do today, or this week or this term.
- ☐ 'Teach' what you have learned to a real or an imaginary person. Imagine you are giving a lecture or instructions.
- ☐ Keep a reflective study journal.
- ☐ Sum up the three most important points of a lecture. Which is the *one* most important point? This helps you to evaluate and select salient points.
- ☐ Make a wallchart or a large plan, linking all you have learned about an aspect of your studies.
- ☐ On your wallchart, in a different coloured ink, link information from another area of your studies.
- ☐ Which is the one best book for the subject you are studying now?
- ☐ Which section of the book you are reading is the most interesting or useful?
- ☐ Pretend you disagree with everything you are reading – how would you argue your case? What examples and evidence would you use?
- ☐ How does what you have learned connect to your work or your everyday life?
- ☐ Invent titles for essays or reports. Give yourself 5 minutes to write a quick outline plan for one of these.
- ☐ List all the key points for one aspect of study.
- ☐ Draw a simple picture or symbol to remind you of each aspect.
- ☐ Discuss your ideas – or your difficulties – with other people.
- ☐ Write key points on index cards or Post-it® labels. Juggle these around to see how many ways you could organise the same information.

© Stella Cottrell 1999, *The Study Skills Handbook*, Macmillan Press Ltd

Motivated learning

Motivation and goal-setting

Your level of motivation will affect your success, especially in slow or difficult patches. It is likely that there will be times when you get bored, frustrated or anxious. You may feel as though you cannot be bothered with a piece of work, or that you are struggling with your studies. You may even feel like giving up altogether. You will need clear motivation to keep yourself going even through such tough times.

Strengthen your motivation

Reflect upon your reasons for pursuing this course of study. Use the two questionnaires (pages 81 and 82) to help focus your thinking. Photocopy them so you can redo the exercise later and compare responses.

For each questionnaire, decide which are the *two* most important factors for you.

> Jot down your thoughts about why these are important to you.

If study becomes a struggle, look back over your answers to boost your motivation.

The peaks are calling me
Victory!

Keep setting yourself new goals and challenges

Set goals

Make tasks more manageable by breaking them down into mini-goals (see page 66). Set yourself small, short-term goals so that you are able to have lots of small successes. In time these add up to greater achievements.

Celebrate successes

Set targets and deadlines which are easy to meet – increase your chances of success. When you achieve a short-term goal (such as two hours' reading), reward yourself (for example, by taking a half-hour's break).

Give yourself bigger rewards for completing whole tasks, to encourage yourself next time.

Mark success

Note down your achievements and successes in your reflective journal – it is important to identify what you do well, so that you can do it again!

After a few months, look back on your early work. Give yourself credit for any improvements you have made.

Aim for higher peaks

When you have met one set of goals, push yourself a bit harder. Make your next set of goals a little more challenging.

Find support

Find someone who encourages you and makes you feel good about yourself. Talk to this person about your goals and ambitions.

Attitude

Attitude is very important. Try to think of *difficulties* as *challenges*. If there is something you have to learn which seems threatening, consider the ways in which it can also be an opportunity to do something new.

> Which aspects of being a student appear like 'threats' or 'problems' to you at the moment? How could these be seen as challenges and opportunities?

Reasons for study

You are more likely to succeed in your study goals if you have a clear sense of purpose. It is useful, at the beginning of your course, to consider all the reasons you may have for undertaking this course of study.

To help clarify your ideas, here are some of the reasons *other* people give. How many of them apply to you?

Reason for study	Very true	True	Not relevant	Untrue	Definitely untrue
I want to have the qualification					
It will help me to get a good job					
The subject will be useful in my job					
I want to prove something to myself					
I want to show my family/friends that I can do it					
I want to experience university life					
I'm bored and need a challenge					
I always wanted the opportunity to study					
I enjoy learning new things					
I missed out on education when I was younger					
I want to get more out of life					
Reasons of your own:					

Choose one or two of the reasons which you feel strongly about. Write down why these are so important to you.

© Stella Cottrell 1999, *The Study Skills Handbook*, Macmillan Press Ltd

What do I aim to achieve at university?

What are the outcomes you hope to achieve through studying at university? These may not be the same as your reasons for studying (page 81). Draw a ring round the number that indicates how important each potential outcome is to you.

Outcome	Less important								Very important
Personal development									
To prove something to myself	1	2	3	4	5	6	7	8	9
To acquire more self-confidence	1	2	3	4	5	6	7	8	9
To broaden my horizons	1	2	3	4	5	6	7	8	9
To get my life out of a rut	1	2	3	4	5	6	7	8	9
To experience university life	1	2	3	4	5	6	7	8	9
Course-related									
To gain a Higher Education qualification	1	2	3	4	5	6	7	8	9
To learn more about a subject that interests me	1	2	3	4	5	6	7	8	9
To have the opportunity to study	1	2	3	4	5	6	7	8	9
To get a good grade	1	2	3	4	5	6	7	8	9
I just want to get through	1	2	3	4	5	6	7	8	9
Work-related									
To improve my career opportunities	1	2	3	4	5	6	7	8	9
To be better at my current job/employment	1	2	3	4	5	6	7	8	9
To improve my chance of promotion/higher salary	1	2	3	4	5	6	7	8	9
Other outcomes									
To show my family/friends that I can do it	1	2	3	4	5	6	7	8	9
To make up for having missed out on education when I was younger	1	2	3	4	5	6	7	8	9
To make new friends with similar interests	1	2	3	4	5	6	7	8	9

Select two outcomes you have decided are important to you. Write in more detail about what you aim to achieve.

Look back at this from time to time to see if your aims, and motivation for studying, are changing. Use pages 83–5 to explore your desired outcomes further.

© Stella Cottrell 1999, *The Study Skills Handbook*, Macmillan Press Ltd

Using desired outcomes to guide study strategy

Your reasons for studying and your desired outcomes can guide the way you proceed with your study, as in the following examples.

Outcome A: to learn about the subject

If learning about the subject is the most important outcome for you, then reading around the subject and doing what interests you may be more important than following the curriculum.

Outcome B: to have a good grade

If your chief priority is getting a good grade, then it is likely to be important that you 'play the game' and find out exactly what is required.

Outcome C: just to get through

If you have many other demands on your time, or gaps in your education, you may have to limit yourself to covering essentials. What is important is that you know how to find and use information to get you through – you can fill gaps in your knowledge later in life.

Stating your desired outcomes

Outcomes are most motivating when stated in the present:

> I am able to achieve a 2.1!

It is also best to state them as positive objectives:

> I am able to gain a good job.

(Negatively formed outcomes, such as 'A degree will help me to escape from my current employment', are less effective in providing motivation.)

> **The effect of thinking negatively**
>
> Having a negative outcome is like going shopping with a list of what you are not going to buy.
>
> O'Connor and McDermott (1996)

Analyse desired outcomes in detail

The following questions are based on an approach known as Neuro-Linguistic Programming (NLP). For each desired outcome, go through the following questions and the resource sheet on page 85.

Are your desired outcomes 'well-formed' ?

- Are the desired outcomes clear and specific?
- Are they at all limiting?
- Do they help you?
- Are they realistic?
- Are they sufficiently motivating?
- Are the outcomes worth it?
- Are they really desirable?
- How will you know you have achieved the outcomes – what will be different?

What are the implications of having these desired outcomes?

- Will you need to put everything else on hold?
- Will you have to change your study options?
- Who else will be affected?
- Other implications?

What are the potential gains?

- Will you feel more in control of your life?
- Will you have more respect for yourself?
- Other potential gains?

What are the potential losses?

- Will you see less of family and friends?
- What sacrifices are involved?
- Other potential losses?

Visualise yourself in the future, having achieved the outcome

- Where are you as a result of your achievement?
- Are there any good or bad consequences?
- What has changed for you?
- Are you as happy as you thought you would be?

What will you do to achieve the outcomes?

Visualise or consider exactly what you will do and when. For example, for an assignment, see the time laid out in your diary; watch yourself doing the required study. Ask yourself:

- Where am I?
- What am I writing on?
- What have I got to drink or eat?

What obstacles might prevent you achieving the outcomes?

Look at problems in advance.

- What could stop you achieving your desired outcomes?
- Have you set yourself too much to do?
- Are there people who would suffer?
- Who might try to stop you?

What other obstacles might there be?

- How will you overcome each of these obstacles? Visualise yourself overcoming obstacles in the same way you did above, in relation to 'achieving the outcomes'.

Fine-tune your outcomes

Keep modifying your outcomes until you have goals that feel, sound and look right for you.

- Use the chart on page 85 to clarify and focus your thinking about each of your desired outcomes.
- Do you need to revise or reword the original outcomes so that they are more realistic and motivating?

Self-sabotage

It can be hard to accept that we may *achieve* our desired study outcomes. Many people have set patterns that they use in their daily life to sabotage their own best-laid plans.

It is not clear exactly why this happens. Sometimes it is simply hard to accept that we might now be successful where once we struggled. If we do succeed, we may start to feel that we should have tried harder in the past. If we fail now, however, this will 'prove' that we were 'right all along' in believing that we could not do something. At other times, we may fear failure so much that we just want it to happen quickly so that it is over with: waiting to see whether we can succeed may be too difficult.

> **Make a clear mental plan**
>
> Create in advance the mental plan for as much of an activity as you can. Your mind will now orientate you to achieve it.

Kinds of self-sabotage

Students sabotage their studies in all kinds of ways. Examples include:

- not turning up to lectures
- leaving work until the last minute and then missing deadlines
- not turning up for exams because they feel they will fail them
- filling their time with any activity *except* study
- refusing to enter a library
- spending all their time in the bar.

There are many more to choose from!

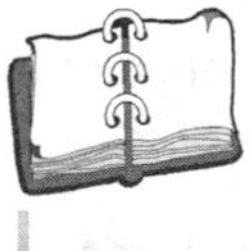

- What kind of self-sabotage are you most like to engage in?
- What kinds of events are most likely to trigger you into self-sabotage?
- How could you recognise that you had started to sabotage your studies?
- Is there anybody whom you would trust to point this out to you?
- What would you do to turn this around?

Achieving desired outcomes

Desired outcome *State this with positive wording, in the present tense*	
Potential gains 	
Potential losses 	
How I'll recognise when the outcomes have been achieved 	
Targets (sub-goals) 	
Possible obstacles 	
Steps to overcoming obstacles 	
How I'll celebrate success 	

The C·R·E·A·M strategy

C·R·E·A·M strategy	How I will incorporate this strategy into my study
Giving more freedom to my imagination	
Finding ways to increase my enjoyment in study	
Personalising what I learn, and the way I study it	
Being flexible in study strategies and having plenty of variety	
Reflecting on my learning, and evaluating my progress	
Organising time and space, and being in the right state of mind for study	
Seeing where I waste effort by being over-virtuous	
Linking learning in one subject to other subjects, and to real-life issues	
Increasing my motivation	
Formulating clear outcomes and sub-goals	

© Stella Cottrell 1999, *The Study Skills Handbook*, Macmillan Press Ltd

Review

Chapter 4 develops themes presented in Chapter 2 on reflection and general approaches to study. It encourages you to consider successful study as something which can be:

- personalised: through particular strategies, your learning preferences, your desired outcomes and your own motivations for study
- individual and varied
- creative, fun and enjoyable
- active and dynamic.

You will also have gained an insight into many ways in which you can study more effectively, through:

- your attitude to learning
- your organisation of space
- an awareness of your time, such that you plan and monitor how you use it
- the optimum use of a computer for study.

The C·R·E·A·M strategy is a general principle or 'meta-strategy' which encourages you to consider your own attitudes and motivation, and to apply strategy to any area of study. It encourages you to look for options and to identify for yourself how you could study more easily and successfully.

It is an open-ended strategy which you can adapt for yourself. How successful you are depends on your own creativity, your powers of self-observation and reflection, your personal effectiveness, your readiness to be actively involved in your learning process, and your level of motivation.

Chapter 5

Working with others

LEARNING OUTCOMES

This chapter offers you opportunities to:

- become aware of some of the advantages of working with others
- develop your communication skills
- develop confidence in participating in discussion groups and seminars
- understand what can make a group work
- develop strategies for making a confident oral presentation
- learn to assess your own performance in groups, seminars and presentations
- become aware of how prejudice can disrupt learning, and of ways to deal with it.

The benefits of working with others

Most courses schedule groupwork of one kind or another because they value the additional learning which takes place.

Contexts

Some of the contexts in which you may be required to work with others include:

- seminars
- group projects
- mentor schemes
- work placements
- discussion groups
- support groups
- lab groups
- art 'crit' groups.

The format of these will vary, but there are basic principles and skills common to many different group contexts. These are addressed in this chapter.

Working co-operatively

Working co-operatively creates opportunities to:

- share ideas – so each of you has more ideas
- gain extra perspectives and points of view, which otherwise you might not have considered
- tap into a wider pool of experience, background knowledge and styles of work
- stimulate each other's thinking

- clarify your own thinking through talking and through answering questions
- gain others' assistance in remaining focused on the main point – freeing you up to explore a thought
- learn to deal with challenge and criticism
- realise there are more dimensions and answers to a question than you can discover on your own.

Ways of working with others

Supportively

Talk through your difficulties and concerns – others may feel the same way. Help each other to find solutions.

Encouragingly

Let others know what they do well. Ask their opinions. If you appreciated a particular contribution or found it helpful, tell them!

Collaboratively

Give each other suggestions about the best things to read for an assignment. Talk about what you have to read. Share strategies for coping with work, children, money, projects.

Divide different aspects of your study between you: for example, you could each check a different library or organisation for information, or you could be guinea pigs for each other's project questionnaires.

Co-operatively

Go through your lecture notes together and see if you picked out different points. Photocopy essays once they have been marked and read each other's. What differences do you notice?

With constructive criticism

If you disagree with another person's ideas and if the issue needs to be addressed, then phrase your suggestions in a positive way. Suggest ways forward for improvement, rather than criticising what is wrong, or was wrong in the past.

Hazards to watch out for

Beware of copying

All completed pieces of written work must be in your own words – so be careful that you don't appear to be copying other people – nor they copying you.

Share work fairly

If you share tasks out, make sure it is on a fair basis. Consider what is fair in the circumstances, and what to do if someone really cannot do what they agreed to do.

Encourage others, but look after yourself

Encourage other people if they are feeling discouraged – but avoid being drawn into anybody else's depression or negativity.

Planning to prevent difficulties

If you are going to work with somebody else over a period of time, it can be helpful to think through what you hope to gain from working together, and what hazards may arise. You could each write down your reflections under three headings.

1. Advantages
2. Potential difficulties
3. Ways we could deal with these difficulties

Go through all the advantages together to encourage you to proceed.

Consider each potential difficulty and brainstorm ideas for ways of dealing with it. Be creative in looking for strategies. If you are truly stuck, speak to another friend, a tutor or a student counsellor.

Talking and listening skills

Good communication is a two-way process. It requires both good listening skills and participation in the discussion.

Do you talk *to* people, or *at* people, or *with* people?

- People who talk *at* you are listening to themselves. They leave no space for a response.
- People who talk *with* you are keen for you to join in.
- People who talk *to* you consider you, and your response, carefully.

Non-verbal communication

We indicate to other people how well we are listening through our verbal responses, and also through non-verbal communication, such as:

How well do you listen?

- Ask someone to watch you while you are listening in a group.
- Ask for comments about your non-verbal signals to various group members.
- Are you surprised at this feedback?
- Do you come across to others in the way you imagined?
- If not, what would you like to change?

In your journal, consider how well you listen to others. Do you:

- take in what other people say?
- give other people room to speak?
- let other people finish before you start?
- use encouraging non-verbal signals?
- 'switch off' when bored or if you dislike the person?

Could you do anything differently to put others more at ease when they are speaking?

Which non-verbal communication are you sensitive to? What do *you* find encouraging? What do you find *discouraging*?

Better listening

Try to tune in to speakers. Some of these techniques may help:

- consider the speakers' feelings
- find ways of encouraging them
- focus on the content – think of some way this could be of value to you
- listen for key words and jot them down
- think of a question you could ask (when they have finished speaking)
- link what they are saying to something you already know
- find one positive comment you could contribute.

Making your point

Speaking in a group

If you are anxious at the idea of speaking out in a group, the following may help.

Before the group

- Make a decision to speak at least once during the group – even if it is only to hear yourself say 'yes' out loud. Build up from a small base.
- Get to know other group members, if possible, so that you feel more at ease.

During the group

- Sit next to somebody you find reassuring.
- Write down what you want to say – if necessary, read it out.
- Think of an example, or evidence, or an illustration to support your point.
- If you are nervous, breathe out slightly more slowly than usual.
- Take your time when speaking – aim to speak more slowly than you feel necessary.
- Make eye contact with at least one person in your audience.
- Be brief. When you have made your point – *stop*. Avoid going back over what you have already said.
- Be clear. If something sounds confused, say 'I'll make that clearer', or check people have understood.
- Speak up so everyone can hear. If people have to strain to hear you, they will be less sympathetic to what you are saying – and you may have to say it all over again.
- Act as though confident, even if you don't feel it.
- Don't apologise – smile!

After the group

- Congratulate yourself on any progress.
- Keep any mistakes or stumbling in proportion – it is not the end of the world.
- Decide what you will do next time.

Being judged by your voice

Many people feel self-conscious about the way they speak, or about their accent. If you feel anxious about your voice, remember:

- your voice is an important part of you – everybody has an accent, and no accent is better than any other
- your voice, or accent, is less important than your ideas and opinions
- other people may be just as self-conscious about the way they speak
- concentrate on getting your message across and making sense, rather than on pronunciation
- there are many successful people with all kinds of accents.

Group sabotage

It is quite easy to sabotage a group. Often this happens unintentionally, because people are nervous or worry about being judged by others.

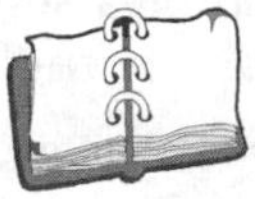

How might you sabotage a group unintentionally – for example, by being late, not preparing, whispering or chatting? What could you do differently?

Making the group work

Although there are many benefits to working in groups, being part of a group is not necessarily easy. Dealing with the challenge of the group develops a range of skills.

The following guidelines are helpful for seminars and group work.

Create a supportive group atmosphere

Remember that people have feelings

Be aware that people are often anxious that they will be criticised or found wanting. Be constructive in your comments and aim to be kind, rather than scoring points.

Address anxieties directly

In the first session, brainstorm how everybody in the group feels about being in it. What were their concerns before arriving? Did other people feel the same way? It helps to know that you are not the only person who has concerns.

Discuss how the group could turn worries into opportunities.

Make ground rules

This is especially important if you are forming your own support or project group. Ground rules should address the anxieties raised above. Include:

- the time you will meet
- what to do if someone dominates or does not pull their weight
- what kinds of behaviour or comments are unacceptable.

Investigate group strengths

Brainstorm the range of skills and experience in the group. Who prefers to do art work, run meetings, write? Be clear and speak out about what *you* would like to do. If several people want to do the same thing, rotate roles or share tasks out. Include all group members.

Create an effective group environment

Set clear agendas and boundaries

Be clear about the purpose of the group and each meeting.

- Set an agenda for group meetings and decide how long to spend on each item.
- Be clear which meetings are for work and which for socialising – and stick to this.
- Arrange meeting times and venues well in advance, so that everyone can attend them.

Check progress

If the group does not seem to be working well, address this directly. Each person in turn should say what they feel could be done to improve things, including assessing what they personally could do differently.

- Does the group need to bond more through a social activity, or by meeting earlier to socialise?
- Are tasks shared fairly?
- Is somebody dominating the group?
- Are you considerate enough about each other's feelings and ideas?

Try to avoid negative criticism or allocating blame.

Task allocation

- Be clear about who is doing what.
- Ensure that tasks are allocated fairly.
- Set clear deadlines for completion.

Group roles

For each session, decide who will take which role.

Chairperson

Although these are everybody's responsibilities, the chair helps the group to form an agenda and keep to it, ensures that everyone gets to speak and that their views are heard, sums up main points, and keeps the group focused on the task.

Timekeeper

The timekeeper ensures that the group keeps to the agenda and the time schedule. Sometimes he or she will time spoken contributions.

Record-keeper

The record-keeper notes who is going to do what and when, and any other decisions made.

Task manager

The task manager checks, between meetings, that everyone is doing what was agreed.

Being an effective group member

The responsibility for the group lies with each member of it. If a problem arises, even if it seems to be the fault of one person, every member shares responsibility for sorting out the problem so that the group can work.

Get the most out of discussion

Before

- Ensure you have done any tasks agreed for the group.
- Read around the subject. Think about it.
- What questions do you want answered?

During

- Check that everyone can see and hear everyone else.
- Be open to hearing something new.
- Jot down useful information.
- Jot down questions to ask.
- If you don't understand something, ask.
- Link what you hear to what you already know.
- Make contributions – for example, raise points that interest you.

After

- Go over your notes and summarise them. Add any new details and thoughts.
- Check that you know exactly when you will do activities arising out of the group. Are they in your diary?

Help the group to succeed

Be encouraging
Encourage others. For instance, you might say, 'I found it interesting that …'.

Include everyone
Speak to everyone in the group, not just particular individuals. Make sure that everybody has a chance to speak.

Use 'body language'
As you listen, show your attention by smiling, by nodding agreement, and so on. If you want to speak, make clear signals.

Listen to other students
Your fellow students deserve your respectful attention as much as does your tutor – just as you deserve theirs.

Indicate when you agree
Express your agreement: 'So do I …'; 'Yes, that's true …'.

If you disagree
Instead of just rejecting the other person's ideas, explore them: 'What makes you think that?'; 'Have you thought about …?'

Help the flow

- Contribute to the discussion – but don't dominate it.
- Ask questions – but not too many.
- Take responsibility: don't leave everything to one person.
- Encourage the group to keep to the subject.

Admit mistakes
Acknowledge your errors, and apologise: 'Sorry, my mistake.'; 'Oh, I see! I misunderstood …'

Make suggestions
Share your ideas: 'Why don't we …?'

Build on other people's ideas
'That's an important point you made, for several reasons. …'

Offer information
Share your knowledge: 'There's some useful information on that in …'.

Sum up for the group
'Well, have we agreed on these two points so far? First, … ? And second, …?'

Dealing with difficult moments in the group

Strong emotions in a group

When strong emotions are expressed, people may feel nervous – yet these emotions are often honest expressions of what someone is feeling.

Emotions arising from strong opinions

A strong attack on somebody's views can be distressing; people often identify themselves with their own opinions. If you reject the *opinion*, the *person* may feel rejected. The group may need a ground rule that *opinions* can be challenged, but not the person who holds them.

Emotions arising from group problems

If the emotion arises out of the group not working properly, then address how the working of the group could be improved.

For example, it might be that some people feel their views are ignored. What would make them feel they were being heard? Would that be realistic? Can a compromise be found?

Emotions arising from outside the group

People bring into any group events or emotions from everyday life. This can be disrupting, as it is not clear where sudden strong emotions are coming from.

It may help to take a minute or two at the start of each session to say what has been going on for group members. You may also need ground rules about strong emotions – such as, 'If one person is aggressive towards another, the rest of the group will intervene.'

Tears

If people are distressed, for whatever reason, let them have a few minutes' quiet or some space to express their emotions. Don't worry about tears – crying can release pent-up stress. Distressed people may need to be alone, or to speak with just one other person quietly for a few minutes. Show kindness.

Silences

Silences often seem longer than they really are. This is because we so rarely experience silence.

Silence can be very productive, however. Sit with it and value it, especially if the group needs to discuss something of weight. Don't feel obliged to fill silences with questions or jokes.

Dead-ends

If silences suggest stagnation or stalemate, try a new approach.

- Think of several different ways to break the task into smaller parts.
- Is there a way of turning the problem on its head?
- Brainstorm crazy ideas – might one work?

Imbalances in group interaction

Group discussions can easily become unbalanced if:

- one or two people dominate
- two people are locked into an exchange
- there are no spaces in which quieter people can get into the discussion.

The chairperson or group members can address these imbalances directly:

- by thanking dominant members for what they have contributed, and reminding them that others may wish to speak
- by asking if anybody who has not spoken would like to
- by pointing out any imbalance so that the group can discuss it and deal with it.

Some contributions – such as updating the group at the start of a session about your day or week – are important, but can drift on too long. Set time limits in such cases.

Group problems can also arise through more serious issues, including discrimination, prejudice and unfairness. These are addressed below.

Prejudice, unfairness and discrimination

Prejudice and unfairness can create stress and ill-health, such that people cannot perform to the best of their abilities. They can also produce tensions and anger, which affect the study of everybody in a group or on a course.

Unfair discrimination, of any kind, should be the concern of *everybody*.

Your experiences of unfair treatment

Most of us have experienced prejudice in some way during our lives. It may have been name-calling, being left out of activities, or bullying. Some such incidents hurt but are soon forgotten. Others cut so deep that they affect us for many years.

Other people's attitudes, especially if combined with restricted opportunities, can make it difficult for a student to achieve his or her full potential. This may have been true, in the past, for many students starting at college now, with you. Their difficulties may have been due to others' racism or sexism, or their attitudes to disability, lesbian and gay people, single parenthood, or other factors.

The atmosphere may become very tense

Challenge 1

Think about an occasion when *you* were treated unfairly, because of somebody else's attitudes. For example, can you recall an occasion when you were blamed for something you did not do, or when people tried to embarrass you for no good reason?

What were your feelings and attitudes then?

Did the incident have any long-term effects – such as on your confidence?

Avoiding unintentional discrimination

Some people set out to hurt others deliberately, but a great deal of discrimination is unintentional, caused by thoughtlessness or awkwardness. Most of us are upset if we realise that we have unintentionally caused distress to somebody else.

Challenge 2

This exercise aims to help you to avoid those moments when you say or do something you know you will regret.

- Think of a group you are in or have been in, or may be in when term begins.
- There are dozens of ways in which some members of a group could discriminate against each other, maybe without anybody realising. What situations can you think of?
- What questions could you ask yourself to monitor whether everybody is being included, or whether prejudice is leading to someone being left out?

When you have completed this exercise, compare your ideas with those on page 96.

Dealing with unfair discrimination

Take responsibility

Sooner or later you may notice that unfair discrimination is taking place, whether against yourself or against other people.

- Find out who has responsibility for equal opportunities or could give you advice, such as a Student Counselling Service.
- Ask the people you think are being discriminated against how they feel. Which course of action would *they* prefer to take – what would *they* wish to happen?
- Make clear what behaviour you find unacceptable.
- Find some support for yourself – other students who agree with you, or a relevant support group or society.

If you witness or are involved in either a serious incident or discrimination over a long period, keep detailed records. Include:

- the time, date and place of each incident
- names of those present and witnesses
- exactly what was said and done.

Be willing to get involved.

- Come forward as a witness.
- Let the people who are being discriminated against know that they have your support.
- Speak out – let other people know you are aware of the harassment or discrimination, and that you don't support it.
- If an issue arises during a tutorial or seminar, ask that it be addressed.
- Make a formal complaint, e.g. through the Student Union or using the college's grievance procedure.

Monitoring what's happening

Ideas from Challenge 2

- Does everybody get a chance to contribute, or do some people (or groups) dominate?
- Is everybody's experience and background included in the way subjects are discussed? Are there assumptions that everybody is heterosexual? or European? or able to get about easily?
- If people have accents, or dialects, or stutters, are they treated with the same respect when they speak?
- When people make comments or ask questions, are they sensitive to the feelings of others – or aware of issues that might cause distress?
- Where does the group meet? Can everybody get there, even in a wheelchair or using a stick?
- Do you know when somebody is trying to lip-read? What might cause interference or pain for someone using a hearing-aid?
- What words or behaviour might other people find offensive?
- Are there people who look left out, or uncomfortable, or angry? Why is this happening?

Coping with unfair discrimination

Some of us know from experience that we are quite likely to meet with some form of discrimination when we meet new people or enter a new situation.

It can be helpful to think through some of the things we fear might happen – and make plans for coping with those situations in case they *do* happen. You may not have the chance to study in Higher Education again: it is important that you have a strategy, where possible, to minimise the effects of other people's prejudices so you can focus on your study.

Look after yourself

Remember: you are right to feel that you should not have to put up with discrimination.

Most universities have an equal opportunities policy, a harassment policy and a grievance procedure, together with staff who have responsibility for enforcing these. The Students' Union may also be able to help if you feel uncomfortable about speaking to college staff in the first instance.

Things you can do

If you feel best when you *do* something:

- See the suggestions under 'Dealing with unfair discrimination' (page 96).
- Make sure you have a strategy for dealing with stress (see page 227).
- Look after your health. Eat and sleep well.
- Try not to think about the stressful episode just before sleeping. Instead, do something that relaxes you – read, have a relaxing bath, listen to music, etc.
- Don't blame yourself.
- Talk to someone you can trust, and who will be able to discuss your options.
- Write down how you feel – acknowledging your feelings may help you to work through them.
- Keep a written record of what has happened, in case you need it as evidence. This gives you something which demonstrates that the discrimination is real. It might also help you to put the episode out of your mind until you can do something constructive about it.

When you experience unfairness or discrimination, what do you usually do?

What kind of personal reaction is most likely to help you as a student, so that you still feel positive about yourself?

Has discrimination prevented you from doing something you wanted to do?

How are you going to prevent that from happening again?

How can you prepare yourself to deal with discriminatory situations?

How well do I contribute to seminars and groups?

Unit/module:	Seminar:

Aim of this evaluation

- To make seminars and groups work more effectively, both for me and for others.
- To ensure that everybody feels included and safe in contributing.
- To ensure that, as a group, we cover the material we need to.

Strategy

- To evaluate my contributions using this chart, discussion and reflection.
- To compare my self-evaluation with a colleague's evaluation of me.
- To use our evaluations to develop a joint strategy for better seminars.

Self-evaluation chart

1 : considerable room for improvement *5 : excellent*

1	Had I done the necessary preparation for the group or seminar?	1	2	3	4	5
2	Did I make contributions during the session?	1	2	3	4	5
3	Did I speak for more than my fair share of the time?	1	2	3	4	5
4	Were my questions and comments relevant to the discussion?	1	2	3	4	5
5	Did I listen to, and consider, points raised by other people?	1	2	3	4	5
6	Was I encouraging to the main presenter or other speakers?	1	2	3	4	5
7	Was I as encouraging as I could have been to the less confident people in the group?	1	2	3	4	5
8	Did I take a full part, or was I shy or withdrawn?	1	2	3	4	5
9	Did I take relevant notes and references?	1	2	3	4	5
10	Did I keep my attention on the session or did I get distracted?	1	2	3	4	5
11	Did I make all my contributions to the group, or were some to my neighbour only?	1	2	3	4	5
12	Am I clear what I have to do for the next seminar/group session?	1	2	3	4	5

© Stella Cottrell 1999, *The Study Skills Handbook*, Macmillan Press Ltd

Other people's evaluation of my contribution to seminars

Discuss your performance with a friend or other group member. Ask this person to tell you three things you do well, and three things you could improve.

> Use the questionnaire (page 98) to stimulate your thinking. How well *do* you contribute? What changes would you like to make? When will you make them?

The functioning of the group

Consider the overall working of the seminar or discussion group.

> Identify three things the group needs to work on as priorities. How will you raise these issues with the group?

Study support networks

Types of support network

Some courses organise a study support group or network. This may be led by a 'mentor' – a student from the year above. If no such group exists, you may like to set one up yourself. You could get together by telephone or e-mail, or meet after class or in somebody's home.

Many of the principles discussed in relation to other groups also apply to study support groups.

What a support group can do

The work of the support group is limited only by your imagination, but the following activities are generally helpful to most students.

Encourage each other

- Arrange to ring each other to encourage work on a particular activity.
- Look for a constructive comment you could make about each group member's progress. Write these out on separate pieces of paper and give them to each other to take home. At home, put your list where you can see it, to encourage yourself.

Review lectures

Review a lecture, clarifying the main points in order. Fill the gaps in your own notes. Each person notes different things, so by sharing information you each end up with a fuller set of lecture notes.

Solve study problems

- Give one person, *A*, five or ten minutes to describe a current study problem, while the rest of the group listen without interrupting.
- As a group, spend ten minutes clarifying the problem. Brainstorm as many ideas as you can for dealing with the problem. Now *A* listens without interrupting.
- Finally, Person *A* has ten minutes to choose an option, decide how and when it will be done, and negotiate support from the group.

Repeat the process for other members of the group. Then, at the next meeting, check that each of you carried out your intentions.

Share background reading

Read different texts around the subject, and summarise the main points for each other. Discuss your ideas about what you read.

Befriend each other

Simply listening to each other can be very helpful – don't underestimate its value.

Making a presentation or giving a talk

What is the purpose of a presentation?

Students are often asked to give presentations. This process is useful because:

- presentations get discussion going
- they produce a variety of perspectives
- some people present themselves better verbally than on paper
- the ability to give presentations is a skill required in many occupations.

How are presentations assessed?

There are many ways of assessing presentations. Find out from your tutors what criteria will be used.

In general, however, the important feature of a presentation is that you have an *audience* – and you need to communicate information to them.

This means that you should be focused in your presentation.

- Make a few main points. Don't swamp the audience with everything you know.
- Select a few concrete examples which are easy for the audience to visualise.
- Structure the talk very clearly, using just a few headings. Know the order in which you are going to make your points.
- Repeat main points, and summarise what you have said. When people take things in by ear they need to be reminded of the direction your talk is taking, and how the major points link up. Use a handout or overhead projector slide, numbering three or four main areas you are going to address.

Preparing your talk

It always takes longer to *say* something than it does to read through it in preparation. Also, you need to speak slowly in a presentation so that people can take in what you say.

- Prepare only what you can deliver at a reasonably slow pace.

The postcard technique

- Break your talk into sections.
- Give each section a heading.
- Write one heading, and a few easily-read prompt words, onto each postcard.
- Number the cards in the order that you want to introduce those points.
- These will give you confidence that you have something to say, and give structure to what you say.

- Divide your material into the *essential* points that you definitely want to make, and *extra* material you can use if there is time.
- Prepare a summary with which to close your talk.

You could type your headings in a large font, such as 32-point, and photocopy them onto acetates for use on an overhead projector. (Library staff can usually help.) Alternatively, you could prepare a large diagram or poster to illustrate your talk.

Practise your talk several times, going slowly and timing yourself. Edit it down if it is too long.

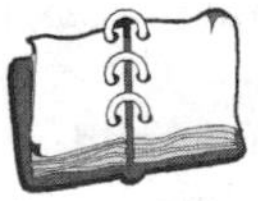

- How confident am I about speaking in groups and making presentations?
- What techniques suggested in this chapter would help me?
- Which three things would be most useful to try out first?

Overcoming nerves

Many people spend so much time worrying about giving a talk that they leave no time to prepare what to say. You can reduce nervousness in the following ways.

- Prepare carefully – be confident about what you are going to say, and how you are going to say it.
- Make a conscious effort to relax (see page 229) – especially 2–3 hours before the talk.
- Arrive early so that you do not need to worry unnecessarily about the journey.
- Be in the room before everybody else. Instead of suddenly being confronted by a sea of faces, it's your space. Smile at your audience as they arrive.
- Have water to drink.

Giving the talk

- Read the section 'Making your point' (page 91).
- Use a clock to time yourself.
- Wait until everybody is settled and quiet before you start speaking.
- Tell the audience whether you would prefer questions at the end or during the talk.
- If possible, speak from your postcards, from a poster or from memory, rather than reading. The talk will flow better and will be easier to listen to. However, if you are unable to give the talk in any other way, write it out in full and read it.
- Remind yourself to speak more slowly and loudly than you would usually.
- Don't apologise for anything you feel could be better. Act as though you are quietly confident that your talk is excellent, and you will be half-way to convincing your listeners.
- Look up. Make eye contact with at least one person in your audience.
- At the beginning, summarise what you are going to say – and in which order.
- Go through your cards in turn. Make each point clearly.
- Pause and take a breath after each point. This gives your audience time to absorb the point. It also makes you look more professional.
- At the end, briefly sum up what you have said.
- Prepare a good line to end with. If you're not sure how to end, simply smile and say 'Thank you'.

SELF-EVALUATION

How effective am I in giving a talk?

Aspects of giving a talk	Rating	How could I improve this aspect?
	low high	
1 Was my main argument clear?	1 2 3 4 5	
2 Did I begin with a brief outline?	1 2 3 4 5	
3 Did I stick to my outline?	1 2 3 4 5	
4 Did I sum up at the end?	1 2 3 4 5	
5 How good was my opening?	1 2 3 4 5	
6 How well did I finish?	1 2 3 4 5	
7 How appropriate were my handouts or audio-visual aids?	1 2 3 4 5	
8 Did I move logically from one point to the next?	1 2 3 4 5	
9 Did I give good examples to support my points?	1 2 3 4 5	
10 Did I answer questions well?	1 2 3 4 5	
11 Did I make eye contact with most of those present?	1 2 3 4 5	
12 Did everybody feel included?	1 2 3 4 5	
13 Did I respect the different viewpoints of those present?	1 2 3 4 5	
What feedback did the audience give me?		

© Stella Cottrell 1999, *The Study Skills Handbook*, Macmillan Press Ltd

Review

It is likely that you will be expected to work with others during your time as a student, whether in seminars, support groups or project groups, and in any case you will find yourself in groups just by being around other students on campus.

If the groups you are in work well, you will gain. You will benefit from different perspectives and views, your own thinking will be stretched and your ideas refined, and you will have a source of support. Whatever groups you are in, it's in your interest to help them function at their best.

Nevertheless, it is quite natural for groups to have problems. For example, they can bring out people's anxieties, some of which may appear as aggression or failure to contribute. In dealing with such difficulties you will develop a wider range of interpersonal and problem-solving skills, which will be useful in work and in life generally.

As in other areas of study, there are strategies which can be applied to specific areas – such as listening to others, getting your point across, working together, and making a presentation. Reflection on, and self-evaluation of, your own contribution is especially important for this area of study.

Overall, it is easier to work with others if it is clear what the boundaries are, what is expected, who is doing what, and when, and if everyone acts with everyday consideration for the feelings of others.

Chapter 6

Research skills

LEARNING OUTCOMES

This chapter offers you opportunities to:

- learn how to undertake general research skills (in addition to any specialist research skills taught on the course)
- become aware of how to find and select the most relevant information from source materials
- develop strategies for adapting your reading flexibly to different contexts
- learn how to make effective notes
- learn what plagiarism is and how to avoid it
- learn how to reference your work
- become aware of how to make effective use of lectures, problem-solving exercises, laboratory work and practicals.

Informed opinions

In Higher Education you will often be told to use your own ideas and express your opinions. This means giving not just 'commonsense' answers but your *informed* opinions, based on knowledge of recent or important texts for your subject area. You are expected to show a deeper understanding of the subject and to use more precise information than the average person in the street.

Identifying the task

Before launching into research for an essay, report or other assignment, make sure you know what is required.

- Read carefully through the assignment guidelines. How many parts are there to the question? What is really being asked of you? (See pages 142–3.)
- What should your work look or sound like when it is finished? (See Chapters 7 and 8.)
- Consider why this particular assignment was set. Is it one that is always set on your course? Or is it topical, related to recent research which has brought the issue into the news? If the latter, make sure you read the relevant recent articles or book.
- Identify the marking criteria. Display them where you can see them.
- How many words are you expected to write? Scale your research to fit your word limit.
- Check how many books or articles you are expected to use. You will not need to read the whole of each book.
- How much time is there to do the research? Break the assignment into parts and set yourself mini-goals with specific deadlines. (See page 66.)

Making the most of the library

There are many more items and facilities than just books in a college library. Visit the library early on and see the range of services available. Typically, there will be:

You did say to make myself at home in the library

- academic journals
- specialist collections
- photocopiers
- laminators
- binding facilities
- computers
- tapes
- slides
- video material
- video-players
- specialist information technology for people with disabilities
- facilities for making audiovisual aids for your presentations
- handouts on how to use library facilities

If the university is split over more than one campus, ask what is available on each and how you can access different facilities.

Catalogues

Catalogues may be on card, microfiche, CD-ROM or computerised. There may also be specialist collections for your subject, as well as indexes for national collections. It is quite usual to need help using these – if you are uncertain, don't be afraid to ask.

Make the library your own

To join the library you will usually need your student number and identity card, so make sure you take these with you.

Walk around the library and become familiar with the atmosphere. Sit at different tables – try different rooms. Where would you work best?

To see how the library works, look up books from your reading list. Try out the technology. It is designed to be easy to use even if you know nothing about computers – have a go!

Find out basic information

- How many items can you take out at once?
- How many items can you take home on loan?
- How long does it take for books to come from the stacks (the store), or from other sites?
- For how long can you have books out?
- Can you reserve books?
- Can you reserve or renew by telephone?
- Are there fines?
- How do you make inter-library loans?
- Are there subject-specialist librarians?

Finding information in the library

Finding books in the library

- Fiction is arranged in alphabetical order by authors' surnames.
- Reference books are arranged by subject. Each subject is given a number, which is shown on the spine of the book.
- All the books on a given subject are together on the shelves.
- You can find a book's reference number by looking it up the in the library catalogue.
- For a computerised catalogue (such as OPAC – the Open Access Public Catalogue), you type in a request and the details appear on-screen. Usually, information and training are available on how to use these.

It helps to find books if you already know:

- the author's surname and initials
- the title of the book.

Journals or periodicals

Journals or periodicals usually contain the latest research for your subject, as well as book reviews. Most journal articles have a short 'abstract' at the beginning which tells you what the articles are about. Browsing through the abstracts and reviews helps to keep you up to date with the subject. You will be expected to refer to articles in most assignments.

Journals are published at regular intervals during the year. They are collected into numbered volumes, usually one for each year. To find a journal article you need to know:

- the title of the journal, the year it was published and its volume number
- the name and initials of the author of the article
- the title of the article.

Indexes and abstracts

Indexes and abstracts are separate publications which give brief details of journal articles, including who wrote what and where to find it. Sometimes reading the abstracts will be sufficient for your assignment; at other times you will need to read the original article also.

In the indexes, you can search by subject heading and by keywords for all the articles on a given subject. They are updated regularly and are well worth using.

Electronic information

An increasing amount of information is being published electronically. This includes anything from mail-order catalogues to academic journals. Electronic information is usually located at an address or site – such as the World Wide Web (www). Your university may have its own intranet, with websites used only within the institution – you may be asked to write your own 'page' on it. Sites used nationally and internationally are on a network such as the Internet.

To locate information on the Internet, you type in the address at which it is stored. This will consist of short abbreviations. Spaces, dots, dashes, oblique strokes and letters must be typed in very precisely. This, for example, is the address of the website of Friends of the Earth:

http://www.foe.co.uk

Having logged on to the Internet, you would simply type this in on the computer screen in the space provided. (You can usually omit 'http://'.)

On your reading list you may be given the name of useful web pages. Type in the address of one and browse the information that comes up on the screen. You can print it out and read or highlight it as printed text.

Making the most of the Internet

The Internet

The Internet had its origin in 1969, when the computers of government, scientific and military bodies were linked. Academic and commercial bodies joined later, and eventually people began to produce information only for the Internet rather than in paper form – there are even novels that are accessible only via the Net.

The Internet connects computers from all over the world, and enables you to communicate by computer directly with people in other countries. There is no owner or central executive for the Internet: it is just a wide, interconnecting set of computers, with some organisations which try to keep it running smoothly.

Advantages of using the Internet

The range of information

Via the Internet you have access to a great deal of information, including:

- newspapers
- government papers
- company data
- magazines
- financial data
- library catalogues.

Types of information

Information on the Internet can include:

- sound – voices and music
- film and video clips
- interactive pages
- computer programs
- virtual-reality pages.

The Net offers you the chance to browse for information across an enormous range of sources without leaving your chair.

Communications

You can send and receive real-time messages from your friends whilst you study, using e-mail. You can also send your essays and assignments to your tutors in the same way, rather than having to deliver them by hand.

When is the best time to use the Internet?

In Britain, it is usually best to use the Internet in the morning. In the afternoon in Britain, it is morning in the USA. When American workers log in, there is much greater demand on Net resources: it can take much longer to access information.

Caution in using the Internet

Is it an authoritative source?

At present there is little editing or censoring of information being sent electronically. Almost anybody can put information on the Net and much of it is of poor quality, from an academic point of view, consisting of chat lines, commercial sites, and advertising. This means it is important that you check for the details of who entered any information you are thinking of using, and consider whether that person is an authoritative source.

When were the data entered?

Information can become out of date very quickly. With books, we are more aware of this: we can see the date of publication and even the appearance of the book may suggest that the information may be old and out of date.

People sometimes assume that if data is accessible on the Net it must be true and up to date. This is far from being the case. For example, an archiving project may have run out of funding for the workers who update information, and the information may since have become out of date, yet the archive may still be accessible on the Net.

Working with the Internet

Getting connected

At most universities, use of the Internet is free.

For home use you need a telephone line, a computer with a recent processor (such as Pentium), and a modem to connect your computer to the telephone. This must carry at least 33,600 bps (bits per second), or using the Net will be slow and costly in phone bills.

Various Internet service providers, such as Microsoft or Compuserve, provide connections to the Net. They charge a fee, but offer a range of services. Choose one with a helpline open in the evenings and at weekends.

Browsers and search tools

Although there is a lot of information on the Internet, it is generally well organised. Software called 'web browsers' helps you to find web pages that interest you.

Internet Explorer

This is Microsoft's web browser. It is free, and easy to use, and there are good manuals.

Yahoo! (at yahoo.com/)

This is a popular search tool. It is a vast directory that covers a wide range of subjects, which are cross-referenced. It is easy to use.

Research-it (at www.iTools.com/research-it/)

This browser is useful for definitions, quotations, maps, language translations, synonyms, and more.

OneLook Dictionaries (at www.onelook.com/)

This checks over 150 dictionaries.

Active channels

Active channels are subscription websites that deliver information in a variety of ways, such as:

- to your own web page
- to your e-mail
- as a screen saver
- to your 'desktop'.

Some websites offer daily updates on news, sports, and other information. You can be informed of updates automatically by e-mail.

Moving around the web

Most web pages have icons, buttons or highlighted text, called links. Clicking on a link takes you to another web page, and there are also 'forward' and 'backward' buttons.

At the start of a search session it is usually simplest to type the address of the first web site, and then click on links to access new sites. This is quicker than typing in lots of addresses.

You can also create permanent pointers to your favourite websites.

Finding what you want

First, use a search tool (such as Yahoo!) to find the *general* topic, such as 'sport'. Then look for the specific topic, such as 'football'. If you're looking for a *specific* person or event, use a search engine such as Alta Vista, Lycos or Excite:

www.altavista.digital.com/
www.lycos.com/
www.excite.co.uk/

Search for keywords that the text is likely to contain. To narrow down the search, look for a *group* of keywords. Be as precise as you can or you may be presented with hundreds of entries.

Useful manuals

If you plan to research via the Internet, it is helpful to use a manual as a starting point. Page 232 lists some manuals which use visual layouts and give clear step-by-step explanations.

Identifying and selecting relevant information

Use the reading list

- Some courses give long reading lists and expect you to select from a range. Others give you a short list and expect you to read everything on it. If in doubt, ask your lecturer what is expected.

Select the latest information

- To keep up to date, look under 'new titles' in bookshops and look for the latest issues of journals on the library shelves or on the computerised catalogue.
- Check whether statistics and similar data are up to date. Are more recent figures available? If so, should you use these?

Select the most relevant information

- Look for the information that relates most exactly to your assignment.
- Draw up a trial essay plan and see what information you will need. Which themes came up in lectures and seminars?
- Check the back cover of the book, the contents list and the index to see what the book covers.
- Quickly scan the introduction or conclusion: these may indicate whether the book is worth reading. They may even provide all the information you need!
- Browse through the headings to get a feel for the book.

Select by reliability

- Is the source a well-known one in the field, such as an academic journal?
- Is the source likely to be biased? If so, does the bias matter in this case?
- Does the text have a good bibliography? Is it clear where any evidence comes from?
- Is the source from a publisher respected in your subject area? (Information in newspapers or from friends is not usually considered reliable.)
- See also 'Critical thinking', Chapter 9.

Select by amount

- Use your essay plan to work out a word limit for each major theme, and then for each topic or example. You will find that you will have very few words to write about any one item.
- Use your word limits to guide you on how much to read and note. If you can only write a line or paragraph about something, you probably don't need to read and note very much.
- Consider whether an article goes into too much depth for your purposes: you may only need to read the abstract or one section.
- Keep asking whether material is relevant to the title of the project, essay, etc.

Reading selectively

If you usually read books from cover to cover, try the following exercise to see how little you could read and still get what you need.

Activity

- Read any information on the back cover. Browse the contents page, section headings, and the last chapter. Make a few quick notes on what seem to be the main points of the book. Record only the gist of what you read.
- Read the introductory and concluding paragraphs of each chapter. When you finish reading, note any extra important information.
- Read the first line of each paragraph. Note any additional important information.
- Now, read the whole book. How much really important *additional* information did you gain by reading the whole book? Which parts of the book were essential? How little could you have read to grasp the essentials?

SELF-EVALUATION

Am I a smart reader?

Do you have strategies for approaching your reading? Which of the following do you do?

Do I know exactly what I'm looking for?

- ☐ Have I considered what questions I'm trying to answer?
- ☐ Have I considered what information I need?

Use reading lists selectively

- ☐ Have I looked at the recommended reading list?
- ☐ Do I know what I *need* to read?

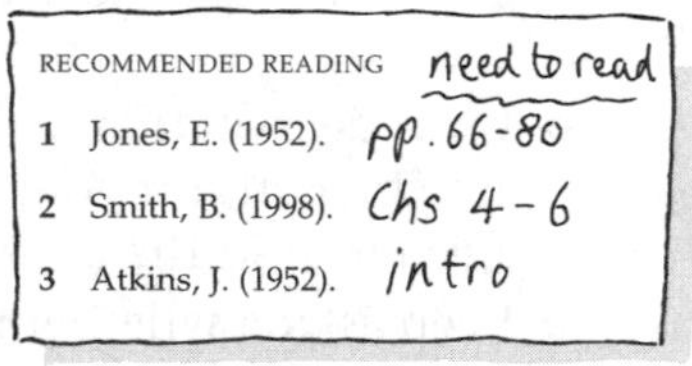

Examine sources for suitability

- ☐ Have I considered each source? Have I considered:
  - whether it's on the reading list?
  - whether it's up to date or fairly recent?
  - whether it looks readable and manageable?
  - whether it has the information I want?

Activity

Practise finding information quickly

Try using an index (at the back of the book).

- Select an item to look up.
- Note the page numbers given.
- Using these, find the item in the book as quickly as you can.

How long did this take you? Could you get faster? Did you notice that when you know what you're looking for, your eyes can pick out information on the page more quickly?

Select relevant parts of the book

- ☐ Do I browse the book quickly?
- ☐ Do I use the contents page, the index, the headings and the sub-headings for guidance?
- ☐ Do I identify which parts of which chapters I need, and put markers in these?

Find information quickly

- ☐ Have I tried using an index?
- ☐ Have I got faster with practice?

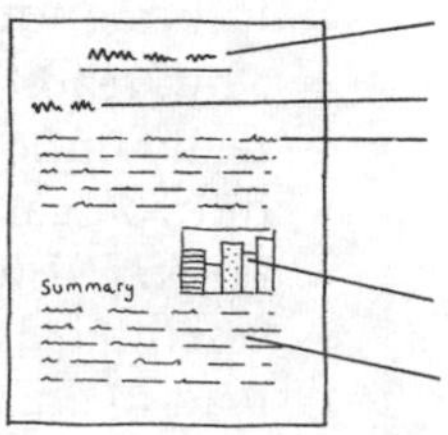

Select relevant parts of the page

- ☐ Do I read the chapter heading?
- ☐ Do I read any sub-headings?
- ☐ Do I read the first sentence of each paragraph (which should introduce the topic or idea)?
- ☐ Do I look at any diagrams, graphs or charts?
- ☐ Do I read any summaries or conclusions?

© Stella Cottrell 1999, *The Study Skills Handbook*, Macmillan Press Ltd

Use photocopies

- ☐ Do I make photocopies of important pages?
- ☐ Do I use marker pens to highlight important words and phrases (only)?
- ☐ Do I jot ideas and thoughts in the margins?
- ☐ Do I make notes about the points I highlighted, to help myself remember them?

> ### Using large photocopies
>
> - For an important diagram or map, make an enlarged photocopy. Attach it to a large poster.
> - As you read, photocopy short key passages.
> - Reduce them in size and attach them to the poster.
> - Link ideas using colour and arrows.
>
> These posters are very useful for revision.

Chart the main ideas

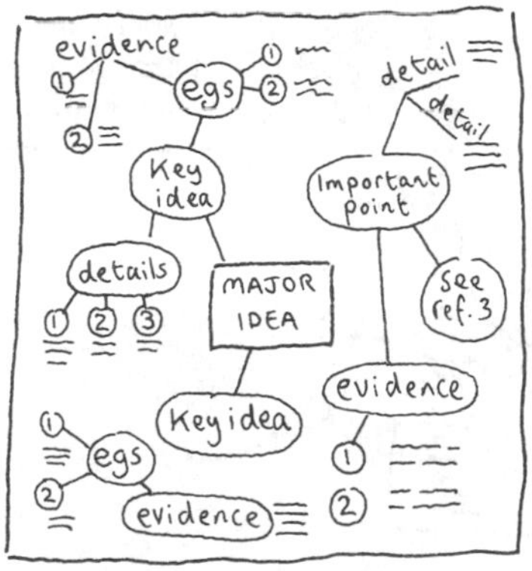

- ☐ Do I map out ideas so that I can see how everything fits together?

Practise second-guessing

- ☐ Do I keep trying to anticipate what is coming next, or what the conclusions will be?

Read interactively

- ☐ Do I think about what I'm reading?
- ☐ Do I question what I'm reading? Do I look for answers to my questions?
- ☐ Do I make notes of the important points, and ideas triggered by what I read?
- ☐ Do I challenge the assumptions of the writer, the logic of the arguments, and the validity of the conclusions?

Vary reading speed and method

- ☐ Do I keep changing the pace, according to the needs of the text? (See page 115.)
- ☐ Do I scan rapidly for specific information?
- ☐ Do I read quickly to get the general sense of a passage, and then read difficult or dense parts slowly?

> ### Engage with your reading
>
> Be active in your reading. As you read, always have paper and pen to hand.

Use markers

- ☐ Do I label a corner of my own texts with a keyword summary?
- ☐ Do I insert labelled bookmarks so that I can find details easily, and need fewer notes?
- ☐ Do I give star ratings to valuable pages, making them easier to find later?

Maintain your attention

I read that three times and I don't remember a word...

- ☐ Do I take in what I read?
- ☐ Do I make sure I'm doing so, by:
  - summing up each section?
  - taking regular breaks?
  - reading interactively?

Listen to yourself read

- ☐ Do I tape-record myself reading important passages?
- ☐ Do I listen to these as I travel, or work around the house?

Using two tape-recorders

- If you have two tape-recorders, speak your ideas into one as you listen with the other.

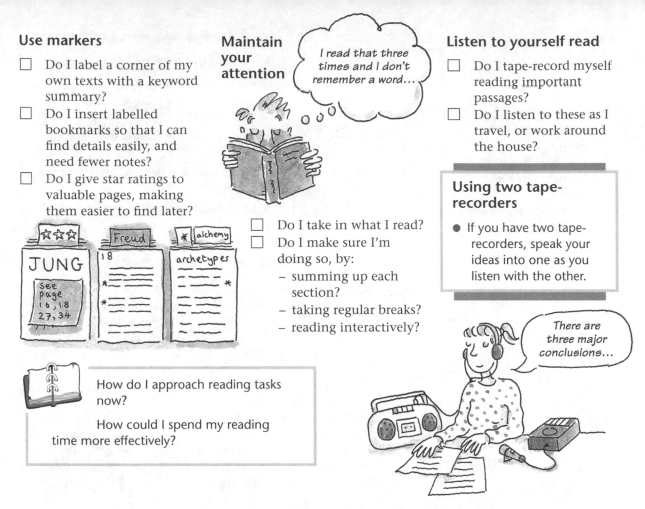

There are three major conclusions...

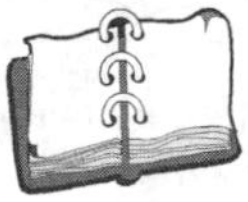

How do I approach reading tasks now?

How could I spend my reading time more effectively?

Improving reading comprehension

Do you:

- ☐ understand most of what you read?
- ☐ know how much you understand?
- ☒ understand uninteresting material?
- ☐ actively monitor your understanding?
- ☒ know how to improve comprehension?

If you answered 'no' to one or more of these questions, experiment with the following active reading strategies to improve your comprehension.

Active reading strategies

Start with something general

Reading is easier if you have a sense of the context and a general overview. Read the most basic text you can find first. Familiarise yourself with the main issues and the vocabulary.

Monitor your comprehension

Read a few sentences, then stop. Without looking back at the text, sum up what you have read in just a few words. Say these words aloud, or jot them down. If you cannot do this, read back over what you have read, using an additional strategy from below.

Guide your reading

Set yourself specific questions to start off your reading. Write them down. Adapt the questions as your reading progresses. The clearer you are about what you are trying to discover, the easier it is to find it in the text.

Re-read difficult passages

Academic texts often contain difficult passages. Don't panic!

You are bound to need to re-read some passages slowly, several times.

Highlight key words and phrases

On your own text or a photocopy, underline in pencil the information you think may be relevant. Look especially at headings, and first and last sentences of paragraphs. Select a few of the key words you underlined and highlight them in colour. Double-underline or star very important points. Make a faint wavy line at the side of fairly important passages. Be selective! If you underline or highlight everything, *nothing* will stand out as important.

Colour-code information

Use different colours for different kinds of information – for example, one colour for reference names and dates, and one for each of the main schools of thought or major theories for the subject. Later, just seeing that colour combination on the page may bring back to you what the page was about.

Ask 'depth questions'

Look for the underlying issues:

- What point is the writer making?
- Why is this detail relevant?
- Is the writer trying to answer a particular question?
- What lessons can be learnt from this text?

Apply the C·R·E·A·M learning strategy

Consider how you can apply the C·R·E·A·M strategy (Chapter 4) to your reading.

Relaxed reading

Reading comprehension is improved when the body is relaxed. Use appropriate lighting; have music or silence, as you prefer; and drink plain water. See Chapter 4 on 'The C·R·E·A·M strategy for learning' and Chapter 10 on 'Memory'.

Improving reading speed

Understanding is the most important aspect of reading, but you will find it helpful if you can also improve your reading *speed*.

How to check your speed

- Find something familiar to read.
- Set the alarm for ten minutes.
- Read for ten minutes at a speed where you can understand what you read.
- Count how many words you read.
- Divide this number by ten, to find out how many words you read in one minute.
- Do this using different texts. If you read fewer than 200–250 words per minute, even on clear and interesting material, it is worth trying to increase your speed.

What is slowing down your reading?

Below is a list of some factors which can slow down reading. Do any apply to you? If so, try the relevant strategies for speeding up your reading (page 114).

- ☐ 1 Do you read advanced texts very infrequently?
- ☐ 2 Do you track with your finger along the line?
- ☐ 3 Do you read out loud under your breath, or mouth the words?
- ☐ 4 Do you read books from cover to cover?
- ☐ 5 Do you start reading before you have worked out what you need to know, or what you are looking for?
- ☐ 6 Do you read word by word?
- ☐ 7 Do you keep checking back along the line, re-reading what you have just read?
- ☐ 8 Do you read difficult sections before you have worked out the general gist?
- ☐ 9 Do you find that the words seem to jump up off the page or that text moves or glares?

Strategies for speeding up your reading

For each of these problems there is something you can do to improve matters.

1 *Read more advanced texts*

Reading improves with practice. Your brain becomes more used to seeing unusual words, and your mind to dealing with complex sentences and ideas. Also, look for subjects that interest you and read more for pleasure.

2 *Finger-tracking*

Move your finger down the page, directly from top to bottom, to train your eye to move more quickly down the text.

3 *Know when to read aloud*

Some people read out loud from habit. Reading silently can speed up reading in such cases.

However, other people can only understand what they read if they *hear* the words. If you read aloud for this reason, try taping yourself so you can re-read 'by ear' rather than by eye.

4 & 5 *Read selectively and actively*

Be choosy in what you read. Use the active readings strategies suggested on pages 110–12, such as working out what you are looking for. You will finish reading more quickly, even though your reading speed may be the same.

6 *Read larger chunks*

Instead of resting your eye on every word, practise reading by resting your eye only two or three times on each line. Your eyes will probably be able to take in several words at once. This is also less tiring for the eyes so you should be able to read for longer periods.

7 *Build up to difficult texts*

Background knowledge of a subject helps to increase reading speed and understanding. If a text looks hard, start with something simpler on the same subject, or read the easiest sections first. You can return to complex sections or more difficult books later.

8 *Keep your eyes moving forward*

Which of these sentences is easier to read?

A Checking back over back over what what you have read makes understanding checking back makes understanding checking back over makes understanding difficult.

B Checking back over what you have read makes understanding more difficult.

Most people find **B** easier to read because they can take in a larger chunk of memorable 'sense'. Encourage your eyes to keep reading forward to the end of a sentence (to the next full stop). You will then be reading larger units of sense rather than just words and phrases. You can read the whole sentence again if necessary.

9 *Jumping and glaring text*

- Coloured filters (such as see-through plastic folders) placed over the page may reduce 'jumping' and 'glaring'. Experiment with different colours and see if one suits you best.
- Consult an optometrist for advice – you may need spectacles with coloured lenses or a particular filter.
- Enlarged photocopies of text can help.
- If the problem is serious and you prefer to 'read by ear', speak to the disability adviser at the university. There may be specialist equipment to enable you to scan texts and have them read aloud to you, or reading services which put books onto tape for you.

Slow reading is sometimes helpful

In some cases slow reading is preferable:

- for texts with condensed information, such as many science and medical texts
- for detailed instructions
- for formulae and equations
- for close analysis of texts, such as for law, literature and history.

Vary your reading strategies

Inspect

Check the title, the contents page, the index, the writing style, the details on the back cover. Flick through to get the feel of the book. Do you *want* to read it? Do you *need* to read it?

Scan rapidly

Scan the page. Which key words leap out at you? You may sense the 'pattern' of the argument or the general subject matter. Is information organised in way that helps you? What can you pick up from section headings, diagrams, the first lines of paragraphs, and conclusions to chapters and the text?

Question

Keep asking questions. What am I trying to find out? What do I need to know? Exactly which parts do I need to read?

Locate specifics quickly

To find a specific piece of information quickly, use the index. Go straight to the right page. Move your eye quickly down the page to find what you are looking for.

Read at the right speed

Read at the appropriate speed for the task. This may be fast for case studies, novels and well-developed arguments, and slowly for texts which condense detailed information into short passages or use unfamiliar specialist vocabulary. As you become more familiar with the ideas and vocabulary used, your speed will increase.

Recall and review

Check that you understand what you have read. What is the basic argument or idea? Does the text answer your questions? Are you convinced by the evidence and the arguments offered?

How does what you have read relate to what you already knew? Does it confirm or challenge your views? What else do you need to find out?

Making notes

Why make notes?

How many reasons can you find for making notes? After you have noted some, look at the diagram on page 117. Are your reasons the same? Which of these matter most to you?

Activity

Note making

Select a passage from a book and make notes on the main points of what you read – or find some notes you have already made.

Compare your notes with the suggestions made below. Do you want to make any changes to how you make notes?

How to make notes

There is no one 'best method', but it is worth considering the following points.

What do you need to note?

Consider:

- Do you really need this information? If so, which bits?
- Will you really use it? When, and how?
- Have you noted similar information already?
- What questions do you want to answer with this information?

A method for making notes

- Put your pen down – so you won't be tempted to copy out of the book.
- Read – to answer your own questions.
- Identify and sum up the main ideas. (Hear them in your own words.)
- Jot down one or two words to remind you.
- Note *exactly* where information comes from.
- Note real names and quotations *exactly* as they are written.
- Leave space to add details later.

Organise your notes

- See 'Recording and using information' (page 121).
- See 'Organising information: plan your writing' (page 146).
- Use a separate file for each subject area.
- Use file dividers to separate major topics.
- Use a separate page for each minor topic.
- Arrange ideas under headings or questions. (Notice how information is organised in this *Handbook*.)
- Label files and dividers clearly.
- Number and label pages so you can find and re-file them easily.
- Keep an updated contents page at the front of each file.

How helpful are your notes?

For each of the following sets of opposite statements, tick along the line depending on how far it is true of your own notes.

Easy to read ✓............... Hard to read

Brief, to the point ✓................ Too detailed

Easy to understand✓........ Hard to understand

Well organised✓ Poorly organised

Pages numbered/labelled✓ No system

Easy to learn from✓.. Difficult to learn from

Well abbreviated✓......... No abbreviations

Important ideas stand out clearly✓... Not easy to see important points

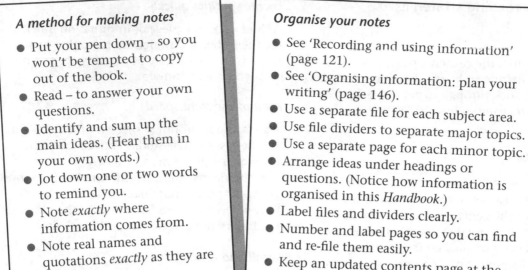

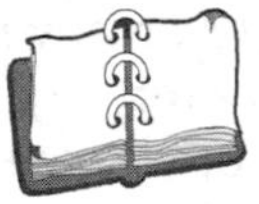

Record your ideas about how to improve your notes. What is the priority?

Note-making styles

Nuclear notes: why take notes?

Is making notes a useful activity? Why make notes at all?

WHY TAKE NOTES?

A. Useful record
1. of important points for future use
2. of where the information comes from

B. Helps writing
1. Helps ideas flow
2. Helps planning – you can see what info. you have
3. Assists organisation – you can rearrange and renumber notes in a different order
4. Helps you get started

C. Helps understanding
1. If you focus on selecting info. to note
2. If you think through where everything fits

D. Helps memory
1. Summing things up briefly helps long-term memory
2. The act of writing helps motor memory
3. Pattern notes can be more memorable visually

E. Helps exam revision
1. Material is well organised
2. More info. is already in memory

Linear notes: strategies for making notes

① Good note-making: general
- 1.1 Think before you write
- 1.2 Keep notes brief
- 1.3 Keep notes organised
- 1.4 Use your own words
- 1.5 Leave a wide margin and spaces – to add notes later

② Useful strategies
- 2.1 Note key words and main ideas
- 2.2 Write phrases – not sentences
- 2.3 Use abbreviations
- 2.4 Use headings
- 2.5 Number points
- 2.6 Make the page memorable – with colour, illustrations, and so on
- 2.7 Link up points – using arrows, dotted lines, colour, numbers, boxes
- 2.8 Note sources of info. exactly
- 2.9 Write quotations in a different colour

③ Unhelpful strategies
- 3.1 Copying chunks and phrases
- 3.2 Writing more notes than you can use again
- 3.3 Writing out notes several times to make them neater

④ Tidying messy notes
- 4.1 Draw a 'square' around sections of notes in different colours to make them stand out
- 4.2 Use a ruler to divide the page up between sections
- 4.3 Draw a ring round floating bits of information
- 4.4 Link stray information by colour-coding it

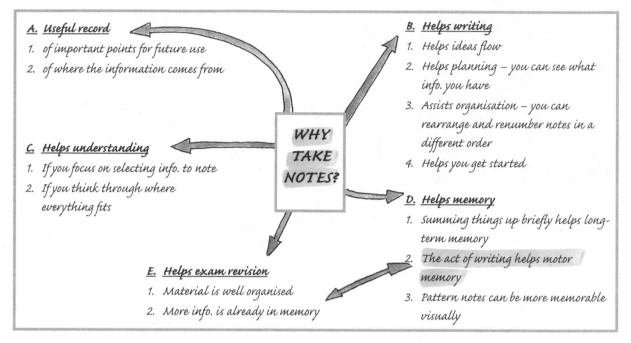

Pattern notes (example)

(See Buzan 1993.)

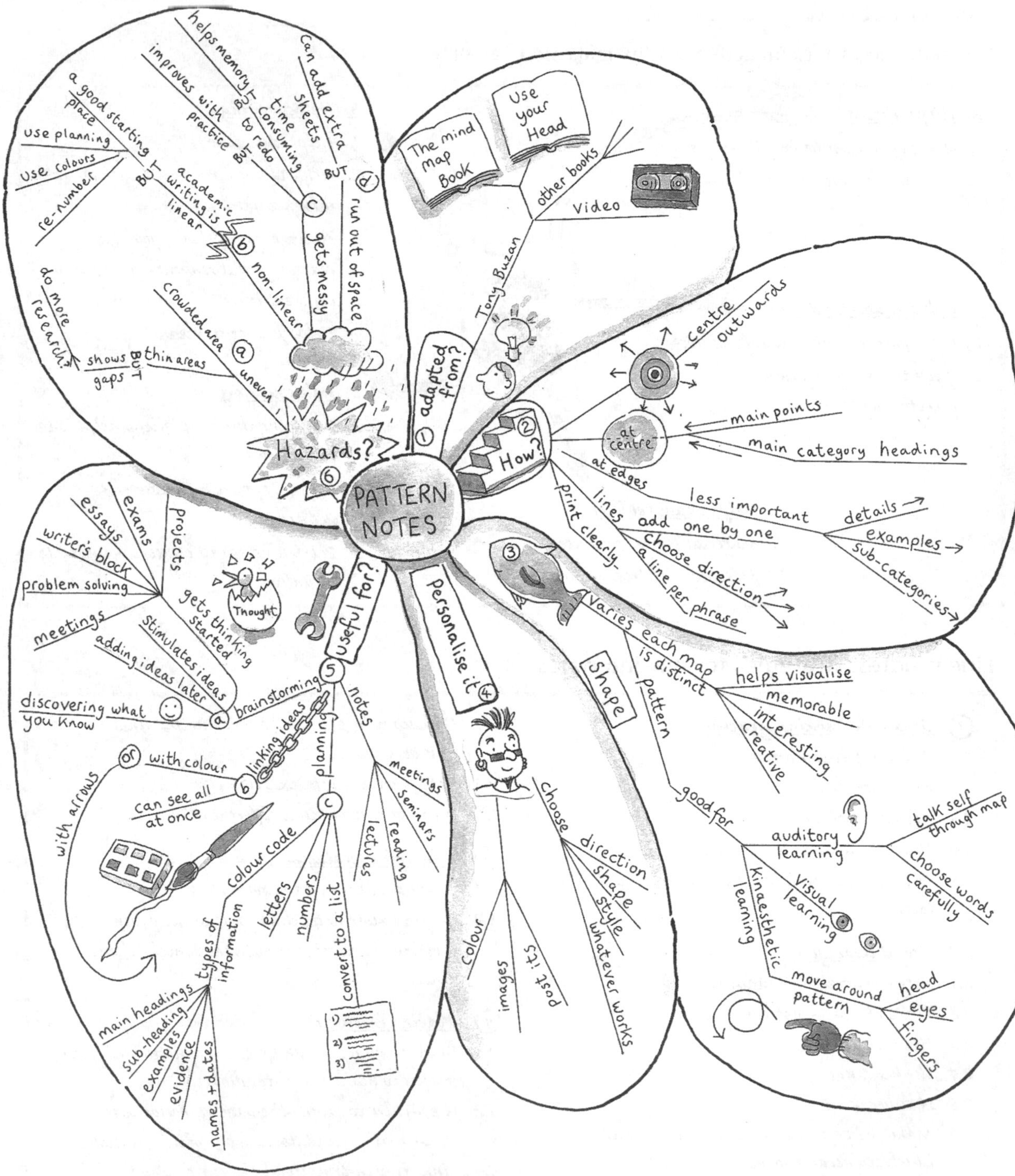

Shortcuts in note-making

Leave space

Leave space in your notes, and a wide margin, so that you can add new information and ideas later. (This much quicker than *rewriting* your notes to incorporate the new information.)

Make just one set of notes

Aim to have just one set of notes. Visual familiarity will make it easier to find information later, and to recall information during exams.

Use labels

Carry Post-it® labels with you. When you have an idea, write it on a label and stick this on a blank sheet in a plastic folder. You can move the labels around as you plan assignments.

Number the pages

Label and number pages. Cross-refer to information already noted elsewhere – for instance, 'see red file, page 24, Amphibians'.

Use abbreviations

Abbreviations save time. Use them in your notes, but not in assignments.

- Work out a system you'll remember.
- Stick to your system.
- Introduce a few at a time, so that your notes make sense.
- Keep a 'key' to your abbreviations near you until you know them.

Useful common symbols

& (+)	and
+	plus, in addition to
>	greater/more than/better than
<	smaller/less than
=	is the same as/equal to
≠	is not the same as
∴	therefore
∵	because
w/	with
♀	woman/female
♂	man/male
→	this leads to/produces/causes

Useful common abbreviations

e.g.	for example
i.e.	that is, that means
etc.	and the rest
NB	important, notice this
p.	page (pp. = pages)
para.	paragraph
Ch.	chapter (Chs. = chapters)
edn	edition
info.	information
cd	could
wd	would
Govt	Government
Educ.	Education
impt	important
devt	development
C19	nineteenth century

Which abbreviations are used in *your* subject areas?

Making notes with confidence

Students' solutions

Sonja and James are two students who used to have great difficulties making notes. Here are their accounts of how they tackled their difficulties, with help from a study-skills tutor.

Sonja

There are two things which I find difficult about making notes. Firstly, I am not very confident about using my own words – the book always seems to say things better. It is very tempting to use nearly the same words as the book. I imagine that I will rewrite them in my own words later – but then I don't have the time, or I forget which bits are taken from the book, and end up with the words of the book in my essay without even realising.

The second thing I find difficult is working out what to take notes about, especially keeping to essentials. I worry in case I miss out information I will need in the future. I can end up with 10 sides of notes from reading only a few pages. It takes ages and there is too much to even look at a second time. When I came to revise for my first exams, I had too many notes to revise – there were simply too many to read, never mind learn.

Now I spend more time thinking and planning before I even touch a book. I try to work out what information I want. I draw a mind-map with everything I already know, and what I need to find out. If I have an essay title I do a rough plan really early, even before I start reading – just to get the shape in my head.

I always start with the easiest book – just to get a picture of what it is all about. With other books, I use the contents page and headings to work out where information is. At this stage I don't write much except something like 'gold – producer countries: p.248 and pp.265–9'.

When I have more idea of what I am looking for, and where that information is, I take more detailed notes. Sometimes, I do this by writing a question and putting the information as an answer. When I am not sure if I want some information, I just write a few lines onto an index card, saying where I can find that information later if I really need it.

James

I find it hard to take notes in lectures. I used to tape lectures and then type out all my notes – which took up all my time and I got very stressed. These days I go quickly through the books before lectures so I know what is likely to come up in the lecture and then I won't worry about noting it all down. I write out obvious headings on the large index cards that I prefer. Then I only have to add in a few words under each heading – to remind myself of something. When I get home, I listen to the tape and add in other bits onto the cards by hand. It's much quicker than the old way. Sometimes I listen to the tape and then speak my ideas to my computer – it has 'speech to text'. I don't do this much as it has problems – you have to be careful not to dictate straight from the tape and end up with the lecture in your essay – but sometimes I summarise things this way.

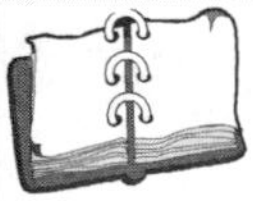

These are just two approaches to dealing with note-taking. Do any of their ideas appeal to you? Or have you a better system?

Recording and using information

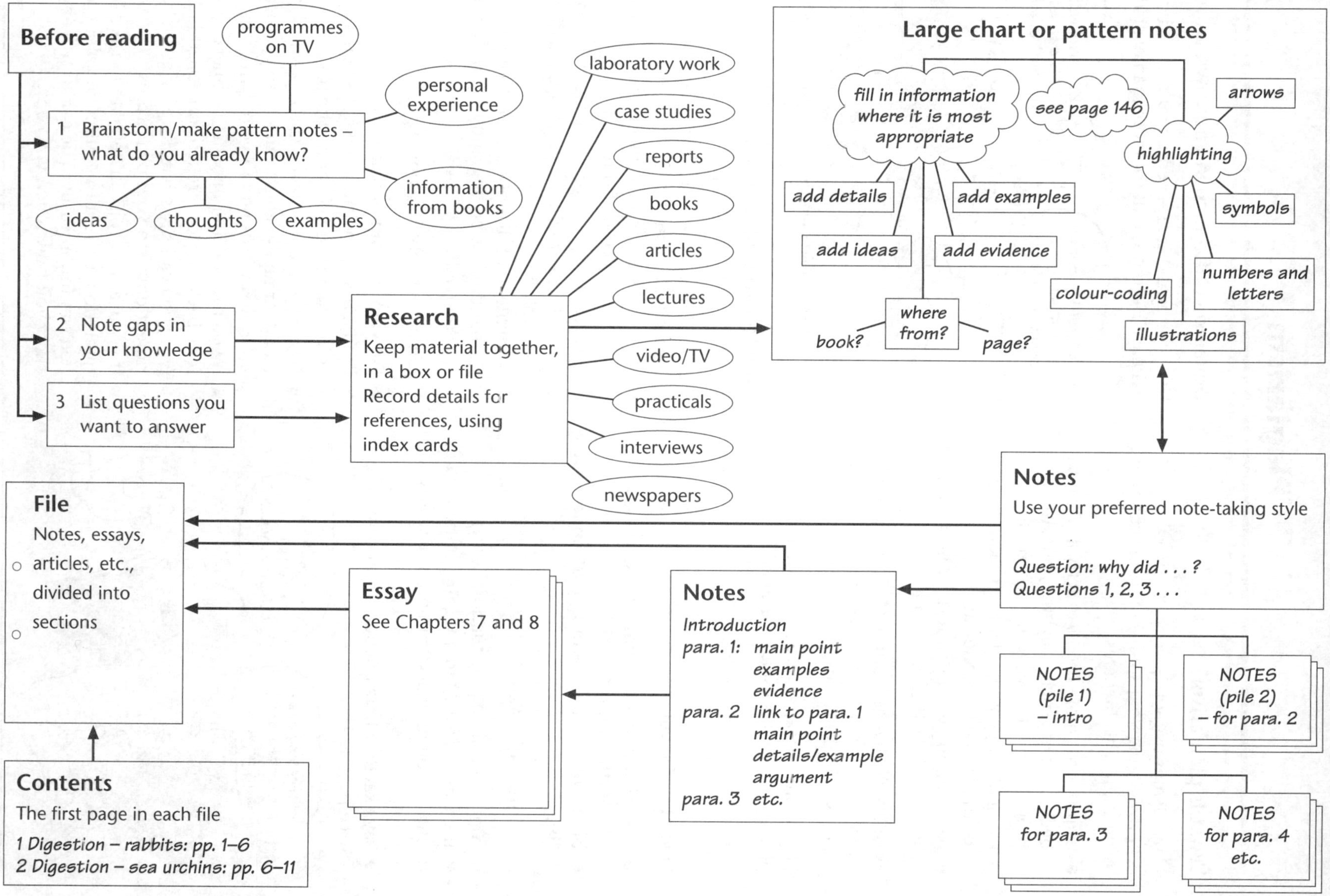

Before reading
programmes on TV
personal experience
1 Brainstorm/make pattern notes – what do you already know?
information from books
ideas
thoughts
examples
2 Note gaps in your knowledge
3 List questions you want to answer
laboratory work
case studies
reports
books
articles
lectures
video/TV
practicals
interviews
newspapers
Research
Keep material together, in a box or file
Record details for references, using index cards
Large chart or pattern notes
fill in information where it is most appropriate
see page 146
arrows
highlighting
symbols
add details
add examples
add ideas
add evidence
numbers and letters
colour-coding
illustrations
where from?
book?
page?
Notes
Use your preferred note-taking style
Question: why did . . . ?
Questions 1, 2, 3 . . .
File
Notes, essays, articles, etc., divided into sections
Essay
See Chapters 7 and 8
Notes
Introduction
para. 1: main point
examples
evidence
para. 2 link to para. 1
main point
details/example
argument
para. 3 etc.
NOTES (pile 1) – intro
NOTES (pile 2) – for para. 2
NOTES for para. 3
NOTES for para. 4 etc.
Contents
The first page in each file
1 Digestion – rabbits: pp. 1–6
2 Digestion – sea urchins: pp. 6–11

Plagiarism

What is plagiarism?

Plagiarism is using the work of others without acknowledging your source of information or inspiration. This includes:

- using words more or less exactly as they have been used in articles, lectures, television programmes, books, or anywhere else
- using other people's ideas or theories without saying whose ideas they are
- paraphrasing what you read or hear without stating where it comes from.

Even if you change words or sentences you have 'borrowed' or put them in a different order, the result is still plagiarism.

Plagiarism is treated very seriously, and plagiarised work is usually disqualified.

Using quotations

Quotations should be:

- used sparingly – and only if the words really are worth quoting
- brief – usually a few words, and at most a few lines.

In writing a quotation you should:

- copy words and punctuation *exactly*
- use three dots (...) to indicate omitted words
- put 'quotation marks' around the words you quote
- say exactly where the quotation comes from (see page 124).

Develop confidence in your own words

Use your own words, even if you don't think you write well – they count for more than copied text.

Other people's words make a poor lifeboat

How to avoid plagiarism

- Write all your notes in your own words.
- Note down *exactly* where you read the information you put in your notes.
- In your assignment, write out where ideas and information come from:
  - reference your work (see pages 123–5)
  - make clear when you are using a direct quotation
  - write a full list of references and, if required, a bibliography (all the books you read).

If you have a habit of copying:

- Put your pen out of reach.
- Read a passage without taking any notes.
- Stop reading and cover up the page.
- Sum up what you have read. If possible, talk aloud, or tape-record yourself, so you hear your own words and in your own voice.
- If you cannot sum up what you have read, look back to 'Comprehension' (page 112).
- Once you can say what the passage is about, note it down in your own words.
- If you want to copy material to use as a quotation, write it in a different colour so that you can find it easily. The colour will also show you how much you copy.

References

Why are references needed?

In academic writing, it is essential to state the sources of ideas and information. Such 'references' allow readers to refer back to the sources for themselves.

There are five main reasons for providing references.

1 Acknowledging a source is a courtesy to the person whose idea or words you have used or referred to.
2 By giving the source you make it clear to the reader that you are not trying to pretend somebody else's work is your own. (You are not 'plagiarising' someone else's work.)
3 The source helps your readers to find the original texts to read themselves, should they wish.
4 If you need to check something later, the reference will help you find it again more easily.
5 People will have more confidence in your assertions if they know where your information comes from. Thoroughness in referencing suggests that you will also have been thorough in checking your facts.

When do you need to give a reference?

You must give the reference whenever you draw on a source of information:

- as your inspiration (in general)
- as the source of a particular theory, argument or viewpoint
- for specific information, such as statistics, examples, or case studies
- for direct quotations (reproducing the writer's exact words)
- for texts which you paraphrase rather than quote.

What information is included in a reference?

Imagine that you wished to read for yourself a source text used by another author. What information would *you* need to locate that source easily? The information usually provided includes:

- the name and initials of the author(s)
- the title, in full
- the year of publication
- for journal articles, the name of the journal and the number of the volume
- the edition, if relevant
- the location of the publisher
- the name of publisher
- relevant page numbers.

You may know that extra information is needed. For example, to find a photograph, print or manuscript you may need the name of the library, the collection, and the catalogue number of the item within the collection. The important question to ask is, 'Could somebody else *find* this source from the information I have given?'

Where do you put this information?

In the body of the text

Whenever you refer to someone else's work, either directly or indirectly, indicate whose work this is.

Use the format recommended by your tutors. Usually this will be simply the surname of the author(s), the year of publication and possibly the page number(s), using brackets in one of these ways:

> ... as noted by Cohen and Smith (1987, p. 56), who said ...
>
> ... two researchers (Cohen and Smith 1987, p. 56) noted ...

At the end of the assignment

Write out full details in a list of 'References' – see page 125 for guidance, and page 233 for an example of such a list.

Giving references

There are various ways of acknowledging your source materials. Check whether you are expected to use a particular system for your course. If not, use the author–date system.

The author–date system

When you have used, quoted or paraphrased a source, acknowledge it. Either within the sentence or at the end of the sentence, write in brackets the author's name, the date of publication and the page numbers. Full details of the source should be written out in the reference section.

Text citations

Here are three different ways of using sources.

Short direct quotation – within the text

> Nonetheless, the film was deliberately inaccurate about the life of José Marti. Jesus Colon (1982, p.82) pointed this out when he wrote, 'José Marti never had a mansion or a hut of his own. Needless to say, he never had slaves.'

Paraphrasing

> Nonetheless, the film was deliberately inaccurate about José Marti, who, contrary to the image depicted in American films, spent much of his life in poverty (Colon 1982, pp. 81–2).

Longer direct quotation

A few words, carefully chosen, make the most powerful quotations, and demonstrate that you can select appropriately. Avoid long quotations; they are rarely needed. If the exact wording of a long quotation is essential, however, indent it and leave space above and below (as shown on the right). Incorporate the quotation clearly into your writing with linking sentences and by discussing its relevance.

> Angry at Hollywood versions of Latin American history, Jesus Colon wrote:
>
> > After pictures like *Zapata* and *Santiago* we can only hope that these Hollywood vulgarisers and distorters, without the least bit of respect for the history and culture of our Latin American nations, won't lay their bovine eyes upon epic themes like the Aztec struggle against Cortes' conquest of Mexico, or Sandino's fight against American imperialism ... (1982, p. 84)
>
> Here we can see that Colon is very critical of versions of Latin American history produced in the USA.

References list

In the 'References' at the end of the essay, the reference to Colon would appear in this form (and in alphabetical order):

> Colon, J. (1982). *A Puerto Rican in New York and Other Sketches*, 2nd edn. New York: International Publishers.

Note that for books you don't give page numbers in the 'References'. For a journal article you give the page numbers for the whole article.

Useful phrases to introduce references

- As *X* points out, ...
- According to *X*, ...
- To quote from *X*, '...'
- *X* states/suggests that ...
- *X* tells/shows us that ...
- In an article entitled *Name of Text*, *X* makes the point that ...
- Referring to ..., *X* says that ...
- As *X* stated/wrote/said, ...
- In *Name of Text*, *X* wrote that ...
- Writing in *Name of Text*, *X* explained that ...
- Writing in 1926, *X* argued that ...

Writing out references

Use index cards

Fill out an index card for each source you use, using paper or cards, or a computer-based equivalent.

TOPIC →	*WRITING STYLE*
Names and initials of author(s) →	*Strunk, W. and White, E. B.*
Year of publication →	*1979*
Title →	*The Elements of Style*
Volume/collection →	*–*
Edition →	*3rd edn*
Location of publisher: Publisher →	*New York and London: Macmillan*
Where to find a copy →	*Barking Library (ref. no. …)*
(brief summary of contents) →	*(information on grammar, writing styles, common errors and misused words)*

The advantages of cards like these are that:

- you will know exactly where to look if you need to double-check some point
- writing the 'References' page is much easier
- if you use a computer, you can simply 'cut and paste' references when you re-use them.

Conventions in writing references

- Don't number the items.
- Begin each source on a new line.
- List alphabetically, by author's surname.
- If you use more than one work by a given author and published in the same year, label these a, b, c … (1999a, 1999b, 1999c, …) in the text and in the 'References'.
- Put information in the same order (author, date, title, location of publisher, publisher) as in the examples below or as your course tutor recommends.
- Underline the title of the book or journal (or use italics, if available).
- Use 'single' quotation marks for the title of an article within a journal.

Include:

- All sources you refer to, including videos, TV, tapes, and the like, but not dictionaries or grammar books.
- Don't include in 'References' materials you have not used in your assignment.
- List additional sources, which you read but did not use, in a 'Bibliography'.

Sample references (see also page 233)

A book:

Bailey, P. (1978). *Leisure and Class in Victorian England.* London: Methuen.

A chapter in a book:

Humm, M. (1991). 'Landscape for a literary feminism: British women writers 1900 to the present'. In Forsas-Scott, H. (ed.). *Textual Liberation: European feminist writing in the twentieth century.* London: Routledge.

A journal article:

Jones, C. (1980). 'The welfare of the French footsoldier.' *History* **65** (no. 214), 193–213.

Material cited within another text, where you have not quoted the original source:

O'Connor, J. and McDermott, I. (1996). *Principles of NLP.* London: Thorsons. Cited in Cottrell, S. M. (1999). *The Study Skills Handbook.* Basingstoke: Macmillan.

An electronic reference (include the date on which you used it):

http://www.foe.co.uk.16 May 1998.

Bibliographies

A bibliography is a list of everything you read for the assignment, whether or not you referred to it in your writing. Your tutor may prefer this to a references list, or may even require both. Use the same style as for references.

Getting the most out of lectures

Lectures are designed to be useful starting points for research, giving a general overview of the subject, its main ideas and theories, and evidence from recent research. Together, these will guide your own reading and reflection.

How to make lectures easier to follow

Before the lecture

- Get a feel for the subject. Read (or just flick through) a book on the subject of the lecture. Look for themes, issues, topics and headings. Look up any technical words you don't understand.
- Write down questions you want answered. Leave space to write the answers under each question either during or after the lecture.
- Jot down your own opinion. Notice if it changes during the lecture.
- Glance through your notes for the previous lecture, and look for links with the next lecture.

During the lecture

Lecturers vary about whether they prefer questions during or after the lecture. They usually go quite quickly, and expect you to jot down main themes and references.

- To focus attention, listen for clues as to where the lecture is going. For example: 'There are five major categories of ...', 'Now, I want to look at ...' or 'Why did this happen?'
- Good lecturers tell you at the beginning which main topics will be covered and in which order, or write up headings.
- Take notes of headings, questions, sub-points, and references.
- Avoid writing details you can easily get later from a textbook. Keep your attention for your listening. If you are not clear where information comes from, ask.
- In your head, challenge what the lecturer says: this will help to focus your attention. Ask, 'Is this always the case?', 'How representative is this?', 'Why is this?' and 'Do I agree?'
- Indicate new questions raised by the lecture in a different colour.

After the lecture

- Label and file your lecture notes and any handouts.
- Read through your notes. Fill in details from your reading or research.

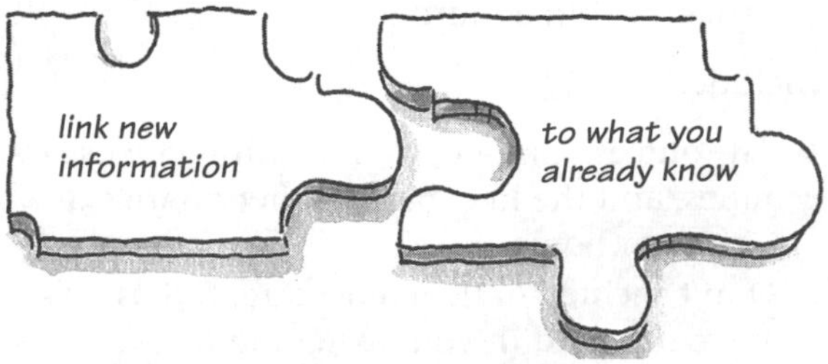

- Discuss the lecture with others. Compare your notes and fill in any gaps.

RECORD SHEET

Lecture notes

Subject area/unit:	**Year:**	**Unit level:**
Subject of lecture:	**Lecturer:**	

Preparation Questions and ideas prompted by reading or discussion prior to the lecture; what do I want to find out during this lecture?

Opening comments by the lecturer Issues, questions, etc., to be addressed during the lecture

Main theme of the lecture

Main points made in the lecture; examples or evidence given

Questions raised by the lecture

References to books, etc.

© Stella Cottrell 1999, *The Study Skills Handbook*, Macmillan Press Ltd

Problem-solving

Why are you given problems to solve?

Exercises in problem-solving are opportunities to learn useful skills with many applications. Such exercises allow you:

- to practise specific procedures
- to put theoretical knowledge to practical use
- to develop reasoning abilities and creativity in finding answers
- to develop your understanding of underlying principles
- to research topics in detail.

You can apply a problem-solving approach to any research or study activity.

Stages in problem-solving

1 *Define the task*

- What exactly is it that you have to solve?
- Is this a particular kind of problem?
- What *sort* of answer is required – a report? formula? a number? action? an essay?
- Is this problem similar in any way to previous problems or tasks you have done? Could solutions from a previous problem apply to this? (See pages 40–1.)

2 *Look at it from different angles*

- Look for similarities with any other kind of problem you have solved. What has it in common with these? How far will previous solutions work here?
- Reword the problem.
- Sketch the problem as a diagram.
- Identify the parts of the problem that you find most difficult. Is there another way of looking at these?
- Talk it through with others.

3 *What information do you need?*

- Would any of your notes be useful?
- Which theories or cases apply?
- What other resources would help?
- Who can you ask for information?

4 *Consider alternative solutions*

- What are the advantages of each solution?
- Would each work?
- What might be the disadvantages of each?
- Which is the best option overall? Why?

5 *Write up the problem*

- Explain clearly how you tried to solve the problem – your methodology. Explain how you arrived at the solution. (In essays, this stage is generally omitted.)

6 *If you didn't succeed, why not?*

- Did you link the new problem to similar problems?
- Did you have enough information?
- Did you 'play' with ideas enough?
- Did you misunderstand what was required?
- Did you consider alternative solutions?

Organise your approach

It may help if you draw up a chart. For example:

Definition of the problem:		
Similarity to other problems:		
Information needed:		
Resources or people who could help:		
Alternative solutions	*Advantages*	*Disadvantages*
1		
2		
3		

(Adapted from Freeman and Mead 1991.)

Practicals and laboratory work

What are practicals and laboratory work for?

These vary a great deal from one subject to another, but some general principles are outlined below.

Practicals

Practicals are designed to help you:

- learn how to use equipment
- practise using equipment and techniques
- see what happens when you put theory into practice
- practise following appropriate procedures
- practise using methods which you may need in professional life.

Health and safety

Make sure you know and understand any Health and Safety Regulations – and follow them carefully.

Laboratory work

Laboratory work is designed to help you:

- develop skills in identifying and clarifying aims
- develop skills in accurate observation
- develop skills in recording data
- practise applying and interpreting data
- practise reporting on your methods, findings and conclusions.

Basic principles

Be assertive

Make sure you get your fair share of time using equipment. Don't be content watching others – have a go yourself.

Ask

If you are concerned about using equipment with which you are not familiar, ask for help.

Find out

Which theory is the practical supposed to be testing?

Discuss

Discuss your findings with your lecturer and with other students.

Read

Read around the subject. How is the theory or the experiment applicable to real life? What kinds of results have other people had?

Record

Record *exactly* what happens. Don't change your results to what you think or know the 'right answer' to be.

Many experiments work only in ideal conditions. Your lecturers will know this and will be looking to see how you record your method and data, and your discussion of why you think you got the results you did.

Write it up

Write up your method, results and conclusions neatly and clearly. Find out the required format for writing up practicals and experiments in your subject area. Are you expected to include diagrams, tables and graphs? Are you expected to use colour?

Review

This chapter has looked at *general* research skills which are common to most subjects, such as identifying and selecting the most relevant information, developing reading strategies, and making clear references to your sources. You need some skills, such as being able to focus your listening, take notes, identify key points, and acknowledge the sources of your information, whether you are in a seminar, on a group project, doing case-study observations or on work placement. Although undergraduate research is generally based on reading, other study activities such as lectures and practical work are part of the research process. For any new study challenge, you can adopt a problem-solving approach.

Some subjects require you to learn very specific research skills, especially in the third year. These skills will vary according to the subject. Some use sophisticated observation techniques, others use statistics or specialist equipment. Undergraduate work does not usually involve gathering entirely new data, or formulating new hypotheses or finding great problems to solve. Whether you are using general or specific research skills, your task as an undergraduate is mainly to develop the basic techniques and demonstrate that you understand the principles involved.

Research is not an activity that can be divorced from other areas of study. Chapters 7 and 8 look at ways of writing up your research, and Chapter 9 goes into more depth about how to take critical, analytical approaches to research. It is also worth browsing again through Chapter 4 to see how you can apply C·R·E·A·M strategies specifically to research.

Chapter 7

Writing for university

LEARNING OUTCOMES

This chapter offers you opportunities to:

- become more aware of writing sub-skills that you need to develop
- get into the writing habit if you have been away from formal education
- learn how to get started on a piece of writing and overcome writer's block
- learn how to examine assignment titles
- develop a procedure for writing essays and reports
- understand what is meant by concepts and 'concept pyramids'
- develop strategies for organising your ideas, planning your writing, and structuring essays and reports
- learn how to complete the basic steps of writing an assignment, such as writing drafts, editing, and presenting your work by hand or computer

Academic writing

Writing a good assignment is both a challenge and one of the most rewarding aspects of study. Almost all students find their writing skills develop significantly at college. This is due partly to the additional practice, and partly to an increase in critical awareness developed by analysing issues from many perspectives.

Writing cannot be separated from other processes such as reflection, goal-setting, organisation and research. Although this *Handbook*, of necessity, addresses these skills in separate chapters, in practice you will find that they are interrelated. You will make best use of this chapter if you are already confident about the material in Chapters 4 and 6. Before you complete your first or second piece of writing, you may find it helpful to browse through Chapters 8 and 9 too.

This chapter looks at skills and stages common to many types of academic writing assignment. It takes you step by step through the different processes involved in writing a piece of course work such as an essay or report.

As your writing skills develop and you become more aware of what is required, you can be more flexible and creative in your approach to writing. However, be wary of tutors who say they value 'individuality': this often means 'be individual within the conventions of our subject area'. Make sure you know what is acceptable and what is not in your subject.

SELF-EVALUATION

How good am I at managing writing tasks?

On the chart below, tick the appropriate box and rate how you well you perform the skill now (9 = excellent, 1 = weak/needs a lot of work).

Do I know …	Yes	Rating	I just need practice	Not sure	No	Page
• how to get into the habit of writing?						133–4
• how to get started on a piece of writing (or overcome 'writer's block')?						136–8
• what an essay is?						139, 183–7
• a procedure for writing essays?						140
• how to analyse assignment questions?						142–3
• how to organise information?						145–6
• how to use and organise concepts?						152–5
• how to structure an essay?						147
• how to structure a report?						149
• how to write good paragraphs?						157–60
• how to write a persuasive argument?						175–6, 196
• about different academic writing styles?						144, 173–80
• how to use personal experience in writing?						180
• how to draft, edit and proof-read?						156, 161–2
• how to present my writing?						163–4
• what gets good marks?						181
• how to use feedback to improve my marks?						182

What are the two main priorities for improvement in your next piece of writing? Highlight these two in colour.

Repeat this self-evaluation when your next piece of writing is returned, using the tutor's feedback.

© Stella Cottrell 1999, *The Study Skills Handbook*, Macmillan Press Ltd

Writing for the fearful

Make any mark rather than worry about a blank page

If your writing skills are *very* rusty, try some of the following short exercises. If you are more confident, skip forward to the next section that you find useful.

Get the writing habit

- Write one word ten times, in different handwriting styles. Which is most comfortable?
- Write out a story you enjoyed as a child.
- Write to a friend saying what you hope to get out of being a student.
- Jot down ten words you like the sound of. Write a short piece which includes all those words. Be as crazy as you like.
- 'Just a minute': give yourself one minute to write about one of the following:
  1. The worst thing I ever ate ...
  2. The most embarrassing thing that ever happened ...
  3. I'm lucky because. . .
  4. What gets on my nerves is ...
  5. Anything you like.

Write for five minutes

1. Choose any subject.
2. Don't stop to think. The idea is to get used to writing continuously, whatever the content. Just write as much as you can.
3. When you can write for five minutes, extend the time to ten minutes and build up your limit.

Write from prompts

- Let yourself be inspired by what you see, hear, think, or dream.

Make a life chart

- Include important events in your childhood, family, education, interests, work, and so on.
- Write a few lines about each item.
- Choose one item and write about this in more detail. Describe what happened, how you felt about the episode at the time, how it affected you in the long term, whether what happened was unusual, and so on.

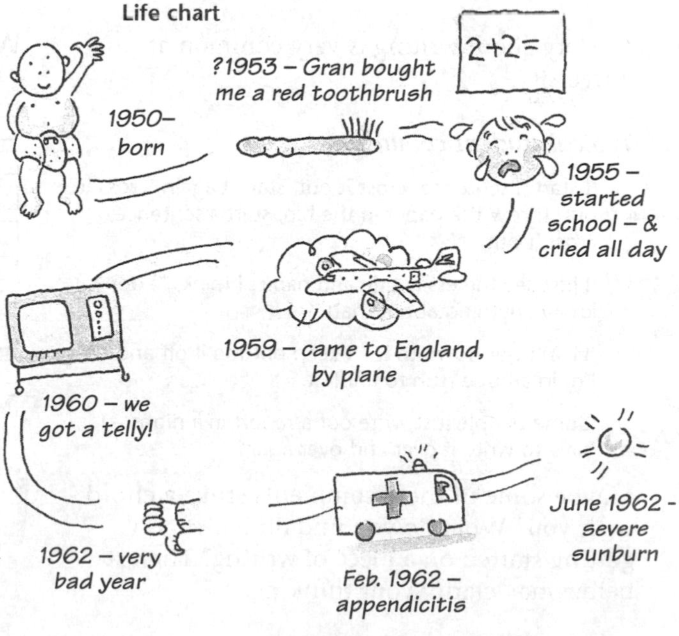

Developing your writing

Most experienced writers rewrite their work over and over, refining their thoughts, finding a better way of saying something, making a long-winded section a bit briefer, or adding more details to develop an idea.

Rewrite 1
Filling out the writing

- Take one piece of writing you have done.
- Jot down a list of five extra details you could add to give a fuller picture.
- Add something you know about someone else's ideas: from television, radio, or reading.
- Add a personal opinion about some aspect of what you wrote.
- Rewrite the piece, adding the new detail.

Rewrite 2
Playing with your ideas

Play around with what you have written. For example, you could:

- change the order of the sentences around
- change some of the words
- add more details
- change the order of the paragraphs around
- ask a question and turn what you have written into the answer
- write from the opposite point of view.

Rewrite 3
Organising your material

- Select one of your pieces of writing.
- Read through it, underlining each major idea in a different colour. For each change of subject, change the colour. If a subject comes up again, use the colour you used before.
- When you have finished, check how often the colour *changes*.
- Rewrite the passage so that all the parts underlined in a given colour are grouped together.

Anxieties about writing

Anxiety about writing is very common at university.

Typical student comments

'I start a sentence, cross it out, start it again, cross it out, throw the paper in the bin, start a sentence, cross it out ...'

'I just see the essay title and panic. I think, "I don't know anything about that!"'

'I can't get down to it – I keep putting it off and then I'm in a huge rush to finish it.'

'Some people just write out a report in a night – I have to write it over and over again.'

Maybe some of these comments strike a chord with you? What do you find difficult about getting started on a piece of writing? The list below may clarify your thinking.

What stops me from writing?

- ☐ The blank page is very off-putting.
- ☐ My mind goes empty.
- ☐ I don't know where to begin.
- ☐ I just can't get down to it.
- ☐ I am not as good as other people.
- ☐ The ideas go round and round in my head.
- ☐ I am embarrassed about my handwriting.
- ☐ I am embarrassed about my spelling.
- ☐ I worry about grammar and punctuation.
- ☐ Other reasons.

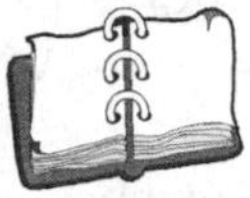

In your journal, note down your thoughts and observations about any difficulties *you* have in getting started.

Similarities between academic writing and other activities

Every day you are involved in situations that require you to plan and to make decisions. Think of one activity you completed recently, such as planning a holiday, choosing this course, or organising a party. On a separate sheet, describe exactly what you did, from start to finish.

The activity probably involved six stages. Tick which stages you went through to complete your activity.

- ☐ 1 Deciding in general what to do.
- ☐ 2 Collecting relevant information or materials to complete the task.
- ☐ 3 Planning the order to do things.
- ☐ 4 Carrying out the plan.
- ☐ 5 Checking that you were going about the task in the right way.
- ☐ 6 Reflecting on how you would do it better next time.

Academic writing follows a similar pattern of planning and decision-making. Suppose you were asked to write about 'The influence of theories on cloning animals'. You may know very little about the subject, and you may have no clear opinion. But you can approach the writing task much as the activity you analysed above.

Activity

Approaching a writing task

To plan a piece of writing you would probably take the steps shown in the table, but not in the order given listed.

- Rearrange the steps in the order you would be likely to carry them out.
- Consider a second order you could use.
- Then look below and compare your responses.
- Would your own suggested order suit you better?

	Steps taken	Order
1	Decide how you would do better next time	
2	Make an outline plan	
3	Put the ideas in order	
4	Research the subject (reading, interviews, experiments, etc.)	
5	Examine the title and decide what is required	
6	Write a rough draft	
7	Take notes from your reading (or interviews, experiments, etc.)	
8	Select the relevant information to include	
9	Write the final draft	
10	Write out the references (books and other sources of information)	
11	Read through the writing, checking for sense and small errors; make corrections	
12	Check if your text is within the word limit	
13	Separate main ideas from supporting detail and examples	

Possible sequences

5 4 8 7 3 13 2 6
10 11 12 9 1

5 4 7 8 3 13 2 6
12 11 9 10 1

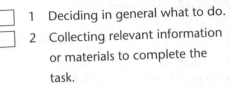

Overcoming writer's block

The following activities can help to overcome writing blocks. Which would be most useful for you?

☐ Scribble

Scribble ideas fast, in any order – whatever comes into your mind – then rearrange what you have written and rewrite it.

☐ 'It's only a draft'

Think of each piece of writing as something you will develop through several drafts. As it's just a draft, it doesn't have to be good – it's just something to work on.

☐ Write in pencil

This will remind you that your draft is a rough one – mistakes are allowed!

☐ Write on loose paper – not in a book

If you don't like what you have written, you can throw it away. Alternatively, you can cut it up and rearrange it.

☐ Ignore mistakes in early drafts

Don't worry about minor corrections, such as spellings – you can sort those out in the final draft.

☐ 'For your eyes only'

Remind yourself that nobody but you needs to see early drafts. Handwriting, untidiness and mistakes don't matter at this stage. Could a trusted friend or relative help you to proof-read, later, for mistakes?

☐ Experiment

Try different starting methods – see 'Tricks for getting started' (page 137). Which ones work best for you?

☐ Start anywhere

Write things in any order that suits you – you can rearrange them later. For example, it may be easier to write the introduction last.

☐ Mark the paper

If blank paper puts you off, make any mark or doodle on it so that it's *not* blank. The paper is only a tool – it can't judge you.

☐ Write by talking

If you find it hard to express yourself in writing, say it out loud and record yourself. Then copy this out and redraft it.

☐ Take one step at a time

Break the task into manageable steps. Look back to the C·R·E·A·M strategies (Chapter 4), such as setting mini-goals.

☐ Use the computer

If you use a computer it is easy to change what you have written. You can use a spellchecker, and nobody sees your handwriting!

☐ Brainstorming on the computer

Brainstorm headings and ideas, typing them quickly on the computer screen. Print them and cut them out. Rearrange them on a large piece of paper (perhaps using Blu-Tack™), until you have the order you want. Use this plan to 'cut and paste' the headings on the computer. Then write the text to go with the headings.

☐ Use specialist software

Use a computer package (such as *Inspiration*) which allows you to brainstorm and organise ideas both as patterns and as linear notes. You can colour-code ideas on screen; if you have a colour printer, you can get a colour printout. This can be very useful if you have difficulties organising your writing.

☐ Rest and relax

If your mind goes blank, you may be tired or stressed. See 'Managing stress' (page 228).

© Stella Cottrell 1999, *The Study Skills Handbook*, Macmillan Press Ltd

Tricks for getting started

Here are some ideas for getting started on a piece of writing.

- You can combine several of these.
- Which ones do you want to try?
- In your journal, keep a record of which work best for you.

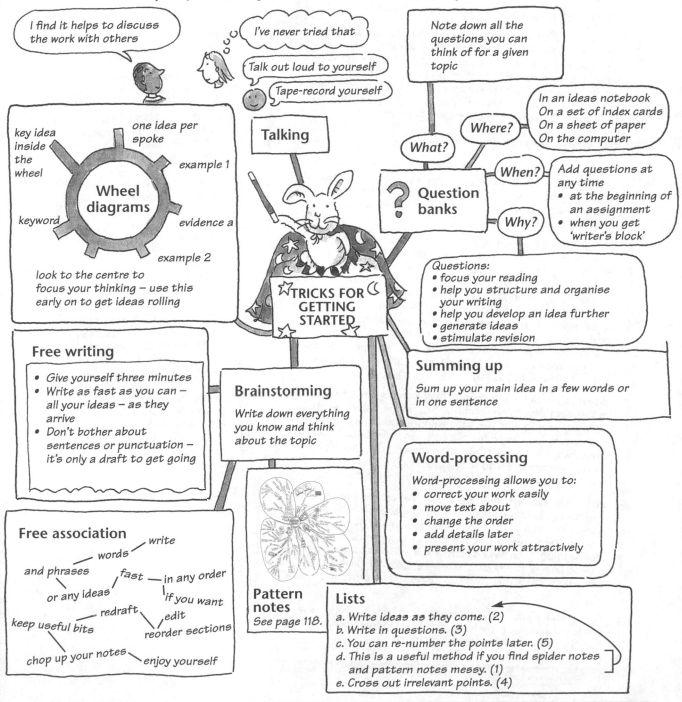

TRICKS FOR GETTING STARTED

Talking

I find it helps to discuss the work with others

I've never tried that

Talk out loud to yourself

Tape-record yourself

Wheel diagrams

key idea inside the wheel

one idea per spoke

example 1

keyword

evidence a

example 2

look to the centre to focus your thinking – use this early on to get ideas rolling

Question banks

Note down all the questions you can think of for a given topic

What?

Where? *In an ideas notebook / On a set of index cards / On a sheet of paper / On the computer*

When? *Add questions at any time*
- *at the beginning of an assignment*
- *when you get 'writer's block'*

Why? *Questions:*
- *focus your reading*
- *help you structure and organise your writing*
- *help you develop an idea further*
- *generate ideas*
- *stimulate revision*

Free writing

- *Give yourself three minutes*
- *Write as fast as you can – all your ideas – as they arrive*
- *Don't bother about sentences or punctuation – it's only a draft to get going*

Brainstorming

Write down everything you know and think about the topic

Summing up

Sum up your main idea in a few words or in one sentence

Word-processing

Word-processing allows you to:
- *correct your work easily*
- *move text about*
- *change the order*
- *add details later*
- *present your work attractively*

Free association

write – words – and phrases – or any ideas – fast – in any order – if you want – redraft – edit – keep useful bits – reorder sections – chop up your notes – enjoy yourself

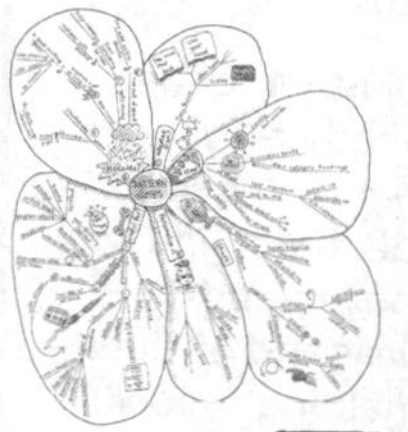

Pattern notes

See page 118.

Lists

a. Write ideas as they come. (2)
b. Write in questions. (3)
c. You can re-number the points later. (5)
d. This is a useful method if you find spider notes and pattern notes messy. (1)
e. Cross out irrelevant points. (4)

Students' solutions to writing blocks

Here two students describe how they incorporate some of the ideas mentioned in this chapter into their own way of working. How would you adapt their methods to suit you?

Marco

WHAT I USED TO DO

I used to find myself staring at the blank page, not knowing where to begin. I had done the reading. I knew in my head what I wanted to say. Nonetheless, getting started on a piece of writing seemed harder than climbing Everest. The page was too empty. Whatever I wrote seemed wrong. I used to write the first line and cross it out twenty or thirty times – maybe more – get a fresh piece of paper, and do the same thing again.

WHAT I DO NOW

I realise now that I used to aim at writing my good draft long before I was ready. My plans were too skimpy to be useful. I was actually trying to develop my ideas, organise information, write a final draft and compose good academic English all at the same time. No wonder I found it hard.

The first thing I do now is draw a face smiling up at me. It reminds me that this is only a draft – not my best copy, so it does not matter if I make mistakes. Next, I look away from the page, and maybe put my pen down. I think of a few things I want to include in my writing and jot them down in a list. When the list is getting long, I turn it into a mind-map – I think other people do it the other way round but it seems to work OK for me like this. I push each part of the map as far as I can take it by asking questions (*who? why? how often? always? everywhere? example? how do I know this?* etc.) As I read or go through my lecture notes, I add bits to the map.

When I have all the information I need on my mind-map, I look at the main themes and number them in the order they should be in my writing. I do the same with the topics I will cover under each theme, and any other material – so I know exactly where everything fits. I draw a different-coloured ring around each theme on the mind-map so it stands out. Sometimes I turn the mind-map back into a list to be clear what I am doing.

I then start with whatever topic looks easiest and just write the basics – not being too fussy at this stage about whether it sounds good – its just a starting place. I remind myself that I am free to write any sentence or bits of sentences in any order that I find easiest to do. I can always correct and edit and move things around later. When I come to rewrite it, lots of ideas and obvious corrections come quite easily, because I have something to look at.

By the time I write my best version, I am already nearly there. By working in stages, there is not that awful moment when writing actually 'begins' – it has developed bit by bit.

Ayeesha

I have revolutionised my writing. I am a 'headings and points' (1, 2, 3) person. I type these straight onto the computer. This organises everything easily. Then it's like joining up the dots. I write a sentence or two about each point. Everything under one heading is a paragraph. Then I write my conclusion, and the introduction. I keep correcting tiny bits as I go along – I am a perfectionist, I suppose. At the end, I print it out, erase the headings, and find a hundred things to correct – mostly quite small. Then I print it out again, and find twenty corrections and so on. I feel like an artist fine-tuning until I am happy with it. Well, I am never a 100% happy. No piece of writing is perfect. You just have to make a decision that 'that's it', the best you can do in the circumstances, and hand it in.

Essays, reports and other academic writing

This section looks at the basics of:

- what essays and reports are
- a seven-point procedure for approaching writing tasks
- analysing the title
- structuring your writing
- drafting, editing, and proof-reading.

The next chapter looks at more advanced features of academic writing: aim to read the two quite close together.

What is an essay?

An essay is a piece of writing which is written to a set of writing conventions. The diagram below gives some brief answers to questions many new students ask.

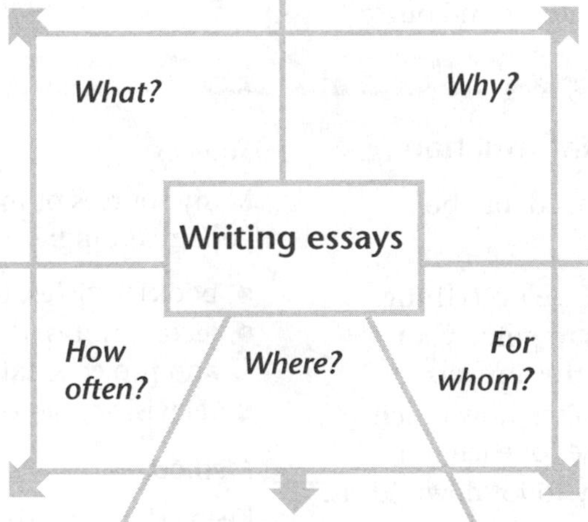

What?

- An essay is a piece of writing with a particular structure and layout (see page 147).
- Usually is is written in a formal, academic style: the language is different from the way you speak, or the way you would write letters to a friend – it is not conversational (see page 173).
- You are expected to keep very strictly to the task set. You are usually given an essay title: often this is referred to as 'the question', even if it isn't actually worded as a question.

Why?

In each essay you can:

- explore a topic in detail
- develop and organise your own ideas through writing
- develop your writing skills
- express your views about a topic

Essays also help tutors to assess your progress, and to assess and grade your work.

Ask your tutors why they give you essays to write – they may have additional reasons.

How often?

- Typically, you may write between two and eight essays each term, but this varies from course to course.

Where?

Write wherever suits you, or as required:

- at home
- in the library
- in the exam room.

For whom?

You write essays for:

- your tutors
- yourself
- examiners
- (sometimes) other students.

A seven-point procedure for writing assignments

Until you develop your own method of writing essays and other assignments, you may find this seven-point procedure helpful.

1 Clarify the task

Before you start research, make sure you know what you are looking for.

- Examine the title and course notes very carefully (page 142). What exactly is required? Ask your tutor early on if you are unsure.
- Write one line to sum up your basic opinion or argument. Adapt it as you proceed.
- Brainstorm or make pattern notes to record what you know.
- What do you need to read or find out?

2 Collect and record information

Get the information you need, but be focused.

- Be selective – you can't use everything.
- Write a set of questions to guide your research – and look for the answers.
- Check the word limit to see how much information you can use for each point.
- Keep a notebook nearby to jot down ideas.

Types of material

You can use any relevant material:

- factual information
- ideas, theories, opinions
- experience.

Sources

Many sources of information are available to you, including:

- books, articles, official reports, surveys
- lecture notes, data from laboratory work and projects, talking to others, interviews
- television, radio, newspapers, videos.

Method

Keep asking yourself:

- 'Do I need the information?'
- 'How will I use this information?'

Recording

Record information as you go along (see page 121):

- where you found information and ideas – for your references list (see page 125)
- notes of themes, theories, dates, names, data, explanations, examples, details, evidence, page numbers (see page 116).

3 Organise and plan

Organise your work as you go along (see page 146).

- Make a big chart to link ideas and details.
- Make a rough outline plan early on – you can refine it as you go along.

Planning

Keep checking what you are doing. Careful planning:

- helps to prevent repetition
- clarifies your thinking
- helps you organise your material.

4 Reflect and evaluate

When you have gathered the information, think about where you have got to.

- What have you discovered ?
- Has your viewpoint changed?
- Have you clarified your argument?
- Have you enough evidence/examples?
- What arguments or evidence oppose your point of view? Are they valid?
- Is it clearer to you why this task was set?

5 Write an outline plan and first draft

Now structure your writing.

- Refine your plan. Work out the order to introduce your ideas, using pattern notes or headings and points.
- Work out how many words you can write on each point. What must you leave out?
- Write a first draft. Write quickly: it is only a draft. You may find it easier to type headings onto the computer first.
- Start with whatever seems easiest.
- Keep going: don't worry about style.
- To begin with, state things clearly and simply in short sentences.

1 Title

2 Introduction

3 Main argument – notes Q (red)
evidence for – notes Q, p. 3–4
evidence against: Q, p. 5 (orange)
evaluation of evidence

4 Alternative theory: notes R (yellow)
example of application
evidence for
evidence against (lemon)
why not convincing

5 Alternative theory 2: notes S (green)
evaluation of evidence
why not convincing

6 Underlying issues – notes T (blue)

7 Conclusions
a
b
c

6 Work on your first draft

Develop your first draft. You may need to do this several times, improving the assignment with each version. Leave time between drafts for your ideas to simmer.

- Rewrite your early draft (see page 156). Adapt the structure (pages 147–9) and organise the writing into paragraphs.
- Make sure your argument is clear to readers.
- Check that you have included evidence and examples to support your points.
- Write out your references (or bibliography).

7 Final drafts

Edit and check your final draft (see page 162).

- Enjoy 'fine-tuning' your writing.
- Read it aloud to check that it is clearly written.
- Keep redrafting until you are happy with the text.

Analysing the title

Pick the title to bits

However they are worded, all assignment titles contain a central question which has to be answered. Your main task is to apply what you know to a particular problem. It is *not* to show how much you know – however brilliant your piece of writing, if it does not 'answer the question' you may get no marks at all.

You are marked partly on how well you select and organise information to meet the requirements of the title or problem – even in exams. Use the title or question to guide you in selecting what to read and note.

Focus on the title

It's essential to take time making sure you understand what is required.

- Read the title aloud slowly three times.
- Underline or highlight words which tell you the *approach* to take (see page 143).
- Underline words which guide you on how to select the *subject matter* of the assignment.
- Write out the title to help you take it in.
- How many sections are there to it?
- Write it out more fully, putting it in your own words. What is the assignment really looking for? What are the central questions?
- What topical issues does it refer to?
- Discuss the title with someone else.
- How does the title link to what you have read or heard in lectures? What else does it ask that you need to find out?

Make notes

Write down in your own words exactly what the question requires. It may form a useful part of your introduction later.

- Note obvious questions prompted by the title: such as 'Why did this happen?', 'How often ...?' or 'How typical ...?'
- Ask yourself why this question was set. Is there some public or academic controversy you should know about? Are there important issues to include?
- Note your reflections on the title, and your opinions.
- What do you already know? Do you have evidence to back up your opinions?
- What do you not know yet? Where or how can you find out more?

Pick the title to bits

Use the title

Keep focused on the title

Put the title where you can see it easily.

Keep checking the exact wording

As you research and write, remind yourself of the *exact wording* of the title. It is easy to forget the focus of the title and drift off on a tangent.

Introductions

In your 'Introduction' (the first paragraph of your writing), refer directly to the title in order to focus your reader. Say how you interpret the title. You can do this by rephrasing the title in your own words. (If you misunderstood the question, at least the reader will be aware of what has happened.)

Conclusions

In your conclusion, refer back to the title to demonstrate to your reader that you are still answering the set question. Link your final sentence to the question contained in the title.

CHECKLIST

Academic keywords used in titles

These words indicate the approach or style expected for the piece of writing.

Account for Give reasons for; explain why something happens.

Analyse Examine in very close detail; identify important points and chief features.

Comment on Identify and write about the main issues, giving your reactions based upon what you have read or heard in lectures. Avoid purely personal opinion.

Compare Show how two or more things are similar. Indicate the relevance or consequences of these similarities.

Contrast Set two or more items or arguments in opposition so as to draw out differences. Indicate whether the differences are significant. If appropriate, give reasons why one item or argument may be preferable (see Chapter 8).

Critically evaluate Weigh arguments for and against something, assessing the strength of the evidence on both sides. Use criteria to guide your assessment of which opinions, theories, models or items are preferable.

Define Give the exact meaning of. Where relevant, show that you understand why the definition may be problematic.

Describe Give the main characteristics or features of something, or outline the main events.

Discuss Write about the most important aspects of (probably including criticism); give arguments for and against; consider the implications of.

Distinguish Bring out the differences between two (possible confusible) items.

Evaluate Assess the worth, importance or usefulness of something, using evidence. There will probably be cases to be made both *for* and *against*.

Examine Put the subject 'under the microscope', looking at it in detail. If appropriate, 'Critically evaluate' it as well.

Explain Make clear why something happens, or why something is the way it is.

Illustrate Make something clear and explicit, giving examples or evidence.

Interpret Give the meaning and relevance of data or other material presented.

Justify Give evidence which supports an argument or idea; show why a decision or conclusions were made, considering objections that others might make.

Narrate Concentrate on saying *what* happened, telling it as a story.

Outline Give only the main points, showing the main structure.

Relate Show similarities and connections between two or more things.

State Give the main features, in very clear English (almost like a simple list but written in full sentences).

Summarise Draw out the main points only (see 'Outline'), omitting details or examples.

To what extent Consider how far something is true, or contributes to a final outcome. Consider also ways in which the proposition is not true. (The answer is usually somewhere between 'completely' and 'not at all'.)

Trace Follow the order of different stages in an event or process.

© Stella Cottrell 1999, *The Study Skills Handbook*, Macmillan Press Ltd

Common features of all academic writing

Although the wording of essay or other assignment titles may differ, almost all academic writing requires you to do certain things.

Use source materials

Do not simply state your personal opinion or say what is in your head. Instead, use material from reading, lecture notes and other sources to give reasons, evidence, examples and case studies.

Compare and contrast

Most assignments require some element of comparing and contrasting, especially of theories, models or research findings. You will probably have to read different opinions and weigh them against each other.

Use criteria to evaluate

State which criteria you use to evaluate evidence: for example, that you are using the most up-to-date figures, or figures drawn from the largest survey, or a well-known expert's opinion for a particular reason (such as that he uses evidence from twenty well-conducted experiments). See Chapter 9, 'Critical analytical thinking'.

Show awareness of complexities

Demonstrate that you are aware that answers are not always clear-cut. For example, although the expert you quote seems to have the best argument, his twenty experiments may all have used small children whereas the question set refers to teenagers. Acknowledge weaknesses in your own argument and strengths in opposing arguments. State clearly why there are difficulties coming to a firm conclusion one way or another.

Follow an argument

In your writing, show a line of reasoning which gives direction to the writing, so that one point follows logically from another. (See Chapters 8 and 9.)

Make a decision

Show which side of the argument, or which model or theory, is best in the final analysis. Even though the case may be fairly evenly weighted, show that you are able to make a decision on the basis of the evidence.

Follow a set structure

There is likely to be a set structure for the type of writing and a particular style for your subject area. (Different styles are considered in the next chapter.) *All* academic writing requires that you group similar points together in one paragraph or section, rather than scattering them through the text.

Be 'discursive'

Link your points so that they feed into sentences and paragraphs, and so that each paragraph follows naturally from the previous one. All should contribute to a central guiding line of reasoning. (This is different from presenting a random set of points, for example, or headings with bullet points under them.)

Be emotionally neutral

Most academic writing requires you to stand back and analyse dispassionately, as an objective onlooker.

Structuring your writing

The structure and organisation of your work is just as important as the content. What matters is not just what you know but the way that you organise it.

How do you structure academic writing?

Like a building, a piece of academic writing gains its structure and shape from several elements.

Design: your argument

What you are trying to say (your argument) should provide the structure for the whole piece of writing. Your reader should be able to follow your line of reasoning easily: how it moves from *a* to *b* to *c*. (See page 175 and Chapter 9.)

Scaffolding: organising and planning

Organise and plan your work before you start.

- Group ideas together, in files or on paper.
- Devise a working plan to guide your research.
- Make an outline plan for your writing.

(See pages 146 and 150.)

Central framework: formal structure

Different formal structures are required for different kinds of writing, such as essays or reports – see pages 147 and 149.

Bricks: paragraphs

Writing is organised into paragraphs, and each paragraph itself has a structure. Clear paragraphing assists the reader. (See pages 157–9.)

Cement: wording

You can use language, such as linking words and emphasis, to highlight your point and show the direction of your argument. (See page 160.)

Organising information: grouping things together

First try this ...

For each box, work out:

- How many circles are there?
- How many triangles?
- How many *types* of triangle?

Box A

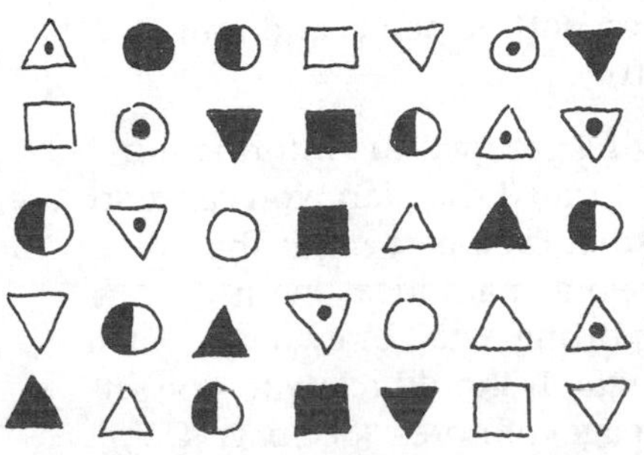

Box B

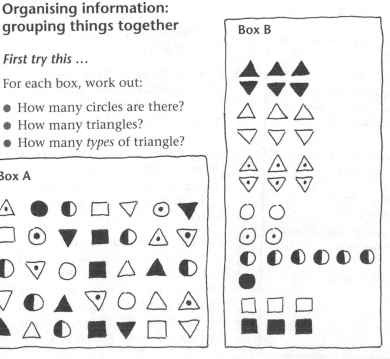

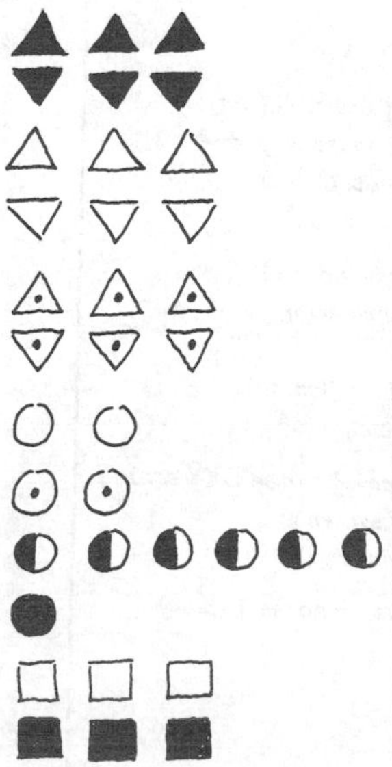

Comment

You probably found it quicker and easier to find the answers for Box B. If so, why was this the case?

Why group information?

Grouping ideas and points has several advantages.

- You will be able to find things more easily.
- You will find it easier to draw up your writing plan and follow it.
- Your thinking will be clearer.
- Your readers will be able to follow your argument more easily.
- You will get in a mess if you don't.

See pages 121 and 146.

Organising information: planning your writing

Below are four steps you will need to take in organising information for an assignment. Each step makes the next one easier. (See also 'Recording and using information', page 121.)

1 *Divide the work into topics*

When making notes, it may be easiest to use a separate sheet for each main point or topic. Or you may like to use a large sheet of paper, writing out points so you can see them all clearly.

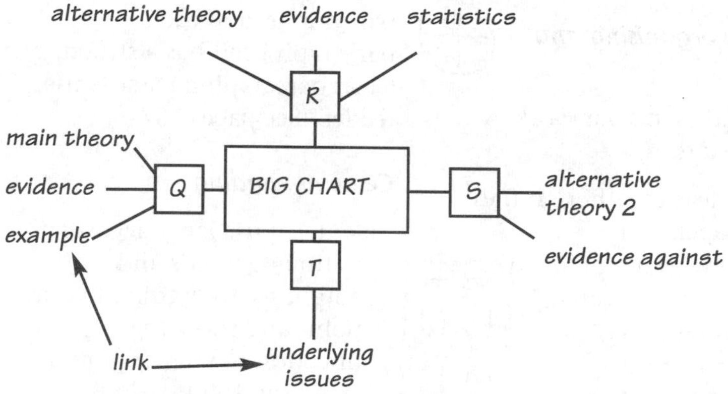

2 *Rearrange your notes*

- Spread your notes out so that you can see them.
- Look at what you have.
- Group related information.
- Arrange the material in the best order.

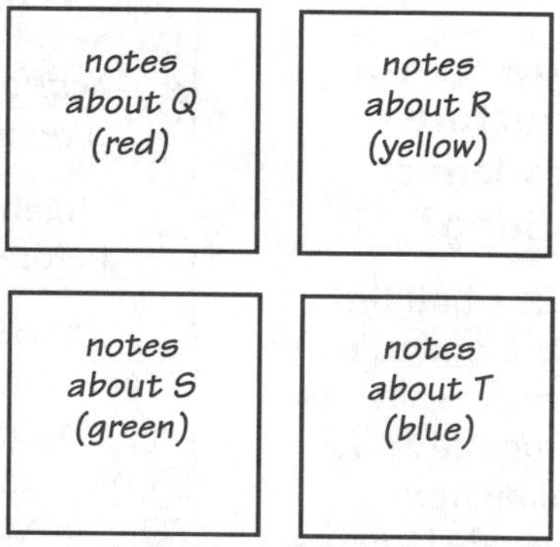

3 *Write an outline plan*

Write your first outline before you have done any research. Often you will find that you know more than you thought. The outline helps to shape your ideas and focus your reading. You can adapt it as you go along.

1 Title
2 Introduction
3 Main argument – notes Q (red)
  evidence for – notes Q, p. 3–4
  evidence against: Q, p. 5 (orange)
  evaluation of evidence
4 Alternative theory: notes R (yellow)
  example of application
  evidence for
  evidence against (lemon)
  why not convincing
5 Alternative theory 2: notes S (green)
  evaluation of evidence
  why not convincing
6 Underlying issues – notes T (blue)
7 Conclusions
  a
  b
  c

4 *Organise information into paragraphs*

Colour-code each pile of notes. The plan shown uses the sequence of colours of the rainbow, to assist memory. Divide your notes with coloured dividers. Give each paragraph a colour: underline main points in this colour. Maintain this colour-coding onto pattern notes, outline plans, and rough drafts.

Having grouped the information and formed the plan, you can start writing. Each paragraph should have one main idea – with supporting detail or evidence. Each paragraph should relate to one set (or page) of notes. (See page 157.)

Structuring an essay

1 Title/question

As stated earlier (page 142), every essay title contains an actual or implied question. The whole of your essay must focus on the title and address that question.

2 Introduction

In your introduction, explain what the essay is going to do.

- Explain how you interpret the question.
- Identify issues that are you going to explore.
- Give a brief outline of how you will deal with each issue, and in which order.

Length: about one-tenth of the essay.

3 Develop your argument or line of reasoning

Paragraph 1

- This paragraph covers the first thing your introduction said you would address.
- The first sentence introduces the main idea of the paragraph.
- Other sentences develop the topic of the paragraph. Include relevant examples, details, evidence, quotations, references.
- Lead up to the next paragraph.

Paragraph 2 and other paragraphs

- The first sentence, or opening sentences, link the paragraph to the previous paragraphs, then introduce the main idea of the paragraph.
- Other sentences develop the paragraph's topic.

(For more about paragraphs, see pages 157–9.)

4 Conclusion

The conclusion contains no *new* material.

- Summarise your argument and the main themes.
- State your general conclusions.
- Make it clear why those conclusions are important or significant.
- In your last sentence, sum up your argument very briefly, linking it to the title.

Length: about one-tenth of the essay.

5 References and/or bibliography

References and bibliography

List all the books, articles and other materials you have referred to within the essay. (See page 125.) If a bibliography is required, list relevant texts, including those you read but did not refer to in the essay.

The structure given here is the most basic. It underlies not just essays but many other types of writing. The structuring of different types of essay is discussed in Chapter 8.

Writing reports

What is a report?

A report is the formal writing up of a piece of research or project work. Reports are usually written in a concise style, giving precise detail. Information is presented under clear headings. Reports are structured in similar ways which can help you to find information quickly when reading them. Dissertations tend to use all the sections listed on page 149. Other reports may not contain all these sections – for example, acknowledgements may not be needed. Your tutors may have preferences, too: they may prefer you to integrate the literature review into the introduction, or the conclusions and recommendations into the discussion section.

Make the job as easy as possible

Write the sections in whichever order is easiest for you. Once written, rearrange them into the structure your subject requires or the order given on page 149.

Use headings

Give each section a heading, to indicate what it covers. Use brief sub-headings to introduce different kinds of subject matter. Number sub-sections.

1 Heading for first section

1.1 Subheading 1

1.1.1 your first point under subheading 1.1
1.1.2 your second point under subheading 1.1
1.1.3 etc.

1.2 Subheading 2

1.2.1 first point under subheading 1.2
1.2.2 second point under subheading 1.2
1.2.3 etc.

2 Heading for next section

Is material in the right place?

Check carefully that each element is under the right heading. It is easy to get absorbed in developing an idea, and include material from a later section.

Be precise

The writing style required is usually very sharp and focused. Omit unnecessary detail or description, especially in the literature review.

The description of your methods must be precise enough to allow somebody else to duplicate your research exactly. (See pages 169–70.)

Data

Data must be clear and accurate, and presented in tables, charts or graphs if appropriate. Tables detailing your main results may be part of the main report: other data is usually put into numbered appendices. In the text, refer the reader to each appendix by number.

Principal differences between essays and reports

- Essays and reports have different structures. Compare pages 147 and 149.
- They have different layouts. Headings and numbering are used in reports, but not in essays.
- Essays flow as continuous text: reports are broken into clear sections.
- Essays present an argument or ideas rather than the findings of new research data. Reports present research data you have collected yourself, for example in a laboratory experiment, a survey or a case study.
- Essays discuss, compare and evaluate ideas. Reports often include recommendations for action.
- Essays use a consistent style throughout. Reports contain a mixture of writing styles: for example, the methods section uses descriptive writing, the abstract is a summary, and the discussion section is analytical.

Structuring reports

Check whether your course uses a particular structure for reports.
If not, then include the following, in this order.

Title Write this on its own in the centre of the first page, with your name, the course title, and the date.

Acknowledgements List people you wish to thank for help given.

Abstract Give a brief summary or overview of your report, including its conclusions. Restrict this (usually) to one paragraph. Omit details or examples, except main experimental data.

Report abstracts may be reproduced and read separately from the rest of the report, so they often contain information also included in other sections.

List of contents List the main sections of the report and the page on which each begins (including any appendices).

List of tables and illustrations List any illustrations, charts, maps and so on, giving the page number for each.

Introduction Briefly discuss what the research is about – why is it important or significant? State your proposals or hypotheses briefly: what are you going to show or prove?

Review of the literature Discuss briefly some of the most important writings on the subject, discussing other researchers' main findings. Do you agree or disagree with them? Focus on how previous research connects with and leads up to your research. Introduce your experimental hypothesis, if you have one.

Method How did you conduct your research? What methods did you use? Did you replicate methods used by other researchers? Even if your tutors told you what methods to use, include these in the report.

Exactly what were the conditions of the experiment? How many people or items were included? How did you select them? What instructions did you give to participants?

Measurement criteria Discuss the kinds of data you gathered. How did you analyse them? How reliable or accurate are your data?

Present the results Present your main findings briefly, under headings if appropriate. Give results in the order in which you conducted any experiments, or start with the most important.

Discuss the results This is a longer section. Analyse and explain your findings. Were they what you had expected? Did they fit the theory or seem to disprove it? Were they consistent with your hypothesis? How are they significant?

How could the research have been improved? What follow-up research would be useful?

Conclusions In some subjects, a conclusion is inappropriate. Otherwise, summarise your key points and show why your hypothesis can be maintained or rejected.

Recommendations In subjects such as social policy or health, you may be asked to give a numbered list of suggestions for action to resolve problems.

References List all your sources, in alphabetical order.

Bibliography If required, list relevant further reading, again in alphabetical order.

Appendices Present together any essential extra material, such as instructions to participants, copies of materials used, or tables and graphs of data. Number each item. Do not include items unless they are mentioned in the report.

© Stella Cottrell 1999, *The Study Skills Handbook*, Macmillan Press Ltd

Planning your writing assignment

As you become more aware of different writing formats, you can use the appropriate structure to guide your planning.

Plan spatially: draw out your pages

Before beginning any research:

- Work out roughly how many words you write or type on one page of A4 paper. (This may be about 300 words.)
- Check the overall word limit for your assignment. (This may be 1200 words.)
- How many pages of your writing or typing will your essay occupy? (For instance, 1200 words at 300 words/page will occupy 4 pages.)
- Take that many pieces of paper. Draw out in pencil how much space you will give to each section, item or topic, as in the sample essay below. How many words can you allocate to each section? Or to each topic or example?
- It may take a few attempts to get the balance right. Note how little you can write for each topic or example.
- If you wish, continue to plan out your essay, point by point, on these sheets. Notice how much space each item can take.

With this spatial plan, can you now see:

- how many pages of your writing your assignment will take?
- where sections or topics will be on the page?
- how your word limit divides up?
- how little or how much you need to read and note for each item?

An outline plan for the essay on pages 183–5 (1000 words)

Page 1

Introduction (c. 100 words)
- *definitions*
- *what the essay will cover and the order*

paragraph 2 (c. 150 words)
- *maternal deprivation theory – early bonding essential*
- *later: 'secure base' + 'exploration' behaviours*
- *opposes child care as harmful*

Page 2

paragraph 3 (c. 150 words)
- *why Bowlby's ideas appealed*
  - *social reasons*
  - *research evidence, then e.g. Goldfarb (1947) Robertson (1967–73)*

paragraph 4 (c. 150 words)
- *later evidence underminded earlier research e.g. Tizard (1970s)*
- *Bowlby seemed less convincing*
- *child care did not seem so bad*

Page 3

paragraph 5 (c. 150 words)
- *Mary Ainsworth (1978) – new research supports Bowlby*
- *but this research also is challenged by some people*

paragraph 6 (c. 200 words)
- *why it is difficult to evaluate the research*
- *depressed mothers: suggest day care can be useful*

Page 4

conclusion (c. 100 words)
- *sum up*
- *theory has been modified*
- *social and day care conditions have changed*
- *under certain conditions, day care may be beneficial*

references

Planning stages

Develop your outline plan

Make a first outline plan

Make pattern notes or a structure plan showing what you know, what at this stage you think are the main issues, your questions, and things to find out.

Action plan

Convert your list of things to find out into an action plan with priorities (page 72).

Plan your time

Use the ***Working backwards from deadlines*** sheet (page 73) and your diary to map out when and where to complete each stage of the writing process. (This becomes easier after the first assignment, when you have a feel for your own pace of working.)

What is the *minimum* you can do? What additional research you would *like* to do, if you have time? Depending on how well you proceed, you can adapt your reading and note-taking to suit.

Rework your plan

If necessary, rework your outline plan as you proceed. You may rework your plan several times as your thinking becomes more sophisticated. This is part of the process of understanding a subject.

Make a clear final outline plan

Clarify your final plan. If necessary use correction fluid to remove unwanted text, use colour to highlight certain areas, or rewrite untidy parts afresh and stick them over the area to be clarified.

Notice whether you use 'neatening the plan' as an excuse to put off writing the first draft.

From pattern notes to linear plan

It's essential to be really clear about the structure of your essay before you start writing. If you're not, your writing and thinking may appear muddled.

Pattern notes are very effective at the planning stage, but you may find it difficult to write assignments directly from them. They illustrate connections and resemble the way the mind organises information in networks, whereas writing is linear and sequential – one point follows another. Pattern notes are also mainly descriptive. On notes of this sort, it is harder to analyse, evaluate and contrast, yet these are what an essay requires.

The following approach can help in translating pattern notes into writing.

- Use the pattern notes to brainstorm what you know and to generate ideas. Encourage your creativity rather than worrying about organising information at this stage.
- Use colour, numbers and connecting lines to link related information on the pattern.
- Redraw the pattern notes, placing together all connected information.
- As a half-way stage between pattern notes and sequential writing, you may like to draw up pyramids (see page 152). On a separate sheet, make a pyramid for each major section of the pattern. With practice, pyramids will clarify how your information is structured.
- From the notes or pyramids, write out your main headings, with main points and items listed under each. Use the colour-code from the pattern notes to guide you. Position these lists on your spatial plan (page 150).

Concept pyramids organise ideas

What is a concept?

A *concept* is a mental representation of a group of items which are similar in some way. For example, the concept 'cutlery' includes objects as different as a four-pronged fork, a hollowed, round-ended spoon, and a sharp-edged knife. Conceptually, these all share the characteristic of being tools used in eating food. Sometimes the phrase *conceptual category* is used instead of 'concept'.

Why concepts are useful

When we come across a new object the brain matches the main features of the new experience against those of previous experiences. It can then make a good guess at what kind of thing the new object is – its concept category:

Once it has identified the category, the brain can second-guess, or infer, other information:

'If it's a tree, it must have roots and sap. It won't leave the area. I don't need to take it for walks. Sorted!'

This ability to identify and share conceptual categories enables us to communicate more easily with other people: we don't need to describe everything in minute detail whenever we speak. In academic writing, if ideas are well organised, the reader can second-guess meaning and other information more easily.

Concept pyramids organise ideas

We can organise concepts into hierarchies – shaped like a triangle or pyramid, as in the simple one for 'tree' below. You don't *have* to use concept pyramids – but they give you an extra analytical tool.

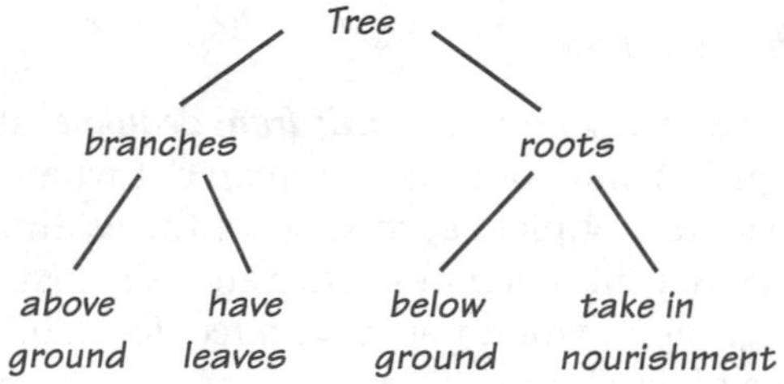

The most general information, or the most inclusive heading, is placed at the top of the pyramid. Aspects of the tree are placed below. Details of those aspects are placed below again – and so on.

Each level of the pyramid shows information of a different category. There are technical names for different category levels, but everyday terms work just as well.

Technical term	Everyday term
Superordinate category	Upper level (*tree*)
Intermediate or basic category	Intermediate level (*oak tree*)
Subordinate category	Lower level (*red oak tree*)
Exemplar	Example (*this red oak tree*)

On another pyramid, *plant* might be the upper-level concept, and *tree* would then be at the intermediate level.

Example: concept pyramid for contrasting birds and mammals

The example below shows a more detailed concept pyramid, showing how different levels of information about animals can be arranged.

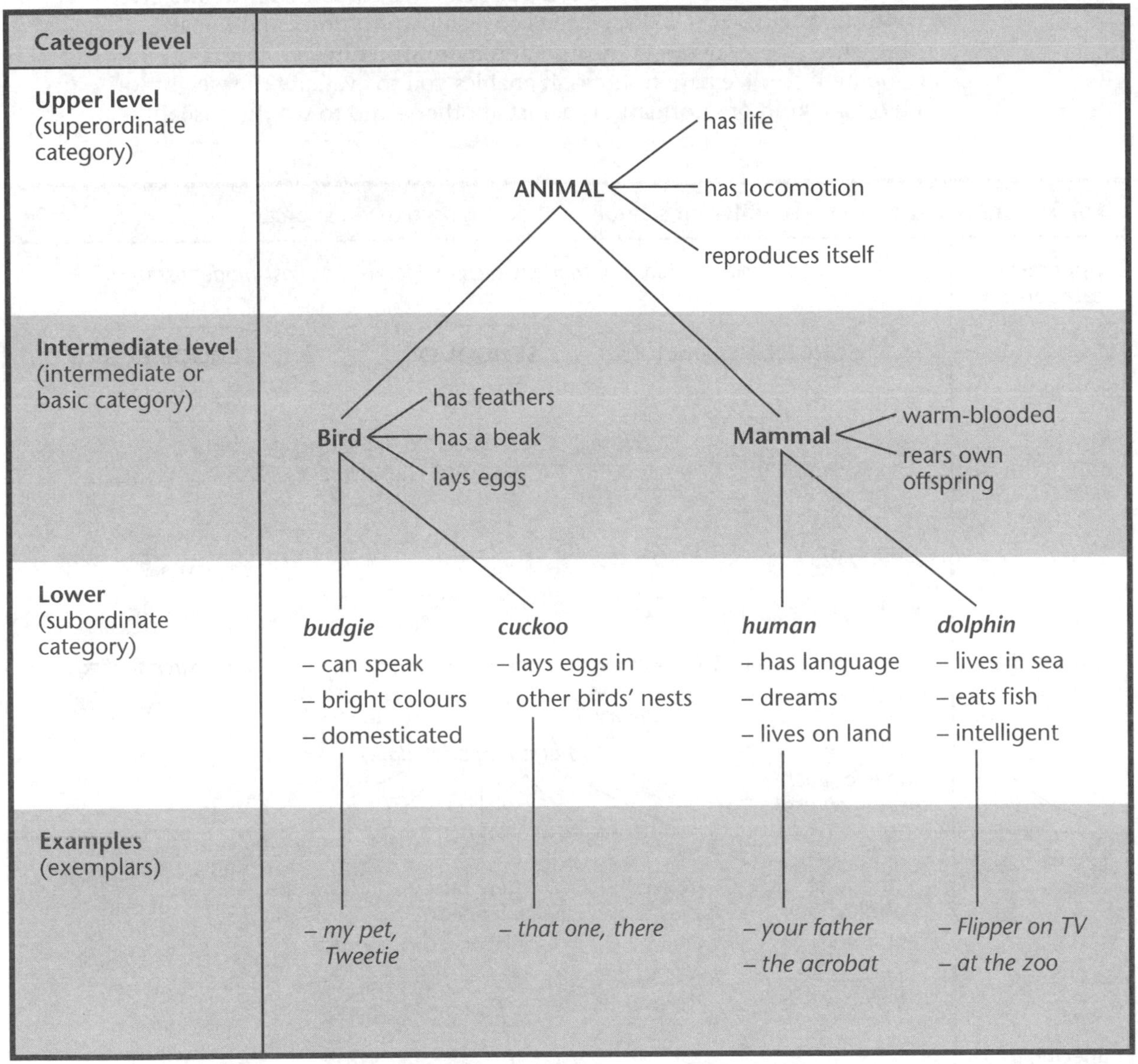

Examples at different levels

If the upper level were *painting*, an intermediate level could be the style, *Impressionism*. A lower level would be painters, such as *Monet*, and examples could be Monet's paintings *Water Lilies*, *Wisteria*, and *Poplars*. You might have separate hierarchies of details of the paintings – with *size*, *colour*, *design*, or *brushwork* as category headings.

If the upper level were *instrument*, an intermediate level could be *drum*, and a lower level might be a *timpani drum* or *African drum*. Specific examples would be *that drum on the table*, or *Gino's new drum-set*.

Essays plans as pyramids

Essay structures consist of several concept pyramids combined into one piece of continuous writing. A halfway step between pattern notes and linear writing, the concept pyramid incorporates more structure and linear development. Unlike pattern notes, it enables you to evaluate the weight (or level) of one kind of information against another – and to see this visually.

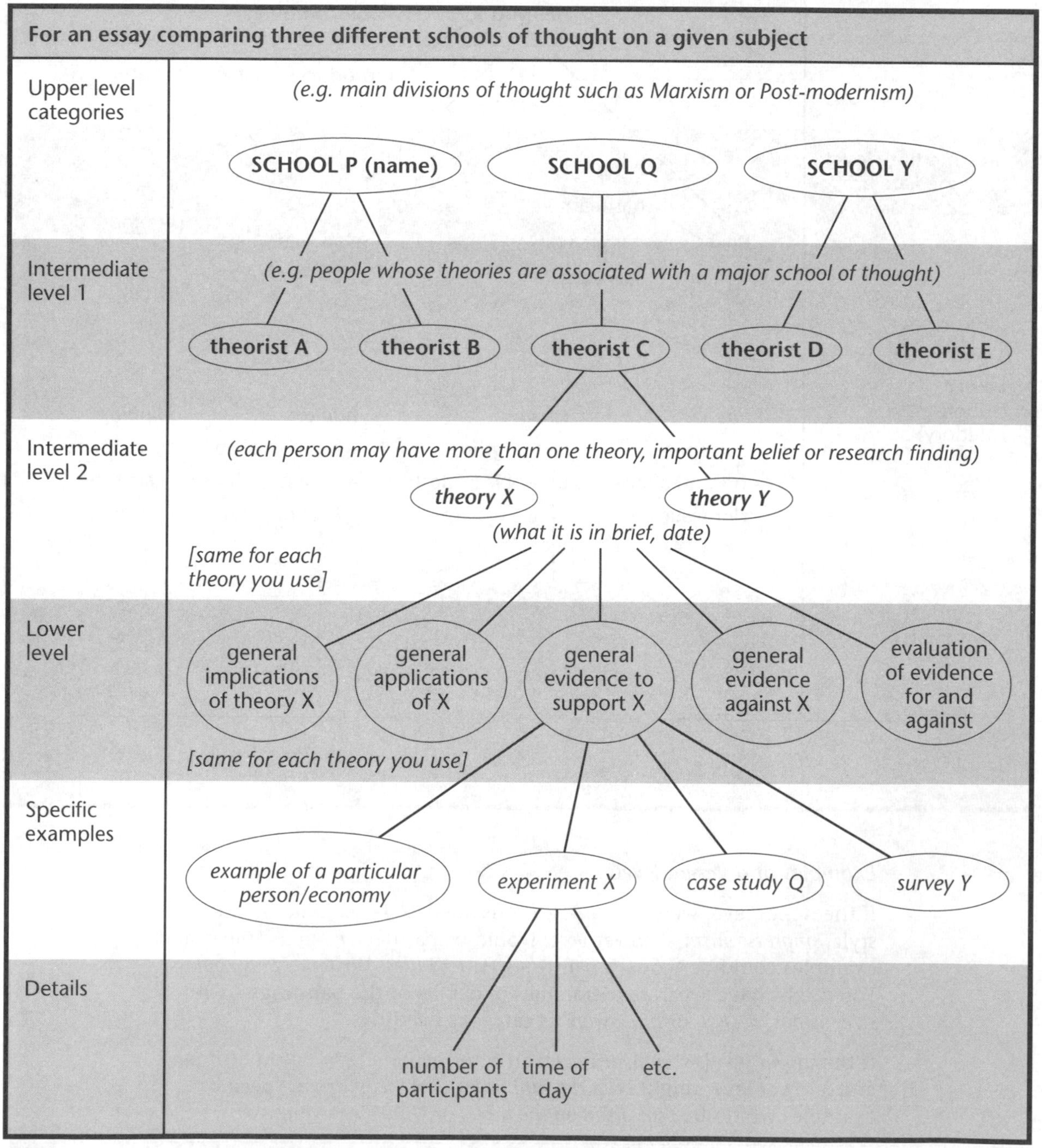

Use pyramid questions to help in planning

Ask yourself key questions to search for or organise the information at each level.

Upper level

- How many major schools of thought are there on this question?
- Which ones are the most relevant and need to be included? (If unsure, go down to the intermediate level and check who said or wrote what.)

Intermediate level

- Which theorist (or judge, writer, or similar) said what, when?
- How can you sum that up briefly?

Lower level

- Overall, how good is the general evidence to support this position or theory?
- What are the general implications of the position or theory?
- What are the general applications of the position or theory?
- What is the general evidence against the position or theory?
- Overall, how good is the evidence for or against?

Exemplar level

- Do you need to include specific examples of applications, implications or evidence? Which are the best examples?
- Given the word limit and the time available, how much detail should you give? For instance, have you space only to mention the name and date and one line about this research? Or are you short of words, in which case you could give more details?

Use pyramids to help with word limits

Having mapped out your information as a pyramid, do you have the right amount for your word limit?

Too much information

If you have too much, you will need to leave something out.

- If you have several examples at any one level, select just one or two examples of them. Do the same with the other levels.
- If you have already used most of your word limit, you may be able to refer to specific examples by name without going into detail. (This depends to some extent on the subject.)

Too little information

If you have too little, you can build up to the word limit.

- Add more examples at the middle or lower levels.
- Write more about your specific examples. Evaluate the significance of the examples for the overall assignment.

Balancing the pyramid

In general, it is more important to explore ideas at the middle and lower levels than to give a lot of detail for specific examples. (See page 212.)

Writing drafts

The art of writing is in the craft of redrafting

Professional writers redraft many times before they are happy: writing rarely flows out 'all at once' in its final version.

Writing is easier if the research, planning and organising is already done and if you focus on different processes in each draft.

Draft 1: a quick draft to get ideas down

Use your plan. Don't worry about style or good English.

- Focus on the assignment question: write out your interpretation of the title.
- What is your core idea? Write out your central idea or the main line of your reasoning.
- Write headings and subheadings from your plan (the pyramid, or whatever), but leave these out of the final draft of an essay.
- Add in details below each heading. Link headings and points into sentences.
- Use your plan: keep looking back to it after writing each paragraph.

Draft 2: fine-tune the structure

Check that information is grouped and ordered – especially into paragraphs (page 157). If not, cut up your text with a scissors and rearrange it, or colour-code and number paragraphs in the order in which you will rewrite them.

Check that the line of argument is clear from one paragraph to the next – if necessary, add in sentences to link ideas. You may need to do this more than once.

Draft 3: fine-tune the style

Read what you have written aloud. How does it sound? Can you improve the flow or style? Add sentences or details where needed.

Draft 4: finishing touches

Aim to leave at least a day between drafts. Your mind will continue to work on your ideas. After a break, you will find it easier to spot passages that need rephrasing. See 'Editing', page 161.

Drafting on the computer

People vary in what they prefer to do on paper, what they do on the computer, and how often they move between the two. Experiment to find out what suits you.

Drafting on the computer is a more continual process – you will probably find you make many small corrections and move text about as you go along. Leave spellchecking until the final draft.

File management

If you intend to make major changes to a draft, save a copy of the document with a number at the end of the name ('Filename2'). Then edit the copy. If you change your mind, you can revert to the earlier draft, or use information from it.

Divide long documents (over about 3000 words or which include graphics) into separate files, adding 'a', 'b', 'c' and so on at the end of the filename. You will be able to move around the file and find information more quickly. Later you can paste the parts together into one long document, or start the page numbers for each part to follow on from the previous file.

Working from a floppy disk is much slower than working from the hard disk. If you can, therefore, copy your essay file onto the hard disk. To save confusion about which copy you are working on, take the floppy out of the computer while you are working. When you finish a session, copy the file from the hard disk onto the floppy.

Listen to your essay

If you have a screen-reader, which turns text into speech, listen to the computer reading your text aloud. Listen for meaning, and for punctuation pauses.

Print your essay

It is easier to read and edit your work on paper printouts rather than working onscreen. The shimmering of the screen may tire your eyes, and you may not always be able to use a computer when you wish.

Paragraphs

Paragraphs are made up of sentences. Usually they are several sentences long.

Each paragraph is organised around a central idea or theme, which is usually made clear in the first sentence of each paragraph. It groups similar ideas and material together. All sentences relate to the main idea of the paragraph.

Successive paragraphs follow each other in a logical order, taking the reader from *a* to *b* to *c*. Words or phrases within them link them to earlier or later paragraphs.

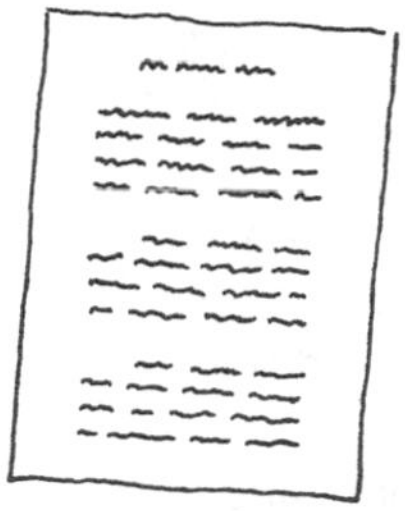

Paragraphs help the reader

Paragraphs break up the text into manageable portions. A page is easier to look at when divided into three, four or five sections.

Paragraphs also organise meaning. They help your readers to think clearly about what you have written.

First sentence

The first sentence of each paragraph:

- is usually the 'topic sentence' which introduces the subject of the paragraph
- starts on a new line
- is preceded by a gap – either an indent on the same line, or a blank line before.

Later sentences

Other sentences of each paragraph:

- develop the theme of the paragraph's 'topic sentence'
- follow each other in a logical order – one sentence leading to the next.

Last sentence

The last sentence:

- sums up the paragraph, or leads into the next paragraph.

Activity 1

Choose two or three pages from one book.

- Read the topic sentences – the ones that sum up the main theme of each paragraph. These are often, but not always, the opening sentences.
- How well do the topic sentences sum up the main ideas of those paragraphs?
- How are the paragraphs linked?
- If paragraphs lacked a clear topic sentence, were they more difficult to read?

Activity 2

How good are *you* at paragraphing? Separate the following passage into sentences and paragraphs.

A Life of Adventure

mary seacole was born in 1805 in kingston jamaica her mother practised as a 'doctress' using medical knowledge which women had brought from africa and developed in the tropics from her mother mary inherited her medical skills as well as her ability to run a boarding house from her father a scottish military man she inherited her fascination with army life marys own medical reputation was established during a series of cholera and yellow fever epidemics she made her own medicines and emphasised high standards of hygiene as well as enforcing strict quarantine on victims by these methods she saved many lives on the outbreak of the crimean war mary volunteered her services to the british army although she had worked for the army before at its own request this time she was turned down undaunted mary made her own way to the war zone once in the crimea she not only nursed the soldiers but also ran a hotel and sold food wine and medicines after the war mary was treated as a celebrity she was decorated by the governments of four countries in england a poem in her honour was published in punch and even the royal family requested her company and medical expertise

Activity 3

- Re-read the paragraphs for Activity 2.
- Decide the main theme of each paragraph. and sum it up in 1–4 words.
- Check your version with the one below.

Suggested answers

Activity 2

A Life of Adventure

Mary Seacole was born in 1805 in Kingston, Jamaica. Her mother practised as a 'doctress', using medical knowledge which women had brought from Africa and developed in the Tropics. From her mother, Mary inherited her medical skills as well as her ability to run a boarding house. From her father, a Scottish military man, she inherited her fascination with army life.

Mary's own medical reputation was established during a series of cholera and yellow fever epidemics. She made her own medicines and emphasised high standards of hygiene as well as enforcing strict quarantine on victims. By these methods she saved many lives.

On the outbreak of the Crimean War, Mary volunteered her services to the British Army. Although she had worked for the army before, at its own request, this time she was turned down. Undaunted, Mary made her own way to the war zone. Once in the Crimea, she not only nursed the soldiers, but also ran a hotel and sold food, wine and medicines.

After the war, Mary was treated as a celebrity. She was decorated by the governments of four countries. In England, a poem in her honour was published in Punch and even the Royal Family requested her company and medical expertise.

Activity 3

The main themes of the paragraphs are:

1 general information: birth and background
2 early medical reputation
3 the Crimean War
4 after the War.

Did you find it easier to read the text for Activity 2? If so, did this increase your appreciation of the value of good paragraphing and punctuation?

Did you have difficulting adding in the punctuation? If so, you could ask your tutors whether any additional support is available.

Writing paragraphs

If you have difficulties with paragraphing, divide your page into three columns:

1 Arguments	*2 Main information*	*3 Supporting detail*

- In column 1, jot down the ideas, theories, opinions and line of reasoning that you want to include in your writing.
- In column 2, jot down the main examples and types of evidence that support your line of reasoning.
- In column 3, write down lesser details, facts, names, statistics, dates and examples that support your main argument.
- Each paragraph should have:
  - one item from column 1
  - one, two or three items from column 2
  - several items from column 3.
- Items selected for each paragraph should all help to make the same point.

Alternatively, using a concept pyramid:

- Each paragraph is likely to need one item at the intermediate level, one at the lower level, examples, and a few details.

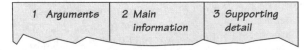

Checking your paragraphs

When you have finished your early drafts, you can check how well you have paragraphed your writing by doing the following exercise.

1 Read each paragraph

Read each of your paragraphs in turn. Decide what is the main topic of each.

2 Sum up the topic

Sum up that topic in about 1–4 words.

3 Give the topic a name and colour

Write the topic in the margin. Give it a colour.

4 Which is the topic sentence?

Which sentence is your topic sentence – the one that sums up the topic? Highlight it. Is it at the beginning of the paragraph? If not, would it be more powerful there?

5 Is everything relevant?

Check whether everything in each paragraph relates to the topic sentence. If you're unsure, put a ring round it and check whether it would be better in a different paragraph. Is anything superfluous? If so, cross it out.

6 Is everything in the right place?

Once you have colour-coded the topic for each paragraph, check each topic in turn: have bits of it have wandered into other paragraphs? Highlight with the topic colour any bits that have gone astray. For example, if you wrote in paragraph 2 about bird habitats and have written more about bird habitats some paragraphs later, highlight both in the same colour. Then cut out separated items of the same colour and paste them together. Rewrite the paragraph, integrating the bits you have moved.

7 Are sentences in the best order?

In each paragraph, are the sentences in the best order? Is it clear how each sentence leads on to the next?

8 Is the line of argument clear?

Is it clear to the reader how each paragraph relates to the others? Is it clear how each paragraph leads on to the next?

9 Is everything relevant?

Is every paragraph relevant to the title?

Make time for relaxation and exercise – you can go on thinking about your assignment!

Linking ideas together

Certain words are used to link ideas and to signpost to the reader the direction your line of reasoning is about to take, such as adding more emphasis, or introducing an alternative viewpoint.

Below is a selection of words used to link ideas, depending on the direction of your argument.

Adding more to a point already made

- also; moreover; furthermore; again; further; what is more; then; in addition
- besides; above all; too; as well (as)
- either; neither … nor; not only … but also; similarly; correspondingly; in the same way; indeed
- in fact; really; in reality, it is found that …
- as for; as to; with respect to; regarding

Writing in lists

- first(ly); second(ly); third(ly)
- another; yet another; in addition; finally
- to begin with; in the second place
- moreover; additionally; also
- next; then; and to conclude; lastly; finally

Putting the same idea in a different way

- in other words; rather; or; better; in that case
- to put it (more) simply
- in view of this; with this in mind
- to look at this another way

Introducing examples

- that is to say; in other words
- for example; for instance; namely; an example of this is
- and; as follows; as in the following examples; such as; including
- especially; particularly; in particular; notably; chiefly; mainly; mostly

Introducing an alternative viewpoint

- by contrast; another way of viewing this is; alternatively; again; rather; one alternative is; another possibility is
- on the one hand … on the other hand
- conversely; in comparison; on the contrary; in fact; though; although

Returning to emphasise your earlier viewpoint

- however; nonetheless; in the final analysis; despite *x*; notwithstanding *x*; in spite of *x*
- while *x* may be true, nonetheless
- although; though; after all; at the same time; on the other hand; all the same; even if *x* is true; although *x* may have a good point

Showing the results of something

- therefore; accordingly; as a result
- so, (then,) it can be seen that
- the result is; the consequence is
- resulting from this; consequently; now
- we can see, then, that; it is evident that
- because of this; thus; hence; for this reason; owing to *x*; this suggests that; it follows that
- in other words; otherwise; in that case; that implies

Summing up or concluding

- therefore; so, my conclusion is
- in short; in conclusion; to conclude; in all; on the whole
- to summarise; to sum up briefly; in brief; altogether; overall; thus; thus we can see that

> ***Activity***
>
> How are these words used in the sample essays on pages 183–6?

Editing your draft

Editing is working on your draft in order to improve it. When you edit, you can …

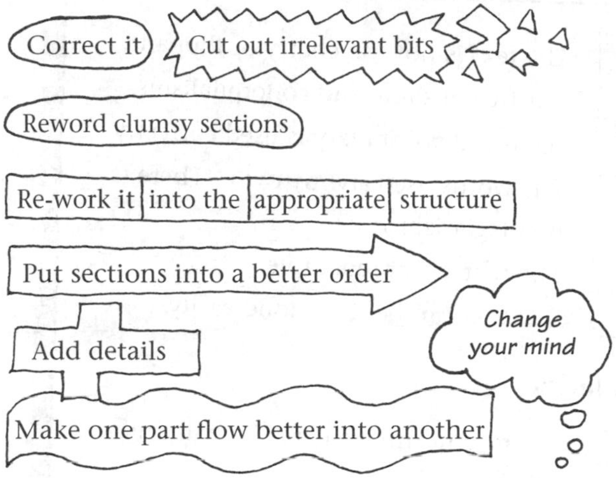

Different kinds of editing

You may need to go through your work several times, checking for different things.

1 *Meaning*

- Does it make sense? Read it aloud slowly.

2 *Organisation and structure*

- Have you used the appropriate structure?
- Is connected information grouped together?
- Is information presented in the best order?
- Is the work well paragraphed? (See page 157.)

3 *Evidence*

- Have you backed your argument with evidence, examples, details, and/or research?

4 *References*

- Is the source of your information clear?
- Are your quotations accurate?
- Are references written correctly? (See pages 124–5.)

5 *Style*

- Is the text easy to read?
- Is it too chatty? Or too stuffy?
- Are any sections confused?
- Is it precise enough? (See page 168.)
- Is the style appropriate? (See Chapter 8.)

6 *Punctuation, spelling and grammar*

- Have you written in sentences? (See 'Proof-reading' below.)

7 *Presentation*

- Is the text legible?
- Does it look neat and well presented?
- Does it follow any presentation guidelines you were given?

Which aspects of editing do you need to spend most time on?

Proof-reading

Edit your draft until you are happy that your draft is written as well as it can be. Then do some final proof-reading.

- Read it once again aloud – does it make sense?
- Look for mistakes such as typing and spelling errors. Look up doubtful spellings or ask someone.
  - If you used the computer's spellchecker, check especially for words that may have been correctly spelt, but which were the wrong words – such as 'there' instead of 'their'.
  - When checking spellings, you may find it helpful to work backwards through your writing, word by word, to avoid drifting into skim-reading.
- Everyone has their own pattern of errors. If there are certain mistakes you make repeatedly, note these down and be particularly careful in checking for them.

CHECKLIST

Editing final drafts

Tick each box below when you have finished checking that point.

Content and argument

- ☐ The text answers the central question(s) posed by the title (page 142).
- ☐ Sufficient space (or words) has been given to the most important points.
- ☐ All the information included is relevant to the set question.
- ☐ The main line of argument is clear, not lost in a sea of detail.

Research material

- ☐ There are sufficient examples and evidence to prove or illustrate my points.
- ☐ My own ideas and opinions are clear to the reader.

Structure and grouping

- ☐ The text is in the appropriate structure or format.
- ☐ Ideas are suitably linked.
- ☐ Each paragraph is well structured.
- ☐ Ideas are presented in the right order.
- ☐ It is clear how each paragraph links to the others (page 160).

Style

- ☐ The style is appropriate for my course (Chapter 8).
- ☐ The text is not too chatty or flippant.
- ☐ It is free of slang and colloquialisms.
- ☐ Technical vocabulary is used correctly.
- ☐ The words used are my own. (There is no plagiarism.)
- ☐ The text is not repetitive.
- ☐ The text can be read aloud easily.

Clarity

- ☐ There is nothing the reader will find confusing.
- ☐ The language is clear and straightforward.
- ☐ The reader will easily follow the line of reasoning (Chapter 9).
- ☐ It is clear which sentence in my introduction summarises my viewpoint or argument.
- ☐ Sentences are of reasonable length and are uncomplicated.

General

- ☐ The introduction is suitable.
- ☐ The conclusion is suitable.
- ☐ Spelling, grammar and punctuation are correct.
- ☐ References are correct.
- ☐ The bibliography (if needed) is accurate.
- ☐ I have taken account of feedback I received for earlier work (page 182).

© Stella Cottrell 1999, *The Study Skills Handbook*, Macmillan Press Ltd

Presenting your writing

The fine details of presentation may vary from one tutor to another. Use the checklist on page 164 to guide you. In general:

- For essays write the title at the top of the first page; for reports and projects write the title on a cover page.
- Write on one side of the page only.
- Make sure your name is on every page.
- Number every page.
- Leave space to one side or between lines so that your tutor can add comments.
- Your final text should be neat and legible. Occasional minor corrections made neatly by hand are acceptable, but if there are a lot of corrections, or sections of text need to be reordered, write the essay out afresh.
- If you are given instructions about binding projects, follow them carefully. Normally, though, most essays don't need special binding or folders – on the contrary, folders often make more work for your tutors.

Using the computer

The computer makes it much easier to produce well-presented work. Below are some facilities you may find useful.

It may suit you to use one font or size while working, and another for the final printout to hand in. For example, you might use very large type on the screen, making it is easier to read, and then reduce the size before printing it out.

For your final draft:

- use only one font throughout
- use only one type size for your main text
- use a clear, simple font for your final draft – not script designed to look like handwriting
- you may like to vary type size for headings, depending on how important they are – if so, be consistent in the way you use them.

Font style and size

Presentation

Presentation

Presentation

Presentation

Presentation

Presentation

Presentation

Presentation

Presentation

Presentation

Presentation

Organise text on the page

You can use tabs and other facilities to indent the text or lay it out in particular ways.

You can centre headings

You can have the text aligned at the left.

You can have the text centred.

You can have the text justified, with straight edges on both sides.

Make text stand out

You can highlight headings or key words using

bold *italics* underlining

Do complicated tasks easily

You can get the computer to do the work for you! It can:

- number pages
- print your name and the title of the assignment in the footer on each page
- produce neat bullet or number points, with indented text
- produce graphics for your statistical information.

CHECKLIST

Lecturers' preferences

Your tutors may have preferences about the technical aspects of presentation listed below. You can use a photocopy of this chart to clarify details with tutors and remind yourself of the appropriate presentation for a given subject or tutor.

Tutor/Subject	Requirements
• Typed, handwritten or word-processed?	
• A4 paper?	
• Use one side or both?	
• Begin each section of a report on a fresh page?	
• Use headings?	
• Number paragraphs?	
• Leave a wide left-hand/right-hand margin?	
• Write my name on each page?	
• Write the title on each page?	
• Use double-spacing (leave every second line blank)?	
• Write as 'one', 'I' or 'we'? (Address the reader as 'you')?	
• Use passive or active voice? (Passive: 'The essay was written'. Active: 'I wrote the essay'.)	
• Which method is to be used for references? Any special layout for references?	
• Bibliography needed? Any special layout?	
• Anything else? (e.g. Use of diagrams, charts, graphs? Standard keys on maps? Use colour in diagrams? Is annotation needed?)	

© Stella Cottrell 1999, *The Study Skills Handbook*, Macmillan Press Ltd

Review

This chapter has looked at how to develop your writing from small beginnings, so as to build your confidence and familiarity with writing. Although academic writing is a distinct kind of writing, you will profit from making *any* kind of writing a daily activity. You will build up speed, become more able to think and write simultaneously, become more aware of how you can improve your writing, and grow in confidence.

The chapter also looked at how to approach a piece of academic writing as a set of manageable steps. This links with the work in Chapter 4, on setting mini-goals. Many of these sub-skills will soon become second nature. With practice, you will find that you combine separate stages quite easily and find quicker ways of doing things.

Check your learning outcomes

- Look carefully at feedback from your tutor. If it is not clear where you have lost marks, ask for an appointment to discuss this. Take with you a copy of the self-evaluation questionnaires on pages 132 and 162.
- Using your tutor's feedback and advice, complete the self-evaluation questionnaire on page 132 again. Notice which areas you now feel confident about, and which you would still like to improve.

You may also find it helpful to browse through Chapters 8 and 9 before your next piece of work.

Basic English skills

It is difficult to get the highest grades at college if your basic English skills, such as grammar and punctuation, are weak. It is worth investigating any language workshops at the university or at a local College of Further Education. Alternatively, some grammar books for adults are listed in the 'Recommended reading' on page 232.

Chapter 8

Developing your writing

LEARNING OUTCOMES

This chapter offers you opportunities to:

- become aware of some of the conventions of academic writing, including
  - basic stylistic conventions
  - being precise
  - distinguishing fact, opinion and argument
- become aware of different approaches to research and academic writing
- understand the influences of the scientific model on most areas of academic writing, including non-science subjects
- understand better what is meant by terms such as 'subjectivity' and 'objectivity', 'quantitative' and 'qualitative'
- learn to use the four main writing styles used in Higher Education:
  - descriptive
  - argumentative
  - evaluative
  - personal/experiential
- know what gains good marks for an assignment, and how to use tutor feedback constructively
- know what a good essay looks like, and gain practice in marking essays yourself.

Browse this chapter before doing your first assignment; then return to look at it in more detail, along with Chapter 9, before later assignments.

Stylistic conventions for academic writing

The following conventions apply to most academic writing. Nevertheless, your tutors may give specific guidance, and if so you should follow it.

Use formal English

Academic English is formal. It avoids slang and colloquialisms, such as these:

- 'The writer is *out of order* when he suggests ...'
- 'The new plans were *just the stuff.*'
- 'These findings need to be *taken with a pinch of salt.*'
- 'The argument was *a bit over the top.*'

Avoid abbreviations and contractions

Write words out in full:

- 'dept.' as 'department'
- 'e.g.' as 'for example'
- 'didn't' as 'did not'
- 'they're' as 'they are'
- 'isn't' as 'is not'

Be impersonal

Most courses prefer you to avoid personal pronouns such as 'I'/'we' and 'you'. Instead, sentences begin in impersonal ways such as:

- It can be seen that …
- There are a number of …
- It has been found that …

Be cautious

Academic writing generally sounds cautious. Writers indicate that they are aware that nothing is completely certain. They use words that express this lack of certainty, such as:

- appears to; seems to; tends to; may; might; possibly; probably; apparently; generally; seemingly.

They may use phrases such as:

- in some cases, this …
- the evidence suggests that …

Avoid conjunctions

The following words are not used at the start of sentences: *or, and, but, yet.*

Numbers

Numbers below a hundred are often written out in full, such as:

- thirty-one per cent
- nineteen members.

However, figures are retained in statistical and scientific work:

- 31 per cent
- 15 °C
- 7.3 newtons.

Be objective

Academic writing avoids personal, subjective words such as 'nice', 'wonderful', 'worthwhile', 'usual' or 'natural', because the reader's understanding of these words may be very different from your own.

Avoid apologies

Don't apologise to the reader for any weaknesses you think there may be in your research or writing, such as that you found the subject difficult or that you had no time to write a conclusion. Write as if you are confident of what you are saying – even if you don't feel it!

Addressing the reader

Avoid asking readers questions or telling them what to think.

Be concise

Edit out unnecessary words:

~~A man called~~ Jay Singh invented …

In ~~a book called~~ *Scottish Pathways*, …

Use continuous prose

Write in full sentences, grouped together into paragraphs (see page 157). For essays and dissertations, avoid lists of points: incorporate the points into sentences. Lists and headings may be acceptable in reports and projects.

Being precise

Example of a vague sentence

Some people did not like the idea at the time and made the politicians stop it but then he attacked him publicly.

Why is it vague?

- 'some people' – who exactly?
- 'the idea' – which idea?
- 'at the time' – when? date?
- 'the politicians' – all politicians? or a certain group? or a political party?
- 'made the politicians' – how did they 'make' them?
- 'stop it' – stop what? how was it stopped?
- 'people did not like the idea' – why not?

It can be confusing to have more than one pronoun (such as 'he', 'she', 'it', 'this' or 'that') in a sentence.

Activity: Which of the following is most precise?

1 A woman ruled the country.
2 Mrs Thatcher served as Prime Minister in Britain between 1979 and 1991.
3 A woman ruled Britain during 1979–1991.
4 Mrs Thatcher ruled Britain for several years and introduced many policies which affected various aspects of people's lives.

Answer

Response 2 – the others all contain vague information.

... rather than sort of not saying quite what you mean, if you know what I mean ...

Using facts, opinions or arguments

I think there should be fewer adverts on TV.

Opinions

Opinions are personal beliefs. These are not always based on good evidence, and may even run *contrary* to the evidence.

What is considered 'natural' or 'normal', for example, is generally a matter of opinion. Even if most people agree with you, it is still opinion, unless you can give *evidence* that what you think is likely to be true.

There were an average of 35 adverts an hour on channel X, on 25th July 1990.

Facts

Facts can usually be checked against evidence. Facts used in academic writing are generally those gathered and recorded in some formal way, such as in journals or official records.

Adverts for toys should not be shown on TV because research by Dr Meehan (1998) suggests that they ...

Arguments

Arguments are *reasons* (which can include facts) given to support a point of view.

As you write, question what you write

As you write, keep checking for precision. Ask yourself questions, such as 'when exactly?', 'why exactly?' or 'who?' Check that you have given your readers enough detail for them to know exactly what you are talking about.

Writing for different subjects

Each academic subject has a slightly different approach regarding:

- *research methodology* – how to conduct research
- *evidence* – what is regarded as appropriate and sufficient
- *writing genre* – the preferred writing styles and conventions
- *objectivity* – how far your approach should be objective or subjective, quantitative or qualitative, scientific or personal.

As a student, you will need to identify the approaches taken by your subject and produce work appropriate to that subject. You will need to be particularly aware of this if you take a 'combined options' course, but even *within* a subject, approaches can vary depending on the area of study.

The influence of the 'scientific' model

Academic writing has been heavily influenced by the notion of being 'scientific' – even when the subject is not obviously about science. Although this view is changing, the approach you are expected to take is likely to be affected by some of the principles of the scientific model, so it is helpful to know what it involves.

The main features of the scientific model are:

- objectivity
- a testable hypothesis
- replicated results
- controlling for variables
- quantitative analysis
- accurate description
- qualitative analysis.

Objectivity

The scientific model values objectivity. This means that instead of relying on personal opinion or common sense, scientists test possible explanations against the available evidence. If data is objective, two people undertaking the same research in the same way should arrive at the same results and conclusions.

A testable hypothesis

A hypothesis is a possible explanation of why or how something occurs, consistent with available evidence. For the purposes of experiment, the hypothesis is formulated in a way that can be tested.

A hypothesis cannot be proved true, but it can be proved *wrong*. If a hypothesis survives many attempts to prove it wrong, it may increasingly be considered reliable and trusted as a 'theory'.

Replicated results

For a piece of scientific research to be taken seriously, another researcher needs to have repeated the research with similar results. This 'replication' indicates that the first results were reliable, and not just a 'one-off' or due to individual opinion or bias. (However, it is still important to think hard about whether bias may be built into the research method itself.)

Controlling for variables

Scientists need to know that what they *think* they are testing is what they are *actually* testing. They need to make sure that 'variables' – all the things that can change, such as the weather, or the time of day, the people involved or the materials used – have not influenced the results unexpectedly.

Usually, research experiments are run many times to check the effects of different variables. The researcher tries to change only one variable at a time, keeping everything else constant. This is known as 'controlling for variables'.

For example, researchers comparing the effect of blue light or red light on plant growth would check that everything *apart* from the colour of the light was identical. For each light colour they would use the same type and size of plant, the same amount of water, the same levels of nutrients, the same temperature, and the same air source.

Quantitative analysis

Scientific research relies heavily on quantitative data. This means it focuses on changes or differences that can be *measured*. Standardised measurements are used – such as number, time, weight and length – so that results are easy to compare objectively. Thus experiments might investigate:

- whether the height (measurable) to which a particular kind of plant grows depends on the temperature of the environment (measurable)
- whether fruit yield (measurable) depends on the amount of light (measurable)
- whether how many words somebody can read in a given amount of time (measurable) depends on the size of print (measurable) or the age of the person (measurable).

The approach is: 'If *this* changes while everything else stays the same, does it have an effect on *that*?' This could also be stated as: 'If X changes while A, B and C stay the same, does it have an effect on Y?' Quantitative analysis involves analysing the relationship between changes in one variable and changes in another.

When changes in X exactly match changes in Y, the changes are said to be 'correlated'. It is important to understand, however, that correlation does not prove that changes in X *cause* changes in Y, or vice versa. Correlation may be due to chance, or both X and Y may be affected by a third variable, Z.

Accurate description

When writing up research, scientists describe their methodology, research conditions and results exactly, so that anyone who wishes to replicate their research can set up near-identical conditions. You will be expected to write accurate descriptions in the same way, such that someone else could replicate your research.

Descriptive writing for reports is very precise: no unnecessary words are used. (See page 174.)

Qualitative analysis

In qualitative research, the data used are not easily measurable. The experiment is not completely objective: some judgement and interpretation are involved. It is acknowledged also that the researcher is in some way part of the experiment itself and may unintentionally influence its results – for example, by having a role in making sense of the research.

Scientists use qualitative analysis in the 'Discussion' part of a report, where they make sense of their results and offer possible reasons for why things did not go as expected. Here they evaluate strengths and weaknesses in the way they designed the experiment or worded the experimental hypothesis.

Nevertheless, science generally regards subjectivity as a 'problem', and often uses language which makes it sound as if no scientists were involved – as if the experiment just happened on its own:

> The experimental design could have been improved by ...

rather than:

> I could have improved the design by ...

Alternatives to the scientific model

Most academic disciplines are influenced by the scientific model. However, subjects vary in how far they value the different aspects of the model. The main differences are in varying attitudes to subjectivity and to qualitative data.

Subjectivity and objectivity

Subjectivity simply means bringing yourself, your own views, opinions, experiences or value judgements into your research or writing. In counselling or fine art, a high value is placed upon subjectivity – that is, upon personal emotions, feelings, intuitions and experiences. It is the opposite of *objectivity*, the aim of the traditional scientific model.

In many subjects, however, you need to combine the two: to analyse both objective criteria, such as the results of independent surveys, market research or case studies, and your subjective response – your feelings, tastes, interests or intuitions.

(See also 'Using personal experience', page 180.)

Quantitative approaches in non-science subjects

Science subjects tend to avoid research where it is difficult to control for variables or to quantify results. For example, issues such as gender, romance or childhood change over time, but as these changes are not easily measurable they would not usually be studied by scientists.

Non-science subjects often find ingenious ways of categorising such information, however, so that it can be roughly standardised according to set criteria. This enables a wider range of issues to be studied in relatively objective ways.

Example: attitudes to children

A researcher interested in how attitudes to children changed over time would aim at finding an objective way of analysing data rather than simply relying on her opinion. She might choose to focus on how often popular magazines referred to themes of 'childhood innocence' and 'goodness' compared to themes on 'disciplining bad children'. One approach could then be to count how often a popular magazine included each theme, and compare data over ten-year intervals to see whether the number of references changed significantly over time. This would give quantitative data.

The researcher here would also have to classify her information carefully to be clear what type of material should be included under her chosen themes ('innocence' and 'discipline'). Classification of words and themes involves some subjectivity, as people mean different things by the same words. For example, someone quoted in one of the magazines as saying 'A good child does as his mother says' might have meant that he obeyed because he was well disciplined, or that he obeyed because he was naturally virtuous – or something else entirely.

Qualitative analysis

It is not always easy to draw a line between what is quantitative and what is qualitative – as you can see from the example above of attitudes to children. In that instance, the researcher needed to make subjective judgements about what was *meant* by innocence or discipline. Usually social science researchers acknowledge their subjective role in the experiment as interpreters of the evidence. Social science and arts subjects may aim at objectivity and quantification where this is possible, but are also interested in the subjective – how decisions and interpretations are arrived at. They are more accepting of overlaps between objectivity and subjectivity.

As a student you may be asked to make qualitative evaluations about project evidence, about decisions made during work placements, or about art or literature. Your lecturers will look for:

- the relevance of the detail you select
- the criteria you use in making decisions
- the aptness of your interpretations.

PLANNER

Polar opposites in academic approaches

For each of the aspects numbered below, find out whether it is the convention in your subject area to be nearer the North or the South Pole. This may vary depending on the type of assignment.

Consider how far each dimension is important for your assignment. You could indicate this by making a tick on the dotted line.

North Pole 		*South Pole* 
1 Every attempt is made to control the conditions under which the research takes place, so that the researcher can decide which variables to manipulate and measure	....	1 Every attempt is made to keep the research true to real life – that is, to give it 'ecological validity'
2 Results can be generalised – that is, they would hold true if the research were repeated	....	2 The unique is considered worthy of study – results may be impossible to repeat exactly
3 Numbers and standardised measurements make it easier to generalise results	....	3 Creative interpretation is highly valued
4 Objective views are formed, based on evidence and facts rather than personal opinion	....	4 Subjective responses, feelings, intuition and creativity are regarded as valuable resources
5 The role of the scientist in the research is minimised and rarely discussed	....	5 The role of the researcher is made explicit – it is considered useful to discuss how the researcher's presence influenced the results
6 Individual differences are not important – generalised findings are valued	....	6 Individual instances, and opportunities for detailed interpretation, are valued
7 Personal experience is regarded as individual and irrelevant: it is not referred to	....	7 Personal experience is highly valued as giving insight and a deeper understanding
8 The language is clinical, neutral, impersonal and dispassionate, even if the researcher is passionate about the subject	....	8 The language used allows the personality and feelings of the writer to shine through

© Stella Cottrell 1999, *The Study Skills Handbook*, Macmillan Press Ltd

Different styles

Compare the following two styles of writing. The first is conversational:

Mount Pepé is going up – it's going to take everything with it when it goes. And I mean everything – villages, farms, trees, the lot. It's frightening to think of how powerful a volcano can be. Think of the damage they cause! Remember Pompeii and Mount Etna!

The second is in a general academic style:

In order to assess whether it is necessary to evacuate the villages on Mount Pepé, three main factors need to be taken into consideration. The first, and most important, of these is the element of safety. According to seismic experts currently working on the volcano, there is likely to be a major eruption within the next ten years (Achebe 1997). According to Achebe, the eruption is likely to destroy villages over a radius of 120 miles (Achebe 1999, p.7).

Notice the differences between the two examples. For each piece, consider questions such as these.

- Does it use full sentences?
- How formal does it sound? (What is the writer's 'voice'?)
- How is emotion expressed?
- Is personal opinion expressed? If so, how?
- How are other people's views included?
- Is the sequence logical?
- Does the piece observe the conventions listed on pages 144 and 166–71?

Styles of academic writing

Although academic writing is distinct from other kinds of writing, it isn't all the same. There are different styles *within* academic writing, including:

- descriptive
- argumentative/analytical
- evaluative/analytical
- personal, drawing on the writer's own experience.

These are explored in more detail below.

Finding the appropriate style

When writing an assignment, it is important to choose the appropriate writing style.

Look at the two examples below, of draft introductions to an essay in response to the questions, 'What problems faced Henri IV on his accession to the throne? How successfully did he solve them?' The first follows the guidance for introductions given on page 147, and analyses the problem set. The second uses descriptive writing, giving background details not relevant to the question.

The first example is of a good introduction:

In 1598, Henri IV was anointed king of a war-torn France, the country having been split by religious and political wars since the death of Henri II almost half a century earlier. The problems Henri IV faced were essentially threefold. He needed to resolve Catholic–Protestant divisions within the country; to curb the power of the Guise, Montmorenci and Bourbons factions which threatened to subvert royal power; and he needed to restore the French economy. This essay will look at the three areas in turn, but will also show how they were interrelated. It will demonstrate how Henri IV tackled each, and argue that ultimately he was extremely successful in solving what had seemed intractable problems.

The second is an example of interesting but irrelevant description (for a *history* essay):

Henri was brought up by his grandfather in the mountains of Navarre. His grandfather was a very religious man and brought his grandson up as a Protestant. Because of his religion, he wanted Henri to appreciate the simple things in life – the fields, the flowers, good wholesome food such as bread and local cheese, and the beauty of the natural surroundings. Henri was allowed a great deal of freedom, and was allowed to roam barefoot in the mountains, and to play with animals ...

Compare each example to the conventions listed on page 144.

Which writer might find it easier to write a good observation case study (page 174)?

Descriptive writing

You are likely to include descriptive writing in most assignments. In some ways it is the easiest style, as we are used to describing things in everyday life. On the other hand, it is easy to give too much detail and forget the underlying purpose of the description. At a Higher Education level you are unlikely to be asked to describe anything just for the sake of describing. There will usually be another purpose, such as:

- being precise about methods used in an experiment
- giving essential background information so that you can analyse significant features in more detail later.

You may be required to:

- *describe what happened* – for example, outlining the main events in a history essay, or your methods and results in a project report
- *describe main features or functions* – for example, different bodily organs in a biology essay
- *summarise the main points of a theory or an article you have read* – for example, in reviewing a book or in introducing the ideas of another author within an assignment.

What gains marks

You will gain marks for:

- identifying relevant themes to include
- identifying the *most* relevant facts in what you include
- clarity, precision and accuracy
- presenting items in the best order
- keeping to the point
- indicating the significance of what you describe.

Examples of descriptive writing

Note the differences between the two following types of descriptive writing. The first is from a cognitive psychology report.

METHODOLOGY

Participants

There were twenty English first-language speakers in each condition, forty subjects in all. These were matched for age and gender across conditions.

Procedure

(See Appendix 1 for instructions.) Each participant was tested separately. They were asked to indicate whether each string of five letters (such as *yongt*) presented on the computer screen was a real word. For real words they pressed the 'y' key on the keyboard; otherwise they pressed the 'n' key …

The second example is from an observation case study from the social sciences.

The man did not appear to be interacting with the child. The train entered Ely station, and he looked to the pushchair, perhaps to see if it was obstructing the exit. He looked out of the window. The child pointed to the door, and leaned towards him; he instantly leaned towards her to listen.

She said, 'Get off soon?'

He replied, 'Not now. In five minutes we're getting off.' The child still leaned towards him, but he didn't say anything else, and looked away. The child turned away and put the teddy on the seat. The man leaned across her, picked up the teddy, and returned it to her lap, saying 'Hold it.' They looked at each other for a moment. The child half-smiled, and they both looked away, so they were looking in opposite directions.

From this you will see how descriptive writing can vary depending on the subject. Look carefully at journal articles and other examples from your subject area to find the appropriate style for your subject.

Argumentative/analytical writing

Most tutors want essays to be analytical, examining 'What exactly?' and 'Why exactly?' in detail. Chapter 9 looks in more detail at analytical thinking.

They also want essays to be 'discursive' – to discuss ideas and opinions, and to show reasoning. In a persuasively argued essay, the writer – that is, you – tries to influence the opinion or thoughts or actions of the reader.

> Find the 'Editorial' section in two quality newspapers. How do the writers try to persuade you to their points of view?

What makes good argumentative writing?

To argue a point of view effectively, you need to do the following.

- State a point of view or opinion, and a clear line of reasoning to support it.
- Offer evidence or examples to support your argument.
- Show where the evidence comes from, and that it is reliable. (For example, it should not *all* be personal experience nor what you have heard somebody else say.)
- Show that you have considered any possible arguments which might *contradict* your case or opinions.
- Be able to demonstrate convincingly why your argument or position is the best (that is, why you think you are right).

Your case will not look very convincing if you merely argue, 'Well, that's my opinion' or 'That's my experience' and fail to consider any alternatives seriously.

Writing the argument

1 *State your position*

- Sum up your argument in one brief, clear sentence.
- Don't be tempted to sit on the fence. You can sound cautious, and show that there are strong arguments on more than one side, but indicate which side *you* find most convincing.

2 *Support your argument*

- Show why your point of view is a good one.
- For each main point, give evidence (dates, names, statistics, examples, opinions from other sources).

Here is the evidence, my Lord...

- Consider: 'Would the evidence stand up in court?' Is it really convincing?

3 *Consider the opposition*

Assume that your reader disagrees with you: you have to convince the reader with good evidence and examples.

- What could your opponents argue?
- What evidence might they have?
- How could you persuade a neutral party that your case and your evidence are better?

> Develop an argument.
>
> - Choose a subject about which you feel strongly.
> - What is your opinion?
> - List your reasons for holding that opinion.
> - List possible arguments against it.
> - How could you reply to those arguments?
> - Use the planner on page 176 to write it out.

Framework for an argumentative essay

Main proposal/hypothesis/argument:

Reasons or arguments in favour	Evidence and examples
1 ______	1 ______
2 ______	2 ______
3 ______	3 ______
4 ______	4 ______

Opposing arguments	Reasons and evidence
1 ______	1 ______
2 ______	2 ______
3 ______	3 ______
4 ______	4 ______

Reasons why my arguments are stronger; weaknesses in the reasoning or evidence for the opposing arguments

1 ______

2 ______

3 ______

Conclusions

© Stella Cottrell 1999, *The Study Skills Handbook*, Macmillan Press Ltd

Evaluative/analytical writing

Most academic writing will also include an element of evaluation, even if this is not obvious from the title of an assignment. You may be required to evaluate:

- two or more schools of thought
- two or more theories or theorists
- which of several items, models or ideas is best for a purpose
- how well another writer has analysed a subject.

Features of evaluative writing

Nearly all evaluative writing involves the following processes.

Comparing

Find the points of similarity, and show that you are aware of any minor points of difference within areas of overall similarity.

Contrasting

Set items in opposition, in order to bring out the points of difference.

Evaluating significance

Evaluate the *significance* of any similarities or differences. Do they matter? Do they have important implications for which model should be used? Or for probable outcomes (which animal is likely to survive, which treatment should be offered, and so on)?

Making a judgement

Indicate which theory or side is preferable. Give the reasons for your opinion, based on an analysis of the evidence.

Showing your criteria

Show the criteria you used in arriving at your opinion, such as that you used data or research evidence as the basis of your decision.

Get the balance right

In evaluative essays – such as 'compare and contrast' essays – it is important to be balanced in the kind of information you use to make a comparison.

'Compare and contrast' at the same category level

Suppose you are asked to compare and contrast two animals in terms of their habitat. First you need to compare them at the basic category level, making it clear you are comparing, for example, birds with mammals (see diagram, page 153). You could then compare cuckoos with dolphins, as these are at the same category level (on this diagram, the lower level). You should not compare cuckoos to mammals, as these are not equivalent concepts – they are at different levels on the pyramid.

Balance

If you use a specific case study about cuckoos, it should be balanced, if possible, by a specific case study of dolphins.

Check your content for balance

When you have completed a draft, make a plan of what you have actually written, using a concept pyramid. You may find that you have spent a disproportionate amount of time on one area, such as one middle-level subject (birds), and included too many examples from a lower level (cuckoos, chaffinches, peacocks). By contrast you may have said very little about mammals as a basic category but referred to ten pieces of specific research on dolphins.

This essay would show imbalance: it would not balance like with like. Use your pattern notes or pyramid to select a similar number of examples at each level.

Organising information for 'compare and contrast' essays

One easy way of organising information for 'compare and contrast' essays is by making a grid and writing information in the appropriate columns.

- Use one column for the information about one theory or item.
- Group similarities together.
- Group differences together.
- At the end, jot the main points in the boxes for the introduction and conclusion.

Introduction: Main themes:		
Areas to be compared and contrasted	A *Birds*	B *Fish*
Similarities		
1 *group behaviours*	*flocks*	*shoals*
2		
3		
4		
5		
Differences		
1 *respiration*		
2 *locomotion*	*flies (wings)*	*swims (fins)*
3		
4		
5		
Significance of similarities or differences. (How did I decide whether something was significant?)		
Conclusion. (Draw the reader's attention to the main points.)		

An empty grid for use is printed on page 179.

Three ways of writing out the essay are given below. Whichever one you use, be consistent with it for that essay. Before you begin writing from the grid, it is a good idea to map out your points spatially (see page 150).

Method 1

This method is straightforward, but tends to use more words than the others.

- Work down the chart.
- Write out all your points for column *A*.
- Write your points for column *B*, in the same order as for column *A*. Highlight the point of similarity or contrast.
- Do the same for any other columns.
- Draw together the significance of the similarities and differences.

Method 2

- Work across the chart.
- Select one item from column *A* and 'compare and contrast' it with column *B* (and any other columns).
- Go onto the next item in column *A* and compare that to column *B* (and any others). Continue until all points are covered.
- Draw together the significance of the similarities and differences.

Method 3

If the similarities are so strong as to make the items almost identical, state in the introduction that you will look at similarities together, and then at points of contrast separately.

- Describe one way in which *A* and *B* are similar.
- Continue until all points of similarity are covered.
- Continue with points of contrast as for either methods 1 or 2 above (depending on which is clearest to read).
- Draw together the significance of the similarities and differences.

PLANNER

Framework for a 'compare and contrast' essay

Introduction: Main themes:		
Areas to be compared and contrasted	A	B
Similarities 1 2 3 4 5		
Differences 1 2 3 4 5		
Significance of similarities or differences. (How did I decide whether something was significant?)		
Conclusion. (Draw the reader's attention to the main points.)		

© Stella Cottrell 1999, *The Study Skills Handbook*, Macmillan Press Ltd

Using personal experience

It is often useful to call upon personal experience in order to make your learning concrete. Reflection on what happened to you, or how you dealt with a similar situation, can help your thinking – even if you don't make a direct reference to it in your writing.

Find out whether your course expects you to write about personal experience. Some subjects expect you to do so, whereas in others it will be inappropriate.

And then I thought that as I had been living in the same address for two years it was time for a change. So, in 1967 I moved down to Essex. I lived in Barr Road, but I soon moved to Small Street ...

Writing from experience

Use your personal experience as a starting point. Consider what lessons can be drawn from your experience, then start your research. Personal experience should not be your main evidence – unless your tutors specifically ask for this.

- If you include personal experience in your writing, consider how typical it is. Has any research been done – do you know of relevant reports or articles? – which shows that *your* experience is true more generally?
- Compare your experience with other people's. If theirs is different, why is that?
- Keep your description short. Avoid long lists and detailed accounts of events.
- Be careful what you say about anyone you mention (by name, or if it is obvious to whom you are referring). Check that they don't mind being included – especially if they are known to those who will read your essay.

Analyse your experience

- How is it relevant to your course?
- How does it link to theories you have studied?
- How does your experience support or contradict the views of a writer or theorist you are covering on the course?
- Can any lessons be drawn from it?
- Can generalisations be drawn from it?
- What evidence is there to show that your experiences are typical or unusual?

Example

Suppose you wrote about your own experience, saying:

Working this way, I found that I was less stressed and my work improved.

You could provisionally generalise this:

It would appear that the absence of stress can produce more effective results.

You would then need to ask questions such as these. How valid is this generalisation? Do other people feel the same way as you? Are there circumstances where stress can produce *better* work?

Personal writing and academic writing

There are some general differences between personal writing and academic writing.

Personal writing	Academic writing
emotional	logical
can be intuitive	uses reasoning
active voice: 'I find that ...'	passive voice: 'It was found that ...'
anecdotal	uses evidence
data from one person	wider database
subjective	objective
tangents may be important	keeps to a logical sequence

What gets good marks?

To get good marks, you do not necessarily have to work longer hours. You *do* need:

- to identify the task or problem correctly
- to discover the underlying issues
- to find out exactly what is expected of you.

Although all subject areas have their own assessment criteria, the following general requirements provide a good guideline as to how marks are allocated.

Lowest marks

The lowest marks are awarded for work which:

- has weak structure
- shows little research, thought or reflection
- is mostly descriptive, with little analysis or argument
- considers only one point of view.

Tutors' comments may resemble these:

> 'You have just written out my lecture notes and paraphrased a few lines out of books, without considering why this is such an important issue.'

> 'The student seems to have written out everything he knows about the subject, in any order, with lots of mistakes, and has not answered the question he was asked.'

Better marks

Better marks are awarded for work which:

- shows some understanding of the underlying issues
- meets the set criteria
- answers the question that was put
- develops an argument or a point of view
- draws conclusions
- shows the relationship between different issues or concepts within the subject area
- reveals some thought and reflection
- organises information into a structure
- gives evidence and examples to support arguments and main points.

Highest marks

Highest marks are awarded for work which includes all of the features necessary for 'better marks', and in addition:

- reveals a good understanding of why the topic is significant, including underlying issues and concerns, and where and why there is controversy
- reveals understanding of how the topic relates to broader issues, beyond the subject area.

'What if I get bad marks for my work ...?'

Although 'marks' such as 'B' or '64%' can be an indicator of how well you are doing, the *comments* you receive are more important. You may feel discouraged and feel inclined to throw your work in the bin if it is returned covered with your tutor's handwriting, but do read the comments – they may be your passport to better marks.

It can be distressing if tutors seem insensitive in their comments. Sometimes this is due to bad tutoring on their part, but try not to be over-sensitive to their remarks. It is best not to take any harsh comments personally. Focus instead on the issues behind the words.

It is also quite usual to have strong feelings about your marks – especially if the amount of effort you put in does not seem to be reflected in the mark. You may feel angry or disappointed, or want to give up altogether.

Don't give up. Wait a day or two, then start an action plan.

Action plan for using tutor feedback

Read through your work and the tutor's comments. Keep asking yourself, 'How can this help me to improve my work?'

1 After each comment, check whether you understand what it was that made the tutor write it. Highlight any comments that you feel are useful to you for your next piece of work.
2 Divide a piece of paper into:
   - major issues: areas which lose a lot of marks, such as not answering the question, lack of evidence, poor argument, weak structure
   - minor errors: spelling, punctuation, grammar.
3 Go through your tutors' comments, listing them under 'Major issues' or 'Minor errors'.
4 Compare this with lists you completed for any previous work. Which comments appear more than once?
5 Number the items in order of priority (with '1' for the most urgent matter to work on), or use the ***Priority organiser*** (page 72).

Action plan	
Major issues	*Minor errors*
2 paragraphing	*(1) spelling authors' names*
3 referencing	*3 commas*
(1) structure	*2 '-ed' endings for past tense*

Making improvements

1 Select one, two or three priority issues from each list to work on in your next piece of work. Set yourself realistic targets.
2 Consider how you will deal with each item on your list. Don't panic! Think constructively.
3 Make sure you understand *why* you received that feedback.
4 Re-read any relevant sections in this guide.
5 Discuss your work with other students.
6 If there are comments you do not understand, or if you are not clear why you received the mark you did, ask your tutor to explain.
7 If you do not know how to improve your 'priority areas', ask your tutor for advice.
8 Find out what gets good marks – *ask*!
9 Ask your tutor for examples of the kind of work they would *like* you to produce.

What is an essay like?

Essay 1

Below is a sample first-year essay for an assignment of 1000 words.

1 Read through it. Essays should be addressed to an 'intelligent reader' who does not know much about the subject, so it should not matter if this is not your area.
2 Once you know what the essay is about, put yourself in the role of a tutor marking it. This will give you a get a better sense of what your tutors are looking for.
3 Even though you may not know the subject, you can still evaluate it according to the criteria set out on the 'Editing your draft' checklist (page 161) or the 'What gets good marks?' list (page 181). Add your comments down the side of the essay or in your journal.
4 Compare your own comments with those on page 185.
5 Has reading these comments changed your view about how *you* marked the essay?

The question set

How has Bowlby's Attachment Theory been modified by the findings of later research? How have theories about attachment affected ideas about child care?

The essay

Page 1

Attachment theory originated in the work of Bowlby (1907–90). The theory was that an infant's ability to form emotional attachments to its mother was essential to its survival and later development. This raises important questions about what circumstances could affect the mother–child bond, and the effects on the child of different kinds of separation. This essay looks in particular at Bowlby's work on maternal deprivation, and at how early research and the later work of Mary Ainsworth seem to support Bowlby's Attachment Theory. It also looks at later challenges to that evidence, which suggest that short spells of separation may not have bad effects upon attachment nor on the child's development. The relative effects of these theories on attitudes towards day-care will be explored throughout the essay and brought together towards the conclusion.

Bowlby's Attachment Theory originally claimed that if bonding was to occur between a child and its carer, there must be continuous loving care from the same carer (the mother or a 'permanent mother substitute'). Without this, he argued, chances of bonding were lost forever, and the child was likely to become delinquent. Originally this was formulated as a theory of 'maternal deprivation'. Later Bowlby focused more specifically on the first year of life when, he believed, the child organises its behaviours to balance two complementary predispositions. These predispositions are firstly, 'proximity-promoting behaviours', which establish the mother as a secure base, and secondly, 'exploration' away from the mother. Bowlby argued that the infant develops 'internal working models' of its relationship with the mother which become the basis of all later relationships. He argued that the mother should be

Page 2

at home with the child for these behaviours to develop, and that day-care was harmful.

Bowlby's ideas were popular with governments at the time, as there was a shortage of jobs for men returning from the Second World War: day-care during the war had enabled many women to work outside the home. There was also other evidence which appeared to support Bowlby. Goldfarb (1947) compared children who had experienced continuous foster care from nine months onwards to those reared in institutions. He found that the foster children were less likely to suffer intellectual, social and emotional difficulties. Similarly, children who stayed in hospital showed distress and little affection to parents when reunited with them (Robertson 1967–73). Bowlby's own research into adolescent delinquency indicated childhood maternal deprivation as a recurring factor.

Much of this research evidence has since been revised. Bowlby's adolescent research was based on evacuees in the post-war years, a time of unusual trauma and disruption. With respect to Goldfarb's research, the Tizards (1970s) found that although children's homes could have a negative effect on development, this could be because of the unstimulating environments, and the high turnover of carers. Some four-year-olds in children's homes had more than fifty carers. Similarly, the hospital conditions of Robertson's research were stark environments where parents were discouraged from visiting and the children were very ill. This is a different situation to pleasant nurseries with healthy children who go home to their parent each evening.

Page 3

Although Bowlby's theory of maternal deprivation has been largely discredited, Mary Ainsworth (1978) built on Bowlby's ideas about exploratory bases and separation anxiety in her now widely used 'Strange Situation' experiment. Findings based on the Strange Situation would appear to support Bowlby and the idea that child-care is undesirable. However, there are criticisms of conclusions drawn from the Strange Situation. Clarke-Stewart argues that the Strange Situation does not take into account how far the mother and child were used to being separated. Cultures such as Japan and the USA vary in how much they value independence in children and so each would interpret the results of the Strange Situation very differently (Super and Harkness 1981).

One of the difficulties in evaluating research based upon Bowlby's theories has been in finding valid comparisons. Most research tends to be based on USA mothers from families under economic and social stress, and who are not representative of all mothers (Burman 1994). One useful comparison group for day-care children would be children whose temperaments prevented their mothers from going to work, and whose mothers then became depressed. It has been found that mothers at home with two children under five are more likely to be depressed. Depression in mothers has also been linked with delinquency in children. This suggests that day-care might benefit both mother and child.

Bowlby's original Attachment Theory has been modified; there is now less emphasis on the 'critical period', on the irreversibility of early weak bonding, and on the necessity of exclusive, continuous maternal care. Separation and reunion behaviours are still regarded as useful indicators of later difficulties, although it is now recognised that many other factors such as marital discord have to be taken into consideration. Modifications in the theory have accompanied changes in child care, hospital and nursery environments. Although there is still popular belief in maternal deprivation, many professionals now agree that day-care can be of some benefit, if both home and day-care environments are of good quality.

References

Burman, E. (1994). *Deconstructing Developmental Psychology.* London: Routledge.
Oates, J. (1995). *The Foundations of Child Development.* Milton Keynes: Open University.
Smith, P. K., and Cowie, H. (1988). *Understanding Children's Development.* Oxford: Blackwell.

Comments

Overall this is a reasonable essay. Good points include:

- the introduction and conclusion (see page 147)
- the clear line of reasoning – the essay follows the introduction on the whole
- ideas are well ordered and paragraphed
- the style is very clear and precise
- the research evidence has been evaluated in terms of its good points and bad points
- the writer's point of view (her general disagreement with Bowlby) is clear, as are her reasons.

The essay could be improved, however, to get a higher mark. For example:

Length The essay is rather short at only 850 words. It should be 950–1050 words for a word limit of 1000 words. The writer could have said more, for example, about the Strange Situation – it is not clear what this is.

Fulfilling undertakings made in the introduction In the introduction, the writer says she will bring together ideas on day-care at the end of the essay, but she has not done so. The area of day-care has been rather neglected compared to her discussion of the theories.

Answering the question Because the writer neglected the day-care side, she has not really answered the second part of the question in full. Look again at the title.

References in the text Although the essay is quite well referenced, paragraph 6 makes several statements without saying where the evidence comes from.

References at the end Although the references given in the text are written out well, only a few of them have been given fully at the end. All references must be written out in full.

Essay 2

Now compare Essay 1 with the first half of another essay on the same subject.

How has Bowlby's Attachment Theory been modified by the findings of later research? How have theories about attachment affected ideas about child care?

The world of psychology contains many theories about children, some more useful than others, although all add something to our overall knowledge about children, so none should be dismissed as unhelpful. One such theory is that of 'attachment', which was the idea of a psychologist called Bowlby. What are the main elements of Bowlby's theory? Well, first, there is his early work about attachment. Second, there are his adaptations of his theory into his later ideas about maternal deprivation. There was a lot of research to support Bowlby at the time, and his ideas were very useful to society so it was not surprising that he had a big following in his day. Later, some of his ideas were discredited but some of his ideas were picked up by Mary Ainsworth. She developed something called the 'Strange Situation' which has been used by many people interested in the welfare of children.

Bowlby actually believed that it was a tragedy for the child if the mother was not with him throughout his early childhood. He was very opposed to the idea of mothers going out to work. During the war, a lot of mothers had left their children in special nurseries set up by the government. These nurseries enabled women to work in factories making armaments or to go out to grow food and any other jobs formerly filled by men. Many women enjoyed this new-found freedom and learning new skills like building bridges, driving buses and being radar operators. Bowlby argued that women's gains were at the expense of the child. He used examples of children who had been abandoned in the war to show that lack of good mothering had led these children into delinquency and other serious life-long problems. Later Bowlby argued that it might be acceptable for the mother to be absent if there was a suitable kind of carer who was always present so the child got continuity. He felt it was from this carer or mother that the baby was able to learn how to form any relationships. So basically, if the baby did not have its mother, it did not have a sense of how to form a relationship, so then it was not able to have the building blocks of any relationships which made relationships in general always difficult. He was actually influenced by the ideas of Lorenz who found that ducklings who lacked their mother at a critical age adopted other objects such as toys to be their mother instead. Bowlby said that human babies also had a critical period for bonding with their mothers – actually up to nine months old. Harlow found that monkeys were also disturbed and when they grew up were not able to look after their babies.

Mary Ainsworth found that if babies were put in a situation with a stranger, they behaved differently depending on whether they had a good relationship with their mother. She said that how babies behaved with a stranger and then afterwards with their mother for leaving them alone with the stranger let you predict whether the baby would be a delinquent later. She said her experiments using this strange situation showed that babies who were in day care were more likely to grow up delinquent.

[continued]

Marking Essay 2

Using the checklists on either page 161 or 181:

1. Underline sections which you think could be improved.
2. Write comments in the margin as if you were a tutor giving the student advice.
3. Are you able to identify why Essay 1 would receive a higher mark than Essay 2?

When you have finished, compare your comments with those below.

Feedback on the exercise

Focus The first sentence is too general and adds nothing to the essay.

Conciseness Overall, too many words are used to say too little. This means that the writer will not cover as much relevant information in the essay as someone who writes in a more concise style, and will therefore lose marks. (See especially lines 3–4 and 23–5.)

Line of argument It is not clear from the introduction what the writer's line of reasoning or main argument will be.

Addressing the question The first half of the essay has not addressed the question – how Bowlby's theories were modified by research findings.

Structure The early comments about the usefulness of Bowlby's ideas could be omitted as the essay looks at this later (lines 6–8).

Detail Too much detail is given about women's activities during the war – this is not strictly relevant to this essay, so wastes valuable words.

Paragraphing Paragraph 2 is far too long – and its central point is not clear.

References There are no dates for references cited, for example for the work of Lorenz (line 26) and Harlow (line 29).

Precision Some of the research evidence cited is rather vague. Essay 1 makes it clear that there were two stages to Bowlby's research, but this is not clear in Essay 2.

Vocabulary Words such as 'actually' and 'basically' are not generally used in academic writing (lines 23 and 25).

Clarity Some sections (such as lines 29–30 and 32–4) could be written more clearly.

Review

Academic writing has certain formal writing conventions, such as not using slang or abbreviations. It is precise – it's difficult to gain marks if your writing is vague.

It is important to be clear in academic writing when you are giving your personal opinion. Academic writing generally values opinion when it is used to support a line of reasoning and is backed up by evidence ('facts').

Most academic writing is influenced by the scientific model, which values objectivity and quantitative data. Different academic subjects vary in how much they value subjectivity (your personal response) and qualitative analysis (your awareness of your role in the process of evaluating evidence).

There are four main styles of writing used within academic writing. Some pieces of work will require you to use several styles within a single assignment. Almost all writing involves an element of argument and evaluation. Descriptive writing and personal writing need to be used with care.

Good marks are allocated for specific reasons – not for general cleverness. It is important to be aware of how marks are allocated in your subject. Use your tutor's feedback constructively, and don't be put off by what seems to be criticism. Tutors want as many students to succeed as possible – and their comments are intended to help you improve your marks.

If you mark essays yourself, using checklists to give you criteria against which to assess them, you will start to see writing through the eyes of your tutor. This will help you to evaluate your own writing: you will become less dependent on getting feedback from someone else before you know whether your writing is good or bad.

Chapter 9

Critical analytical thinking

LEARNING OUTCOMES

This chapter offers you opportunities to:

- understand what is meant by taking a critical or analytical approach
- become more aware of how to use critical and analytical thinking when reading and writing
- develop criteria for evaluating an argument or a line of reasoning in a piece of writing
- develop criteria for evaluating the evidence given in a piece of writing
- learn how to identify and draw valid conclusions.

Critical thinking

Critical thinking means weighing up the arguments and evidence *for* and *against*. Edward Glaser, who developed a test of critical thinking, defined it in this way (1941):

> Critical thinking calls for a persistent effort to examine any belief or supposed form of knowledge in the light of the evidence that supports it and the futher conclusions to which it tends.

In other words, Glaser emphasises the importance of:

- *persistence*: considering an issue carefully, and more than once
- *evidence*: evaluating the evidence put forward in support of the belief or viewpoint
- *implications*: considering where the belief or viewpoint leads – what conclusions would follow; are these suitable and rational; and if not, should the belief or viewpoint be reconsidered?

Analytical thinking

Analytical thinking involves additional processes:

- standing back from the information given
- examining it in detail from many angles
- checking closely whether it is completely accurate
- checking whether each statement follows logically from what went before
- looking for possible flaws in the reasoning, the evidence, or the way that conclusions are drawn
- comparing the same issue from the point of view of other theorists or writers
- being able to see and explain why different people arrived at different conclusions
- being able to argue why one set of opinions, results or conclusions is preferable to another
- being on guard for literary or statistical devices that encourage the reader to take questionable statements at face value
- checking for hidden assumptions
- checking for attempts to lure the reader into agreement.

Develop a detective-like mind

To develop critical and analytical thinking ability, you might imagine that you are developing a detective-like mind.

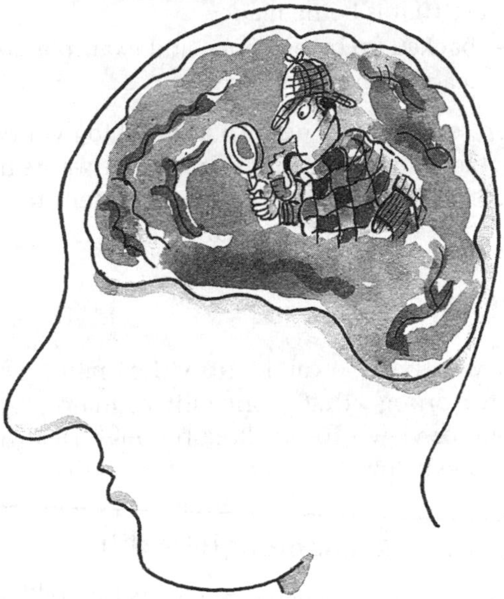

Reading

Critical thinking when *reading* involves the following:

1 identifying the line of reasoning in the text
2 critically evaluating the line of reasoning
3 questioning surface appearances and checking for hidden assumptions or agendas
4 identifying evidence in the text
5 evaluating the evidence according to valid criteria
6 identifying the writer's conclusions
7 deciding whether the evidence given supports these conclusions.

Writing

Critical thinking when writing involves comparable processes:

1 being clear what your conclusions are
2 showing a clear line of reasoning – an 'argument' leading to your conclusion
3 presenting evidence to support your reasoning
4 reading your own writing critically, as above, as well as your sources
5 viewing your subject from multiple perspectives.

Listening

Critical thinking when *listening* involves the same awareness as when reading, plus:

1 checking for consistency in what the speaker is saying – does the speaker appear to contradict herself; and if so, what is going on beneath that contradiction?
2 checking that body language, eye contact, and speed and tone of voice are consistent ('congruent') with what is being said – does the speaker look and sound as though he believes what he is saying?

These issues have been touched on in earlier chapters: the following pages explore them in more detail, and include some basic exercises so that you can try out your critical thinking skills.

Critical thinking when reading

Critical thinking when reading is essential to academic success as much of the writing you do for assignments will include critical analysis of the work of other people.

1 Identify the line of reasoning

Most of the texts you are required to read as a student will include an argument. In academic writing, an 'argument' is:

- a line of reasoning *or*
- an angle or a point of view *or*
- a position that is being defended *or*
- a case that is being made
  - backed up by evidence and examples *and*
  - leading to conclusions.

When reading, you need to keep asking yourself, 'What are the main things this writer wants me to accept? What reasons does she present to encourage me to accept this?'

Activity 1

See whether you can identify the main line of reasoning – that is, the writer's main point of view – in the 'Rochborough Health' passage below. (See page 197 for feedback.)

Passage 1: Rochborough Health

Outdoor play has beneficial effects for children in terms of both their health and their levels of social interaction. According to clinical trials carried out by Rochborough's Health Council Advisory Body in September this year, children who played outside for over fifty days in the year had a 20% higher lung capacity, and 30% lower incidence of asthma and bronchial conditions than children who played indoors. Children who played outdoors also reported having more friends than those who played indoors. A survey of 30 families by Rochborough Social Amenities Committee found that parents were more likely to let their children play outdoors if they had their own gardens or if there were supervised play areas nearby. Mr Arkash of Milton Road said his children did not feel safe playing on the Children's Meadow on the outskirts of Rochborough, as his son had been frightened by a fox there in the past. His little son looked quite tearful as his father spoke. 'He often cries because he has nowhere to play,' said his father. Supervised play areas can be expensive to provide. However, only 18% of homes in Rochborough have gardens. Therefore, to improve the health of all its children, Rochborough needs to provide more supervised outdoor play areas.

Rochborough Playcouncil Newsletter

2 Critically evaluate the line of reasoning

An argument can be critically evaluated in terms of whether it contains:

- relevant, contributing and sufficient propositions (reasons)
- logical progression
- false premises
- flawed reasoning.

Each of these is explored below.

Relevant, contributing and sufficient propositions

The Rochborough Health passage makes a number of statements or *propositions*. For example:

- Outdoor play improves levels of social interaction.
- Only 18% of Rochborough homes have gardens.

These are some of the reasons it gives to support its argument. When examining the line of reasoning, you need to consider whether the reasons given are relevant and whether they support (that is, contribute to) the overall argument. For example:

- the reference to the isolated incident of a fox is not very relevant to the argument about health
- the reference to the expense of supervised play areas *is* relevant to the argument – however, it weakens or undermines the argument rather than contributing to it because the piece does not make clear how the expense could be met.

It is important to check that reasons and evidence are both relevant and supportive of the main argument, as this helps you to identify whether the writer's conclusion is valid. Even if the writer has given relevant reasons that contribute to the argument, however, she may not have given sufficient reasons to prove this is the *only* conclusion that could be drawn.

Passage 2: Injuries

There has been a tremendous rise in the rate of industrial injury. This year there were over thirty reports of repetitive strain injury in the factory (Millex Injuries Report 1999). All those injured worked in the fibre department. Ten years ago there were no reported injuries. This shows that our work conditions are taking a more serious toll upon our health than in the past. *Millex News*

The writer of Passage 2 begins from the premise (starting point) that there has been a great rise in industrial injury. The conclusion is that work conditions are having a more serious effect on health than in the past. He gives a relevant and contributory reason: the rise in the number of reported injuries. However, he does not consider other reasons why the number of reported injuries might have increased – such as whether repetitive strain injury was known about thirty years ago, or whether people were less likely to report accidents in the past.

In addition, the writer has not looked at figures for any other types of injury nor at the health of workers in other departments. He makes generalisations based on only one kind of injury and one part of the factory. He may still be *right* about the rise in industrial injury, but he has not proved his case. He has not given sufficient reasons (or evidence) to justify the conclusion.

Logical progression

In everyday conversation, it is common practice when someone is speaking to assume that there is a logical connection between one thing that is said and the next. For written arguments and in academic contexts in general, you need to question whether one point does indeed follow logically from another. A line of reasoning will:

- begin from a premise
- follow in logical stages (*A* leads to *B*; *B* leads to *C*; *C* leads to *D* …)
- lead to a conclusion that follows directly from what has gone before (there are relevant reasons, in a logical order, which build towards the stated conclusion).

The premise in Passage 1 is that outdoor play is good for children's health. The logical progression is:

- local evidence supports the health argument (that outdoor play is desirable)
- parents' attitudes support this argument
- a lack of facilities prevents outdoor play
- more outdoor play facilities are needed.

False premises

If there were a reason why outdoor play was *not* good for Rochborough children, the writer of Passage 1 would have started from a 'false premise'. The writer of Passage 2 may indeed have begun from a 'false premise' – believing that industrial injury is on the rise in the Millex factory. No conclusive evidence of this is given, so it may not be true.

It is useful to be on the lookout for false premises: many arguments are based on weak foundations of this kind.

Flawed reasoning

Here are some examples of 'flawed reasoning'.

Assuming a causal connection

If two things occur at the same time or place, it is easy to assume either that they must be connected, or that one must have caused the other. For example:

> I revised really well for that exam and got a low mark, so next time I won't revise and I should get a better mark.

This assumes a connection between revision and failure, without considering other possible reasons for failure. Similarly:

> The number of cows in Britain has gone down, and the amount of cheese consumed is on the increase. Psychologically, people seem to eat more cheese when they feel that it will run out.

This assumes that the increase in cheese consumption is related to the number of British cows, whereas it may have been for other reasons such as increased vegetarianism, or a rise in cheese imports. The decrease in the cow population might relate only to herds reared for meat – perhaps the number of milking cows is unaltered.

These examples are chosen to highlight the faulty logic, but flawed reasoning of this sort is not always easy to spot.

Drawing general conclusions based on one or few examples

> The woollen jacket caused a serious skin reaction in the three-year-old, so sale of woollen clothing should be banned.

Here a generalised conclusion is made on the basis of a very small sample of experience – just one example. (The importance of using an adequate sample is explored further below.) There may have been reasons for the reaction unique to that child.

Inappropriate comparisons

In the Passage 1 a comparison is drawn between children who play indoors and those who play outdoors. However, it may have been that the children who played outdoors were already healthier, and those who played indoors did so because of poor health which might get worse if they played outdoors. For example, asthma sufferers are often allergic to pollen and might have been discouraged from playing outdoors.

3 Question surface appearances

Critical thinking requires that you examine these factors:

- Is the evidence what it appears to be?
- Might there be other explanations apart from the obvious one?
- Has all necessary information been given, or might other details lead to a different conclusion?
- Are there interested parties who would gain if the conclusions were accepted?
- Are there hidden assumptions or agendas?
- Does the evidence comes from a reliable, disinterested source?

Activity 2

Look again at the 'Rochborough Health' passage.

- What hidden agendas might there be in this piece?
- What information may be missing that might lead to a different conclusion?

(See page 197 for feedback.)

4 Identifying evidence in the text

Identifying evidence in the text is usually fairly straightforward. Look for statistics, examples, case histories, findings from experiments, surveys, questionnaires or case studies. The evidence may be anecdotal – that is, stories told by one or a few people about their experiences.

Activity 3

What evidence is given in the 'Rochborough Health' passage? (See page 197 for feedback.)

5 Evaluate the evidence

It is not enough for a student to write in an essay or report: 'There is evidence on both sides.' Evidence is not all of equal weight. How can we decide which evidence is better? Some basic guidelines are outlined below.

Use valid criteria to evaluate evidence

Critical thinking involves identifying valid criteria against which something can be evaluated.

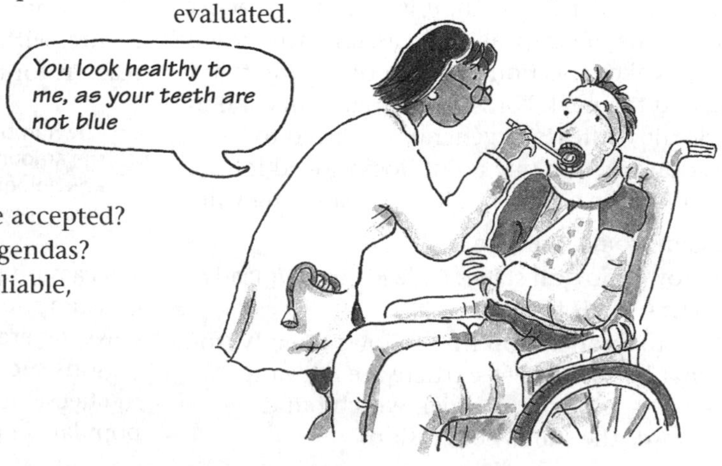

You look healthy to me, as your teeth are not blue

For example, when a doctor declares that somebody is healthy, she takes into account certain criteria, such as body temperature, blood measurements, and the absence of known (or common) symptoms of illness. She evaluates whether signs of potential ill-health are matters for concern and, based on her experience and established medical knowledge, comes to a conclusion about whether the evidence points more towards good health than to sickness.

The following sections give some criteria against which you can evaluate evidence in academic texts and for your own research.

Check the date of the research

Data may be out of date or conclusions based upon it may have been revised. How would your attitude to the 'Rochborough Health' article change if you found out that it was written in 1300, or 1927, or 1999?

Check the source of your information

Articles in academic or professional journals and in recommended textbooks are usually based on in-depth research, and are regarded as more reliable than findings recorded in magazines and newspapers. Newspapers and magazines may be useful primary sources for some subjects such as cultural studies, but are not generally regarded as 'authorities' to quote in essays.

Check for bias in your sources

Bias may not be obvious, and it does not necessarily mean that your source was being 'dishonest' or 'prejudiced'. If somebody has a strong interest in the survival of a particular hospital, for example, the evidence they present may be accurate, yet not the whole story. When thinking critically, we need to be continually questioning in our minds whether there may be hidden agendas, or reasons why the evidence appears to point one way rather than another.

It is always worth considering what political or economic interests might prevent the whole truth from emerging. Consider also how easy it would be, or would have been, for alternative views to be printed and circulated. For example, in some societies, such as sixteenth-century Britain, people who spoke, printed or sold certain viewpoints could be punished by death or loss of limb.

Today, it can be difficult for small organisations or individuals to get the funding they need to research and validate an alternative viewpoint. The overall picture may be distorted if not all the evidence has come to light.

Whilst it is not necessary for you to write about issues of economics, politics and media access in every essay, it is important to be aware of who has access to power, resources and information, who does not, and the possible implications.

Beware the allure of numbers and statistics

It is important to check numerical data, and words that *imply* numerical data, as these are often misused and amounts misrepresented in order to sway the reader.

Most/many Notice words such as 'most' and 'many':

> Most people said that they preferred oranges to apples.

'Most' is a very vague amount. If it *mattered* whether this statement were true or false, we would need more details. How many people were asked? How many preferred oranges? Under what circumstances?

Percentages Notice when percentages are given. Supposing, instead, the statement above read:

> 60% of people preferred oranges; 40% said they preferred apples.

This looks convincing: numerical quantities are given. But is the difference between 60% and 40% *significant*? Here we would need to know how many people were asked. If 1000 people were asked, of whom 600 preferred oranges, the number would be persuasive. However, if only 10 people were asked, 60% simply means that 6 people preferred oranges. '60%' sounds convincing in a way that '6 out of 10' does not. As a critical reader you need to be on the lookout for percentages being used to make insufficient data look impressive.

Sample size Notice also that if just 2 more people arrived who preferred apples, there would be 6 of each. A very small increase in the *sample* (the database of people asked) could easily overturn the original percentage, changing it to 50% for apples and 50% for oranges – no difference at all.

The sample size is the number of people, animals or objects used in the research, whether it's an experiment, a survey or whatever. Small samples give very unreliable information. All other things being equal, the bigger the sample, the more reliable the data. A thousand participants is often taken as a reasonable number for considering statistics to be 'significant'.

Representativeness The sample should be representative of the overall group being studied. If all those asked about fruit preference came from Seville and made their living from oranges, we might not consider them to be either typical or reliable as a sample. Similarly, if all those asked about their preferences were women, or aged ten, or from the South of England, it would not be safe to generalise from them to the rest of the population. To make the sample representative, researchers aim for a good mix of men and women, of different ages, backgrounds and interests.

Conditions of data collection If you found out that those who said they preferred oranges had each been given one free by the person conducting the survey, you might wonder whether the participants had had an ulterior motive in giving their answers, and whether the data were reliable.

Similarly, if the data were collected in face-to-face interviews by personnel wearing the logo of a company known for its orange juice, it is possible that some participants wished to please the interviewers. It is important to find out, where possible, about the conditions in which data were collected, to determine how trustworthy they are. Articles in academic journals usually give full details about the research conditions.

Emotive language and persuader words

Certain words can be very persuasive, and can trigger a position of trust in the reader. Which words they are will vary from subject to subject. For example, for some people the word 'experiment' summons up notions of scientific accuracy and reliability. However, the fact that an experimental approach was used does not in itself mean that the evidence is sound.

Emotive words The use of words and phrases such as 'cruel', 'unfair', 'abuse', 'natural', 'normal', 'commonsense', 'innocent child', 'old', 'little', 'massive', 'unique', 'extremist', 'radical', 'youth', 'new' and even 'final offer' can prompt emotional responses that may lead the reader away from an accurate appraisal of the evidence presented. Emotive images, such as people crying, can be used in a similar way.

Persuader words These words and phrases draw you in by appealing to what they claim is evident. It may be true that what follows is evident, but you still need to be on the alert when you see such words. They include 'surely', 'clearly', 'obviously', 'it is evident that', 'it is plain to see that', 'naturally' and 'of course'.

Activity 4

Evaluate the evidence given in the 'Rochborough Health' passage, using the criteria outlined above. (See page 197 for feedback.)

6 Identify the writer's conclusions

Conclusions generally come at the end of the piece of writing. However, they may also be found at the beginning of the text or even in the middle. They are then are harder to find and tend to be less effective.

Often conclusions are indicated by 'trigger words', such as 'therefore', 'so', 'hence' or 'thus'; or by the use of imperatives – words indicating that something *has* to be done, such as 'must', 'should' or 'need to'.

> ***Activity 5***
>
> Identify the conclusion in the 'Rochborough Health' passage. (See page 197 for feedback.)

7 Evaluating whether the evidence supports the conclusions

A writer may present evidence which could be considered reliable, being based on good research, but then draw conclusions which are not warranted by the evidence. An exaggerated example illustrates this:

- Proposition 1 *The karate champion is a woman.* (Verifiable fact.)
- Proposition 2 *My mother is a woman.* (Verifiable fact.)
- Conclusion *My mother is a woman, therefore she is a karate champion.* (False conclusion.)

Check for hidden false assumptions

In the above example, the faulty reasoning was based on the false assumption that if *one* woman is a karate champion, then *all* women are karate champions. This false assumption is easy to spot, but it is not always so simple. Researchers may try to be objective, but it is very difficult to stand completely outside of the commonsense views and ideological context of the society in which one is writing.

Example

Consider the ideas discussed in the student essays about Bowlby's influential studies of the 1950s (pages 183–6). Bowlby's findings (1951, 1969) suggested that infants who were separated from their mothers at an early age had behavioural and emotional difficulties later. This was used to argue the case against mothers working outside the home. The argument for mothers to stay home was no doubt based on genuine concerns for children's well-being, but the conclusion also suited the economic conditions of the time, in which there was a shortage of jobs for men returned from the Second World War (1939–45).

Later, the conclusion that children were damaged by absent mothers and childcare was heavily criticised (Clarke and Clarke 1976; Clarke-Stewart 1988; Tizard 1991). For example, it was argued that Bowlby's data was based on children in very extreme conditions, such as frightened war orphans and sick children in bleak hospitals and institutions of the 1950s. These children were not typical, and needed to be compared with average, healthy children attending friendly, well-run nurseries, who see their mothers every day. However accurate Bowlby's research may have been, his findings may not have justified the conclusions drawn from them. It is quite likely that Bowlby was affected by the dominant belief system of his day, that a woman's place was at home with the children, and that this influenced his interpretation of the data. It is also likely that his opponents were influenced in their research by changing ideas such as feminism, or by the rising number of women in part-time work.

It is quite typical for research to progress in this way, with advances being made as later researchers question aspects of earlier research, such as whether the sample was representative or whether the research contained assumptions which were invisible to the researchers at the time.

> ***Activity 6***
>
> Do you consider that the evidence in the 'Rochborough Health' passage supports the conclusion drawn? What assumptions are made in the passage? (See page 198 for feedback.)

Critical analytical thinking

Now that you have worked through one passage step by step, try analysing Passage 3, 'Children at Play'. This writer covers issues similar to those in Passage 2, so you can compare the passages.

Activity 7

- Is the line of reasoning good?
- What is the conclusion?
- How strong is the evidence?
- What are the underlying assumptions?
- How well do the reasoning and the evidence support the conclusion?

(See page 198 for feedback.)

Passage 3: Children at Play

Children need to play outdoors and yet it is amazing how few children get that opportunity today. Although Smith (1982) argues that 48% of children prefer to play inside, Jones (1964) found that 98% of children in Britain prefer to play outdoors. I spoke to some parents in Rochborough who said their children missed out by not being able to play down by the river or roam the countryside in safety. Most children are now television addicts, or worse, are addicted to computer games. Everybody knows that this is damaging children educationally, and yet nothing is done about it. This is certainly true of Rochborough's children, and the main reason is that they do not have anywhere to play. Hardly anybody in Rochborough has a garden. It would be better for their health if they played outdoors but parents say they won't let them unless supervised play areas are provided. The parents are worried that they cannot see their children when they are playing. What chance is there for the health of citizens in Rochborough if its children do not get to play outdoors and end up as TV addicts?

Critical thinking when writing

Critical thinking when *writing* includes most of the elements of critical thinking when *reading*. It can be more difficult to analyse your own work critically, however, and to recognise and admit to your own opinions and bias.

Students' writing is often weakened because their thinking is not clear before they start to write their final draft. This is partly a question of planning (see Chapter 7), and partly of spending enough time critically evaluating both what they have read and their own ideas and writing. Time spent in critical analysis is equivalent to 'elaborating the problem' – a process which, as we saw in Chapter 3, was one way in which those who achieved good marks differed from those with poor marks.

Be clear about your conclusions

It is surprising how often students hand in work which shows that although they have done the necessary reading and even given their work considerable thought, they are not sure of their conclusions. The whole of the piece of writing should lead to its conclusion: if the conclusions are vague or understated, *all* of the writing loses its force.

As soon as you are given a piece of work to do, write down what you think your conclusion will be. Put this where you can see it. Whenever you find out something that requires you to revise or fine-tune your conclusion, write out a new one. It may seem paradoxical (or back to front), but your writing will be clearer if you write your conclusions first.

Have a clear line of reasoning

If your conclusions are clear, your argument or line of reasoning is likely to be clear also. The conclusion gives you goalposts at which to direct your shots.

Keep your writing focused, rather than rambling. Bear in mind four guidelines:

- Early drafts may be helpful in elaborating and refining your thinking. However, be sure that your final version says what you really think.
- Work to a writing plan which sets out the reasons, examples and evidence in the most logical order.

- Consider how best to link ideas and pieces of information, so that your writing is not just a list of facts but a line of reasoning.
- Keep your argument clear. From the sea of information gathered at the research stage, select the points that best support your argument and signpost them clearly.

Use evidence to support your reasoning

Use evidence selectively: too many examples may obscure your line of reasoning. Choose a few items that clearly support your case.

Evaluate your own writing through critical reading

As a student, you also have 'readers'. Your tutors or examiners will take a critical reading approach when marking your work. Examine your own writing in the same way you would examine someone else's, as outlined above.

Take multiple perspectives

Whether you are reading, listening, observing or writing, you will be expected to be able to analyse your own and others' arguments – and indeed work, designs or proposals – from more than one perspective. This will mean considering *both* their good *and* their bad points, *both* their strengths *and* their weaknesses.

When you think critically and analyse things from several perspectives, the answer is seldom a straightforward one of right or wrong. Usually there are many contradictory pieces of evidence to weigh up and evaluate against each other.

Feedback on the activities

Passage 1: Rochborough Health

Activity 1: The main line of reasoning

'Outdoor play is good for children's health, so Rochborough needs better facilities for it.'

Activity 2: Vested interests

The article was published by the Playcouncil, who are likely to have a vested interest in arguing for more supervised play spaces.

Activity 3: Types of evidence used

The main evidence is of two kinds: surveys and anecdotes. The detail about the Arkash family is anecdotal (it is just one person's experience). There is also a statistic about garden ownership.

Activity 4: Evaluating the evidence

The evidence about health and parental attitudes comes from official sources which could be considered relatively good 'authorities' and thus reliable. This evidence is relevant and contributes to the argument.

On the other hand, the writer generalises from only one set of health factors (those related to the lungs). It is possible that children who play outdoors have *different* health problems – such as skin complaints or broken ankles. Alternatively, it is possible that the children who played indoors did so because they were more prone to sickness already (such as asthma and pollen allergies). Sickness may have been the *cause* of their playing indoors, rather than the *effect*.

We don't know how representative the children in the survey were of all Rochborough children.

The anecdotal details about the Arkash child and the fox are emotive, and not really relevant to the main argument. The anecdote provides human interest for journalistic writing, but would be unacceptable in most academic writing.

No source is given for the figure of 18% home ownership: we can't judge whether it is reliable.

The writer twice mentions the effects of outdoor play on social interaction, but gives no evidence or details. She or he could link this in more to the main argument.

Activity 5: Conclusion

The conclusion is that Rochborough should provide more supervised outdoor play areas.

Activity 6: Evidence supporting the conclusion

The writer makes a reasonable case and gives supporting evidence. However, there is insufficient evidence to support the conclusion that 'in order to improve the health of its children, Rochborough needs to provide more supervised outdoor play areas'. We don't know what it is about playing outdoors that led to the health improvements. For example, it may be that children ran about more when they were outdoors, and that an indoor running area would have the same effect.

Underlying assumptions

The passage assumes:

1 That playing outdoors is better for all children's health. This may not be the case.
2 That the health of children who play indoors at present would necessarily improve by playing outdoors. This may not be true.
3 That playing outside decreases the incidence of asthma and bronchial conditions.
4 That beneficial effects are available only from outdoor play areas. In fact it may have been other factors about the outdoor play, such as space to run or things to climb, that led to improved health indicators.
5 That there are not enough supervised play areas already for Rochborough children. No figures are quoted for existing supervised play areas so we do not know whether more spaces are needed. The sources the writer quoted don't mention a need for more play spaces. We do not know what percentage of children already play outdoors. All these gaps mean that writer has not given sufficient evidence to support the conclusion.

Activity 7: Critical analytical thinking

On the right is Passage 3 again, with reference numbers added.

Logical progression: the line of reasoning

This kind of writing is likely to receive a comment such as 'What is your point?' It is difficult to identify the thread running through the passage: the line of reasoning is weak. The writer hops backwards and forwards between different types of information, as at (8), having already mentioned these points earlier. The final sentence does not add to what has been stated earlier, at (4).

The conclusion

The conclusion is not clear. The nearest approximation to a conclusion is at (1), 'Children need to play outdoors', as this largely sums up the passage. The writing does not draw its information towards a final conclusion, and the final lines of the passage don't lead anywhere. Compare this to the 'Rochborough Health' passage, which leads to a clear conclusion.

> **Passage 3: Children at Play**
>
> Children need to play outdoors (1) and yet it is amazing how few children (2) get that opportunity today. Although Smith (1982) argues that 48% of children prefer to play inside, Jones (1964) found that 98% of children in Britain prefer to play outdoors (2b). I spoke to some parents in Rochborough (2) who said their children missed out by not being able to play down by the river or roam the countryside in safety (3). Most children are now television addicts, or are addicted to computer games (4). Everybody knows that this is damaging children educationally (5), and yet nothing is done about it. This is certainly true of Rochborough's children (4), and the main reason is that they don't have anywhere to play (6). Hardly anybody in Rochborough has a garden (2). It would be better for their health if they played outdoors (7) but parents say they won't let them unless supervised play areas are provided (2). The parents are worried that they cannot see their children when they are playing. What chance is there for the health of citizens in Rochborough if its children don't get to play outdoors and end up as TV addicts? (8)

The evidence

The evidence is weak, with insufficient detail. The places marked (2) all require further evaluation of the evidence: 'How many children? How many parents? How representative are they of Rochborough parents as a whole? What other views were expressed? How many exactly have gardens? How do we know this?'

A tutor might also comment that the writer has not analysed the sources. At (2b), although the writer uses statistics, these are not recent. She or he offers no possible explanations for why Smith and Jones' research had different findings – such as that they were looking at two different generations of children. The evidence cited confuses the argument rather than supporting it.

Offering evidence to support reasoning

At (7) and (5) issues about health or education could be developed into interesting points, but no evidence or details are given so the reasoning is weak. Compare (7) to the same point in the 'Rochborough Health' passage, which is more convincing.

The evidence: emotive language

At (3) the writer appeals to a 'golden age' when childhood was safer or better. Referring to children as 'addicts' is also very emotive.

The evidence: sources of information

The assertions at (4) may or may not be true. No reliable sources are quoted, so it may be just speculation.

Underlying assumptions

That 'Everybody knows' (5) is an assumption on the part of the writer. How does he or she know what 'Everybody knows'? Our own experience might suggest to us that most children are not 'addicts'.

Does the reasoning support the conclusion?

The main conclusion, that children need to play outdoors, is poorly supported by the reasoning. Although some reasons are given, these are in a jumbled order, without supporting evidence, and are mixed in with irrelevancies such as computer addiction. It is not clear whether an argument is being made on grounds of children's health.

Review

This chapter has looked at ways of developing your critical analytical thinking skills, building on what you learnt from earlier chapters.

You should now be able to link critical reading with analytical writing. Tutors often use terms such as 'critical analysis' or 'analytical writing' interchangeably. They are referring to the 'detective-like' approach outlined on page 188, and to your ability to explain how people arrived at different conclusions or different results.

You need to read, write and think with increasingly critical awareness. You will be expected to examine arguments, evidence and conclusions closely, as well as the links between them. You will be asked to evaluate other people's reasoning and evidence, using criteria to guide you.

Be aware of how easy it is for readers to be swayed by an emotive style. Appreciate the importance of standing back and evaluating in detail.

If you are interested in developing your critical thinking further, you may find it useful to look at Thompson (1996) – see page 232 in this *Handbook*.

Chapter 10

Memory

LEARNING OUTCOMES

This chapter offers you opportunities to:

- understand more about your own memory style and about strategies that suit you
- learn general strategies that assist memory
- become aware of the strengths associated with the different hemispheres of the brain, and how to use these to improve memory
- discover how to optimise the 'triune' brain for learning and memory
- understand how 'stages' of the memory process can be used to assist memory
- develop ideas on how to 'encode' information so as to make it memorable
- learn the importance of organising and 'chunking' information
- understand more about memory in general, and how to use it to your advantage.

Remember, remember …

People generally underestimate their memory. They focus on what they forget rather than what they remember, and rarely appreciate how sophisticated the memory is.

For example, to read this paragraph requires extraordinarily complex feats of memory. You have to remember the complex workings of a language which took you years to learn; you call upon a memory of thousands of known words; you match the look, sound and meaning of particular written symbols to a memory store of thousands of symbols. You integrate all of this in memory and make sense of what you read. You do all of this within fractions of seconds.

People worry about memory deteriorating with age. Research by Harris and Sunderland (1981) suggests that older people remember some things better than the young. Older people often expect that their memory will be worse, so notice more when they do forget – yet greater age means that they also have more to remember. Buzan and Keene (1996) argue that learning *improves* with age – and learning involves memory.

Our brains take in much more information than we need: if we don't make active use of the information, it is as if the path to it becomes lost or overgrown, making it hard to access. The *way* we take in information also affects what we remember.

The more you know about how the brain and memory works, the more you can develop techniques to remember *what* you want to remember, *when* you need it.

Individual memory styles

e each have a combination of memory ategies that work best for us. We each use ried strategies to remember different kinds of information.

> *Activity: how do you remember things?*
>
> Try to recall each of the items 1–6 below. After each one, note down what you did to help you remember.
>
> 1 What is your best friend's phone number?
> 2 How do you use a pencil sharpener ?
> 3 What was your first day at school like?
> 4 What did you wear yesterday?
> 5 Where are your best clothes now?
> 6 How do you get to the nearest postbox?

You probably used different strategies to remember the phone number than to recall your first day at school. You may have used some of the followings strategies – if not, experiment with them now.

Fact strategies

Many techniques may help in learning a fact such as a telephone number. You might try:

- chanting the rhythm of the number
- using your fingers to map out the pattern of movements needed to dial the number
- seeing the number in your mind
- hearing your voice saying the number
- drawing out the digits with your finger
- writing the number down quickly
- noting any memorable peculiarity of the number, such as a repeated pattern (2727) or a reversible number (1331)
- noting any smaller numbers of personal significance to you, such as the year you were born or a relative's house number, contained within the number.

Event strategies

Trying to recall your first day at school may have called up different types of memory.

- The emotional memory of the event may have come to mind – your excitement at starting school, or your distress at being left by your mother, or your fear of the teacher. You might experience this physically in your body, as a tightening of the stomach muscles, for example, or a change in your breathing.
- You may have a strong visual memory of the journey to the school, or of moments during the first day. These may run through your head like a film or a series of snapshots.
- You may be able to hear the noises of the school – the shouts in the playground, or the school bell. You may remember certain smells, or even the taste of chalk on your fingers.

Other strategies

In remembering the six items above you may have used quite different strategies.

- To remember how to use a pencil sharpener you may have moved your hands to guide you through the sequence of movements.
- To remember what you wore, you may have recalled the place where you were.
- To remember where your clothes are now, you probably used a mixture: visual recall of where they usually are, and a check through your memory of recent events to see if there was any reason why they might be somewhere else.
- For the postbox, you may have visualised the local geography, or remembered a time you posted a letter, or imagined the walk to the box, or repeated instructions under your breath.

Check your memory style

What helps *you* remember things? Here's a simple way to find out.

- Colour in 10 words on the word chart on the right.
- Read through the chart for 2 minutes, then cover it completely.
- Write down all the words you can remember.
- Read the following section as you check your results.

sea	Lenin	dog	merry	PINK	chair
saucer	cog	kitchen	LOG	hobby	butter
cheese	circus	green	Spain	essay	harp
windy	glink	student	jog	pills	sandwich
	walnut				
sick	Fred	pong	doctor	Gandhi	plate
JAM	happy	sneeze	sad	maybe	holiday
fog	lost	tutor	INDIA	hand	bandage
blue	bread	table	blook	kneel	gloom

What helps you remember?

Look at the words you recalled. Does the selection of words you remembered suggest that you used any of the strategies below? If so, you have valuable clues about how you can arrange information you *want* to recall.

Your memory may be assisted by any or all of the following.

Recency effect ☐

You may have remembered best the words you learnt last.

Primacy effect ☐

You may have remembered best the words you learnt first.

Sound ☐

You may have remembered rhyming words, odd-sounding words, or words that you heard together in your head.

Locus (place) ☐

You may have associated a word with a place you know.

Real names ☐

You may have a particularly good memory for names.

Visual features ☐

You may have noticed the look of a word (such as the words in capitals or those with shapes around them).

Visual association ☐

You may have linked words with pictures or mental images.

Visual arrangement ☐

You may have remembered where items were on the page. (If so, you may find it easy to recall flowcharts or pattern notes, or be helped by visual spacing or making links with a picture.)

Semantic association ☐

You may have remembered words with meaningful associations, such as bread, butter, sandwich.

Being bizarre and unusual ☐

You may have noticed odd things, such as the words 'pong' and 'glink' which stand out. (If you did, you may find it helpful to link ordinary things with bizarre images.)

Stories ☐

You may have linked unrelated items so that they made a story. (This can help with the letters of a difficult spelling. For example, 'liaise': Liam Is Always In Such Ecstasy.)

Colour and activity ☐

If you remembered several of the words you coloured in, you may be sensitive to colour; or perhaps you benefit from *doing* things with information you are learning.

Musical association ☐

Did you try singing or chanting information to tunes you know?

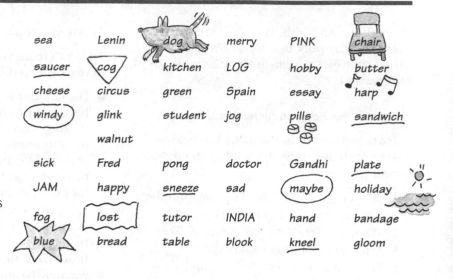

Improve your memory

Particular practices can help you remember things. Below are some that are well known, and you may have others of your own.

Self-awareness

Know what tricks and methods you *already* use to remember things.

Repetition or over-learning

This is essential. Go over information at least three times. Check back often, for short lengths of time (rather than once for a long time).

Association

Link what you need to remember with something you already know. See also 'Active learning' (Chapter 4).

Mnemonics

Any trick to help you remember is a mnemonic (pronounced *nem-on-ic*). One common mnemonic is to use the first letter of each keyword to make a new 'word' that sums up the whole subject – just as 'CREAM' sums up Chapter 4. It doesn't matter if the letters don't make a real word.

Active listening

Discuss what you're trying to learn with friends. Listen to your voice saying or reading it. Tape yourself. Exaggerate. Use accents. Be dramatic.

Writing things down

In your own words, write things out over and over again.

Personalising it

Relate what you learn to yourself. (For example in what way does it *affect* you? Does it remind you of someone you know, or somewhere you have been?)

Play

Play with information. Look for the fun in it. Relax and enjoy the process.

Think about advertisements

Advertising agencies deliberately set out to make us remember their advertisements. The 'tricks' and 'devices' they employ to prompt our memory can also be used to help us to remember what we study.

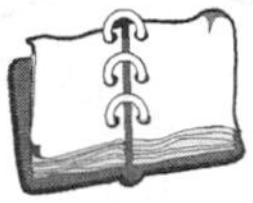

Think of three adverts (from TV, magazine, hoardings, etc.). What makes these three memorable for you?

Devices used by advertisers

Which of these devices are most effective in helping *you* remember?

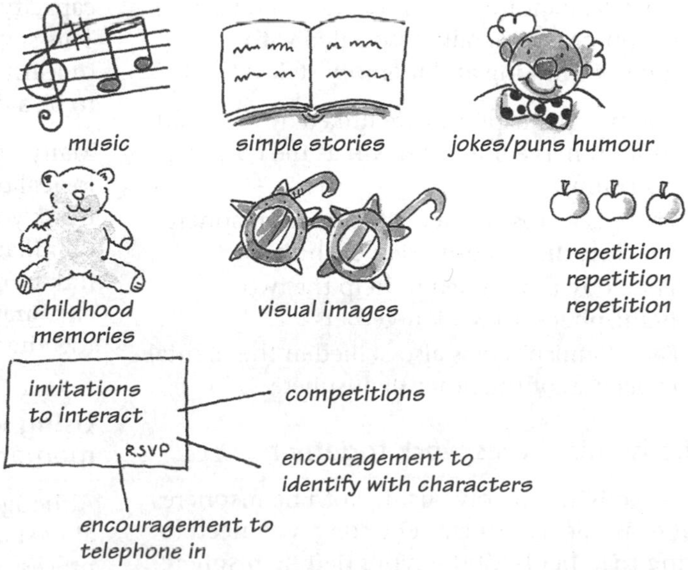

Using the brain

Left brain

Logical thinking style

sequence
logic
analysis
numbers
lyrics of songs
language
names
calculation
sense of time
reasoning
chemical formulae

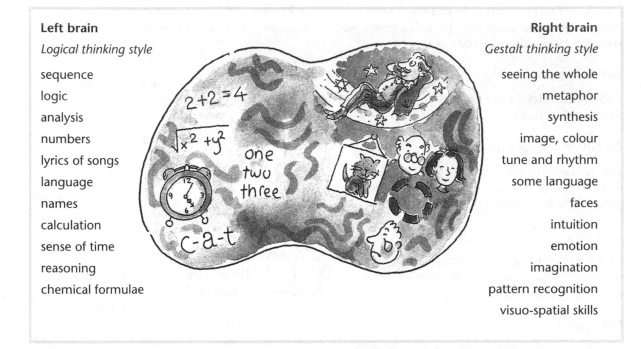

Right brain

Gestalt thinking style

seeing the whole
metaphor
synthesis
image, colour
tune and rhythm
some language
faces
intuition
emotion
imagination
pattern recognition
visuo-spatial skills

Left brain – right brain

The brain is divided into two hemispheres, left and right. Research into brain damage shows that different mental functions are affected depending on which hemisphere is damaged. This understanding led to the idea that each hemisphere is generally associated with particular thinking and memory styles.

- The two hemispheres are linked by over 200 million nerve fibres (known as the corpus callosum).
- There is a crossover effect: each hemisphere controls the opposite side of the body.
- The body is designed to help the two hemispheres to work together.
- Each hemisphere is also skilled in the mental capacities of the other hemisphere.

The hemispheres work together

Most activities involve using both hemispheres. For example, to remember a song, you need to bring together both the lyrics (left hemisphere) and the tune (right hemisphere). To remember a person, you need to link the face (right hemisphere) and the name (left hemisphere).

If something in one part of the brain makes learning difficult, the brain has a tremendous capacity for finding a different route to learning. This suggests that if something proves difficult to learn or memorise in one way, there is likely to be a different way your brain could learn it.

Many people identify more with either the logical or the Gestalt thinking style. Do you think you are more 'left brain' or 'right brain' dominant? You can use your preferred style to link information across the hemispheres. This encourages the parts of the brain to work better together and makes learning easier.

Using left and right brain to improve memory

Although the brain uses both hemispheres for almost any activity, you can encourage this process, giving greater brain integration, and making use of more of your brain.

If you have a 'right brain' preference

- Draw a diagram or picture to show how varied information links up.
- Personalise information – find a way to make it relevant to your own life or experience.
- Use shape and colour to highlight and organise information.
- Use different colours for different topics.
- Sing the information you have to learn.
- Move around as you learn – try to recall what you have just learnt as you do the housework or walk to the bus stop.

If you have a 'left brain' preference

- Write out the information by hand.
- Turn the information into lists.
- Number items of information so that the sequence is clear.
- Use headings to break up the information into different categories.
- Turn information into flow diagrams so you can see progression.
- Build up from details until you get the whole picture.

Locate the information in the brain

Make an experiment. While trying to visualise or recall information, first look up and to the left; then do the same but looking up and to the right. Also try looking left, then right, and then down to each side.

Which direction worked best? Look in that direction when you try to recall information.

For optimum memory, combine different methods

Whatever your left- or right-brain preference, find a way of linking those skills to the skills associated with the other side. For example, if you are a picture thinker, number and sequence your pictures. If you use lists, then sing or colour them. Left-brain thinkers need to ensure they have the whole picture and can see how everything fits together. Right-brain thinkers need to ensure they appreciate the sequence, order, and hierarchy of importance.

When learning something, combine a mixture of memory strategies:

- look at it
- repeat it with rhythm
- write it
- number it
- give it a shape
- turn it into a diagram
- say it aloud
- sing it
- draw it
- colour it
- act it out
- make it bizarre

and use any other device you find useful from pages 202–3 and below.

The triune brain

The brain is also divided 'top-down' into three main areas of activity: reptile brain, limbic system and neo-cortex. McLean (1973, cited in Rose 1985) referred to this as the 'triune brain'.

The neo-cortex

The neo-cortex is what people generally think of when they speak of 'grey matter' or imagine a brain. It controls intellectual processes such as language, thinking, and handling numbers.

However, the neo-cortex is only part of the story: other parts of the triune brain also affect what can be learnt and remembered.

The mammalian brain (or limbic system)

The mammalian brain is located above the brain stem, roughly in the middle of the brain, and consists of a number of organs which control functions such as emotions, pleasure, moods, romance, and immunity to disease.

The reptile brain also affects study

In evolutionary terms the reptile brain is the oldest part of the brain. It is situated in the brainstem at the base of the head, and manages our basic instinctual and survival responses.

The reptile brain interprets stress or anxiety as a danger to our survival. It tries to help us 'escape' by drawing the main resources of the body to the large muscles and producing extra adrenalin so that we are in a heightened, alert state, ready to run away. Resources are taken away from the areas of the brain that we use for academic study: logical argument is not needed for basic survival. Being in 'survival mode' is not very helpful to study – if we don't use up the adrenalin by moving the big muscles, we may feel tense, over-alert, easily distracted and unable to concentrate.

The triune brain

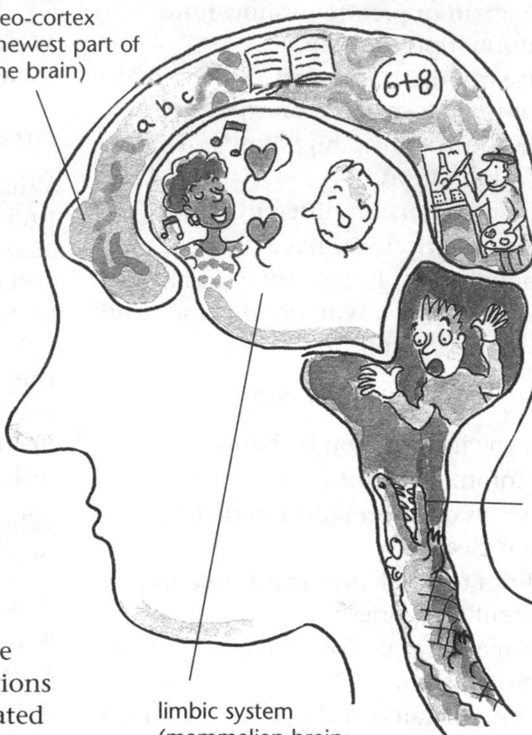

Learning

Learning involves interaction between these three aspects of the brain, which are linked through the limbic system.

Some psychologists believe that emotions are the main link between the three areas. Emotions are a great stimulus to memory. The Accelerated Learning Movement uses music, images, colour and associations to create unconscious emotional arousal, facilitating faster learning.

A state of 'relaxed alertness' helps the imagination, and increases suggestibility and openness to new information. It can also stimulate left–right brain interaction (Rose 1985).

Optimising study with the triune brain

The following guidelines will help you study as effectively as possible.

- Stay relaxed, so that you avoid 'survival mode'. If you feel tense, go for a walk, stamp your feet, exercise or move around as you learn: this will use up excess adrenalin.
- Once you are relaxed, give yourself a positive emotional outlook on the task in hand: that it is easy, enjoyable, exciting, fun, interesting, full of surprises.
- Use your imagination to 'reframe' difficult or boring subjects as challenges. Set yourself targets, such as 'I'll learn three pages in the next half-hour' or 'This will be the most creative set of pattern notes I have made so far', so that your interest and emotions are involved.
- When studying, listen to music which has an expressive and recognisable melody played on string instruments, and has a steady bass rhythm of about 60 beats per minute. Possibilities include classical Baroque music (such as Bach or Vivaldi), classical Indian music, and New Age healing tapes.
- Use your imagination to make strong visual links between ideas.
- Make your notes visually striking, pleasant and appealing to the eye.

Stages of the memory process

Another way of using the brain to improve memory is to work with the different stages in the memory process (see page 208).

Four stages in the memory process

1. *Taking in information* – noticing or attending to information, and absorbing it.
2. *Retaining it* – in short-term memory.
3. *Encoding it* – interacting with the information in working memory so that the brain can store it in long-term memory.
4. *Recalling it* – retrieving or remembering information, whether on purpose, by accident, or in dreams. Recall can seem accurate even when it is not.

Stage 1: Taking information in

What we already know and have a name for affects how we direct our attention, what we notice, and therefore what goes into memory. We need to maintain our attention in order to remember.

If you study on 'automatic pilot', little attention is involved so you will remember less. You will remember more if you:

- direct your attention consciously and purposefully
- focus in a relaxed way – not with hard concentration
- take breaks and make changes in what you are doing, so as to maintain relaxed attention – a few minutes moving around or doing something different is sufficient
- link information to what you know
- give names and labels to information
- deliberately arrange or adapt information so that it is structured and yet stands out as odd, distinct, different or more interesting – so that it grabs your attention.

Stage 2: Retaining information long enough to remember it

Rehearsing new information in short-term memory helps the working memory hold onto it. Repeating it gives the brain time to call up stored memories to help you make sense of the information and encode it for storage.

Rehearsal must start within a few seconds, as information fades quickly. Rehearsal is a useful strategy for holding onto names, dates, numbers, formulae and instructions for long enough to write them down. You can then employ other memory strategies to remember the information long term.

Stage 3: Encoding information – the key to memory?

The brain encodes new information so that it can be represented in the memory. Codes may be oral, auditory, kinaesthetic (using touch and feelings), verbal, semantic (related to meaning), visual, emotional, or motor (using a muscle sequence).

For example, when you tell a story, the brain encodes the pattern of fine-muscle movements you used to speak and stores them. It can also encode and store the sound of your speech on your own ear; the images and emotions which the story brought to mind; the look of the text; and details such as who was in the room or the buzzing of a neon light. The brain links information it has encoded – so any one aspect could trigger the whole memory later. The more facets of an experience the brain has encoded, the more triggers to memory.

It follows that you can assist your memory by *choosing* to encode information in several ways. Some are suggested below, but create your own too.

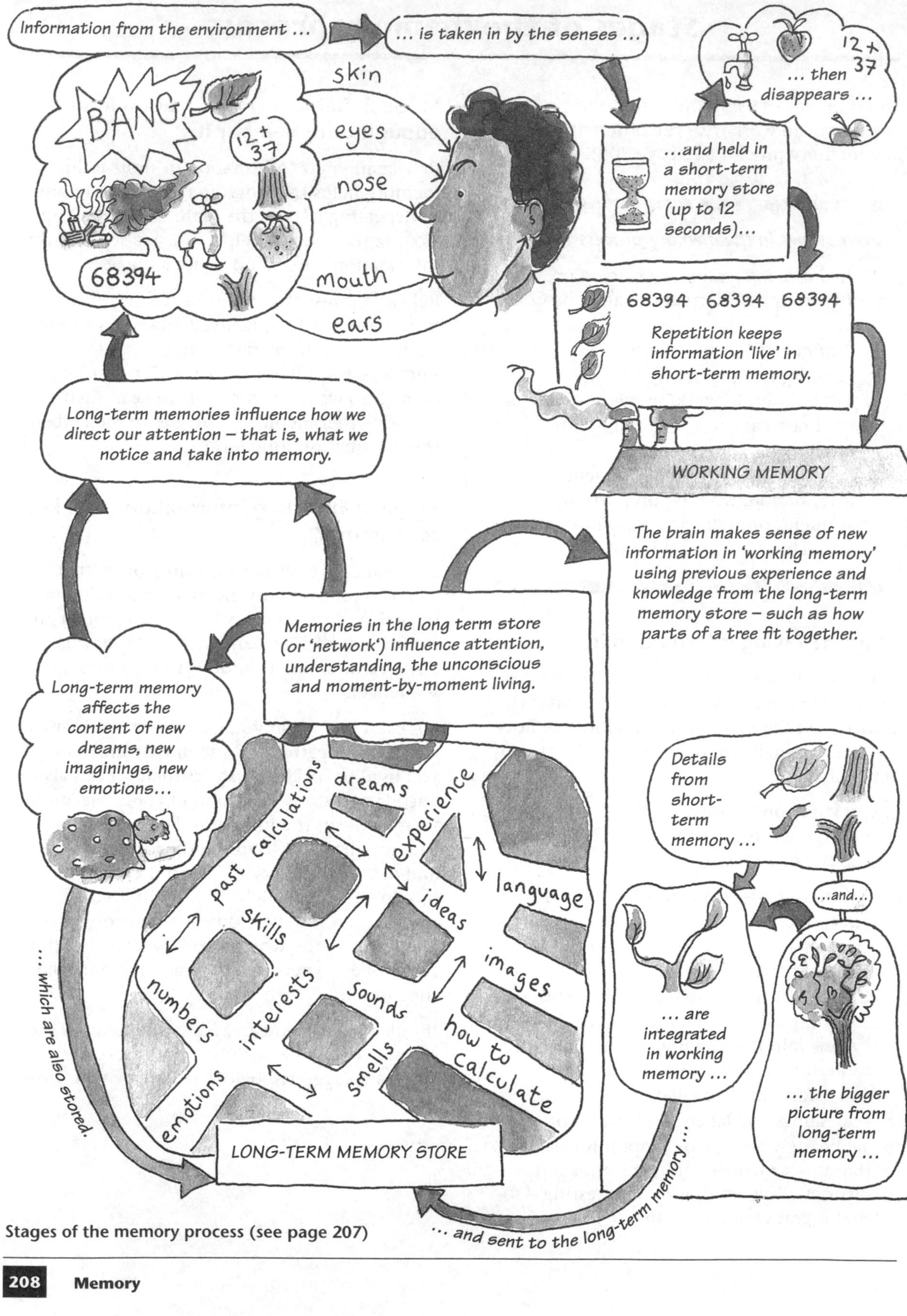

Information from the environment …
… is taken in by the senses …
BANG
12 + 37
68394
skin
eyes
nose
mouth
ears
… then disappears …
12 + 37
…and held in a short-term memory store (up to 12 seconds)…
68394 68394 68394
Repetition keeps information 'live' in short-term memory.
WORKING MEMORY
The brain makes sense of new information in 'working memory' using previous experience and knowledge from the long-term memory store – such as how parts of a tree fit together.
Long-term memories influence how we direct our attention – that is, what we notice and take into memory.
Memories in the long term store (or 'network') influence attention, understanding, the unconscious and moment-by-moment living.
Long-term memory affects the content of new dreams, new imaginings, new emotions…
Details from short-term memory …
…and…
… are integrated in working memory …
… the bigger picture from long-term memory …
dreams
past calculations
experience
language
ideas
skills
images
numbers
interests
sounds
how to calculate
smells
emotions
LONG-TERM MEMORY STORE
… which are also stored.
… and sent to the long-term memory …

Stages of the memory process (see page 207)

Suggestions for multiple encoding

Use your environment

- Use a different room for each subject.
- Notice aspects of the environment such as the light or feel of the room – how do you feel in that place?
- Attach your notes to the furniture. Notice their location.
- Associate a different location with each subject. Associate furniture, windows, plants and ornaments with particular topics.

Use your clothes

- Associate items of clothing with topics in your learning – a shoe could represent one aspect of foreign policy; each button on a shirt could represent a quotation. Clothes with patterns, pockets and buttons are especially useful.
- Wear these clothes into the exam room as a memory trigger.

Use the parts of your body

Parts of your body are especially helpful as triggers to memory, as your body will be there in the exam room!

For example, each hand could represent an essay plan – each finger one major topic; each segment of each finger a principal reference you would use. The fingernails could represent counter-arguments; the knuckles could be associated with relevant quotations.

Use motor memory

- Study on the move. If you exercise, associate each movement with something you wish to remember. To refresh the memory, go through the exercise in your mind.
- Writing, drawing and speaking also use motor memory: the fine-muscle sequence is recorded by the brain.

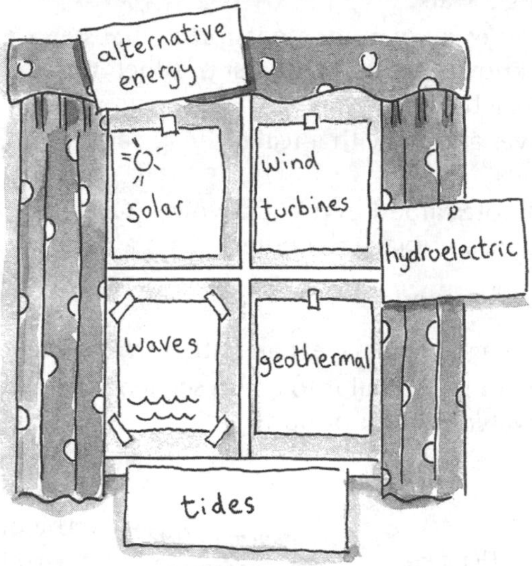

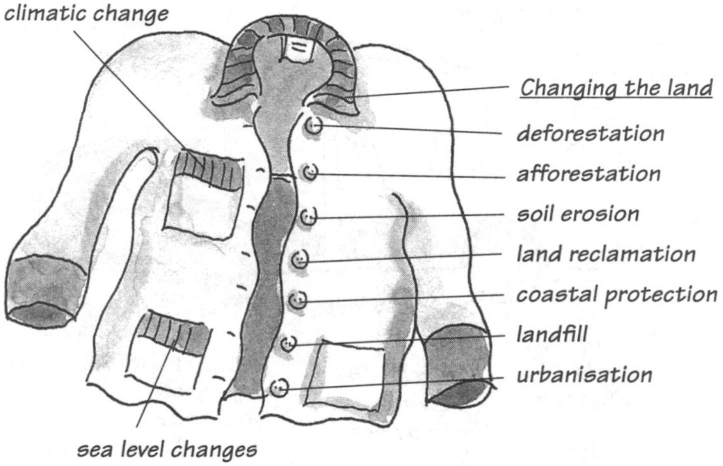

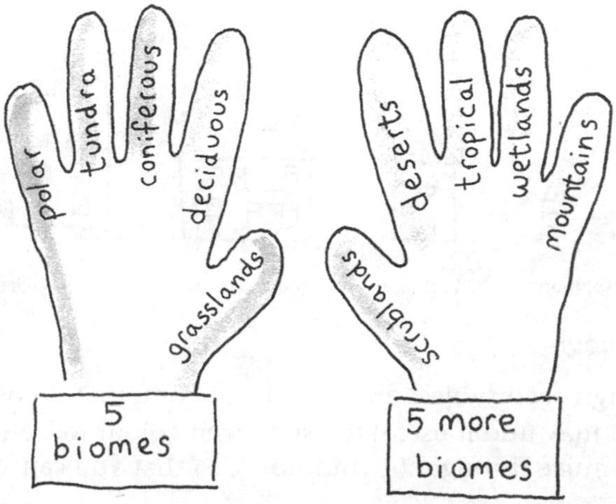

Use auditory memory

- Speak your ideas onto tape and listen to them during a walk.
- Sing an essay plan for a possible exam essay to a well-known tune. Make a list of which tunes go with each subject.
- Go over a topic with a real or imaginary friend, or your cat.
- Read notes aloud in peculiar voices. Over-dramatise to make the notes memorable.

Use visual memory

- Make page layouts clear and attractive.
- Turn your material into a film sequence that you can watch in your mind's eye.
- Assign to a topic an object such as a car, and label different bits of the object with the things you need to remember: the driving wheel with your main point; the four wheels with four main theorists; the doors with examples of practical applications of the theory; items in the boot could remind you of background information or historical development; and parts of the engine or objects on the front seat could indicate future developments.

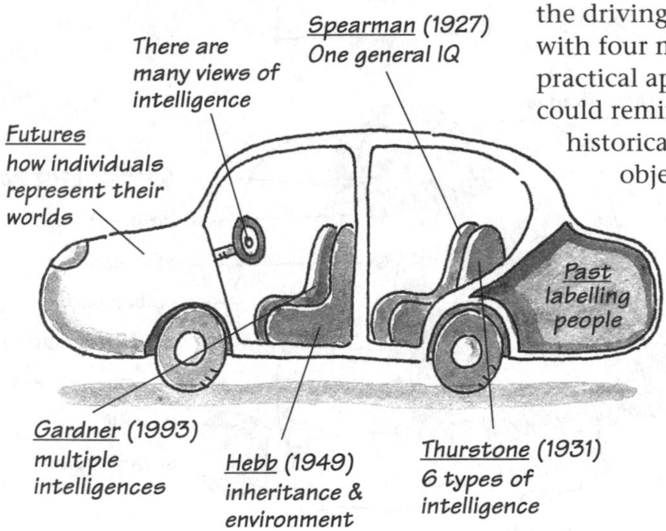

- To remember complex lists and formulae, such as accountancy balance sheets, use a sequence of images, linked by a story.
- Use scale (size) and visually distinct images to separate out similar or confusing material, such as information about similar theories. Arrange these in a visual hierarchy.

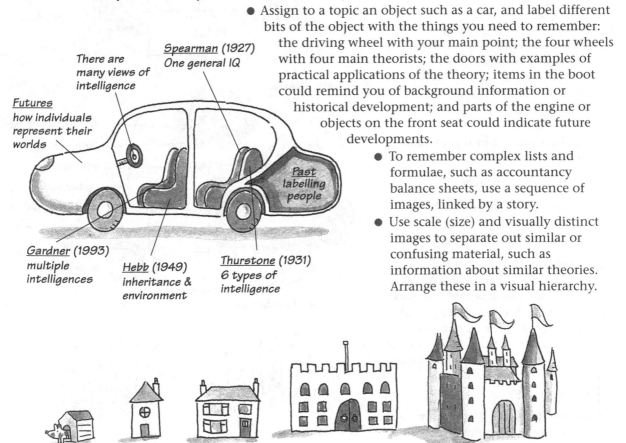

Use colour

- Assign each subject area a different combination of colours.
- You may find it useful to use a given colour for references or for formulae throughout your notes, so that you can spot them easily.

- Give each theme a different colour. You can then see at a glance which pages cover what, and which combinations of themes come up together. This makes reading more interactive, and finding information faster.

Use verbal memory

- Reduce information to keywords.
- Organise information into hierarchies under headings (see concept pyramids, page 152).
- Write out your information in the fewest words possible – this process encourages interaction with the material.

Use semantic memory

- Spend time considering the *implications* of what you have found out. For example, who is affected? What would it mean for the future? What changes might arise? What theories could this information overturn? What are the moral, legal or ethical consequences?
- Think of a different way of saying what you have already written.
- Decide which are the three most important aspects of the subject, or the most important theories or ideas. Then decide which is the *one* most important.
- Consider all the ways in which one area of a subject is similar to another.

Stage 4: Recall

Good recall is linked to how much attention and awareness you bring to the process of taking in the information and encoding it.

Overlearning to aid recall

If you want to recall information at will, such as for exams or for complicated sequences that you use regularly, you may need to 'overlearn'. Overlearning is a combination of:

- active learning
- using the techniques from this chapter
- checking back over and over again what you have learnt, without looking at prompts.

Strategy for overlearning

1. Make a set of pattern notes or an outline for an essay plan on a large index card or on paper, so that you have an overview.
2. Write names, dates and keywords for the references for each topic on index cards. Check that you can recite or reproduce the information on the card from memory.
3. If you can't, put the prompt card into a plastic folder (so it won't get smudged) and carry it around with you. Glance at it briefly in spare moments, such as at the bus stop or while doing the dishes.
4. Do this several times over a few days. Just looking at the prompt from time to time, or running the information through your head, will keep the memory fresh. Little and often is more effective than simply repeating the information over and over on one occasion.

If the information is hard to remember, there is probably a better way of encoding it.

Memory thrives on organisation

Activity

1. Read List A for 15 seconds, then cover it.
2. Recite a nursery rhyme (to prevent rehearsal).
3. Write down the words you remember.
4. Check List A and jot down your score.

List A

plum	elbow	giraffe	caravan
puppy	banana	foot	apple
pony	cherry	barge	bungalow

Now do the same with List B, including the underlined words. Even if you did not do well with the first list, have a go.

List B

Fruit	Animal	Home	Body
plum	giraffe	house	foot
banana	puppy	apartment	knee
apple	donkey	bungalow	elbow
cherry	pony	caravan	hand

You probably remembered many more items from List B. List B is more memorable because:

- grouping similar items together helps recall
- using group headings helps recall
- being able to see that there were only four types of information gives the task manageable boundaries
- many of the items on List B were also in List A – and going over information again helps recall.

Organising information into pyramids

Concept pyramids (see Chapter 7) organise associated information into hierarchies. They are excellent memory aids.

In an experiment in 1969, Bower and other psychologists asked a group of people to learn 112 words. The words were grouped and linked meaningfully, as in List B above, and organised into four pyramids. People remembered 100% of the words by the third attempt.

By contrast, a second group of people were given the same words, also arranged into pyramid shapes, but this time with the words randomly assigned to each pyramid – they were not meaningfully (or semantically) linked. The second group remembered only 47% of the words by the third attempt.

This suggests the importance of both:

- linking information meaningfully, *and*
- organising the ideas into hierarchies or concept pyramids.

Pyramids, pattern notes and pictures

Some people prefer to organise information as pattern notes or other images. Combining pattern notes, concept pyramids and pictures can give a great boost to your powers of recall.

Pattern notes and pyramids

Pattern notes work best when generating ideas and for recalling information from memory. Well-organised notes will be easier to remember.

- Let your imagination wander when you make the initial pattern. Let the ideas flow (page 118).
- If the initial pattern shows no clear hierarchy of ideas, reorganise the words to fit into a concept pyramid. This may take some time, but it clarifies your thinking (see Chapter 7).
- Colour-code the different levels of the hierarchy. For example:

- red for main headings
  - pink for less important headings
  - yellow and orange for intermediate-level information
  - dark green for key evidence, and light green for details about evidence
  - dark blue for specific examples, and light blue for details about examples
  - violet for references (names and dates).
- Draw rings, boxes or other shapes around crucial information, so that it stands out.

You may find it helpful to build up pattern notes as a series of concept pyramids, or to work back and forth between a pattern and pyramids. You may wish to rework only some parts of the pattern into concept pyramids, and then to stick these pyramids back onto the original pattern with glue or Blu-Tack®. There is scope for all kinds of imaginative adaptations.

Pattern notes can be as big as you want – just keep adding and linking information.

Pictures and pattern notes

- You can select any image to anchor your memory – like the car suggested on page 210.
- Associate each part of the picture with one aspect of the topic you wish to remember.
- You can incorporate images into patterns and pyramids. Draw them, or cut images out of magazines and stick them on.
- Add small pictures, to increase your interaction with the material and to make it more visually memorable. The better, brighter, odder, and more exaggerated the pictures, the more memorable the pattern.

'Chunking' information

Short-term memory is the aspect of memory that allows us to store away some information for a few seconds whilst we focus on a different aspect of the problem, such as keeping a phone number in our head whilst we find a pen to write it down, or remembering to carry and add a digit to the next column when we add up numbers larger than 10.

Nobel-prize winner Herbert Simon found that we can generally hold five 'chunks' of information in short-term memory (1974). However, the 'chunk' can vary enormously in size: it could be a single word or number, or a phrase, or a whole story, or how to count up to a million. Try this out for yourself.

- Read the list under 'Small chunks'.
- Cover the list, then try to remember each phrase exactly.
- Do the same for the 'Bigger chunks' list.

You should be able to remember roughly the same number of chunks, irrespective of their size – for example, five sets of two words and five sets of longer sentences.

Small chunks (2 words)

Happy Birthday	No Smoking
No way	Buckingham Palace
Mouth-watering	Photograph album
Small change	New Year

Bigger chunks (7–10-word sentences)

The rain in Spain falls mainly on the plain.

There is no business like show business.

Once upon a time there were three little pigs.

There is no escaping from your conscience.

Somewhere over the rainbow, way up high.

I hope you know what you are doing.

To be or not to be, that is the question.

Postman Pat has a very nice hat.

'Chunking' helps long-term memory

The same principle can be used to help organise information in your long-term memory. This is especially useful for exam revision. For example, if for one topic you have ten references to remember, arrange the names in the order in which you are likely to use them, and then make up a story to link them together into one chunk. Give the story a simple name. The crazier the story, the easier to remember. Good English does not matter. In the example, the names are printed in bold.

Example

Names to revise

Gordon	Pilkington	Snodgrass
Collins	Rowbottams	Rider
Manchu	Ellis	Webster

Linking story

Bike story

Mr **Gordon**, drinking gin, shouted at glassy Mr **Pilkington**, that the **Snodgrass** needed cutting before the colicky **Collins** children slipped off their bikes onto their Row**bottams**. The first bike **Rider** was **Manchu**-ing [chewing] a toffee and fell off because his W-**Ellis** [wellies] got caught in the spokes. He fell into a spider's **Web**ster.

This is a useful tactic to use whenever you have information that does not link up easily. Most of your course material links up more naturally, and understanding how it fits together as a whole reduces it to a single chunk or fewer chunks.

What do we remember?

Flanagan (1997) argues that we remember:

- 20% of what we read
- 30% of what we hear
- 40% of what we see
- 50% of what we say
- 60% of what we do

  and
- 90% of what we read, hear, see, say *and* do.

These are clearly not scientific figures, but they suggest the importance of interaction with the material and of using all your senses. This chapter has aimed to give you ideas on how to work towards that 90% – or better. Participants in Bower's research (see page 212) were able to gain 100% recall, and that was without multi-sensory involvement. By combining all of these strategies, you can greatly enhance your memory potential.

Review

Memory is an active process. There are innumerable ways of enhancing it: if one doesn't work, try another approach which might suit you better.

Work with your own learning style and memory preferences to try out new ways of remembering things. Creativity and imagination are essential ingredients. To remember well, it helps to be relaxed, have fun with the memory process, and play with information until you find a helpful mnemonic. Be aware that what works for one kind of information might not work for another – some trial and error is involved.

You can enhance your memory by using your brain fully. Be aware of your left–right preference, the action of the three parts of your triune brain, and the different stages of the memory process. The way you encode and organise information is particularly important.

Take charge of your conscious memories. You may achieve remarkable improvements!

Chapter 11

Revision and exams

LEARNING OUTCOMES

This chapter offers you opportunities to:

- consider some advantages of examinations
- become aware of some common pitfalls – and learn how to avoid them
- develop ideas for approaching revision in the long term and in the build-up to exams
- consider other preparation needed apart from revision
- develop strategies and techniques to help during the exam itself
- learn ways of managing stress in order to facilitate your learning
- feel you have some control over the exam experience.

The prospect of examinations can be extremely stressful, whether you have performed well or badly in the past. You may even feel resentful – that it is a waste of your time, or that you know the material but cannot show your knowledge under exam conditions. Understanding the reasons for exams, being aware of ways that exams can be an advantage to you, and knowing you have some control over the process, can help to create the positive mindset needed for a successful exam experience.

The purpose of exams

The main purpose of exams is for lecturers to check that you have understood the work covered on the course and that the work which demonstrates this is entirely your own.

Preparing for exams involves a high release of energy and an unusual degree of focus, which produces a very intense kind of learning. That focus and intensity are not easy to reproduce under any other conditions.

Some advantages of examinations

There are some positive benefits in exams!

- You cannot be expected to give very long or detailed answers in exams: you need to use less information than in a comparable piece of coursework. As a result, less in-depth research and reading may be needed than if you were set additional coursework.
- You don't have to write out references or bibliographies in full at the end.
- Exaxminers are generally more sympathetic about scrawled handwriting, minor grammatical errors, spellings, and forgotten details than lecturers are for coursework.
- Compared with continual assessment, there is less pressure on you throughout the year.

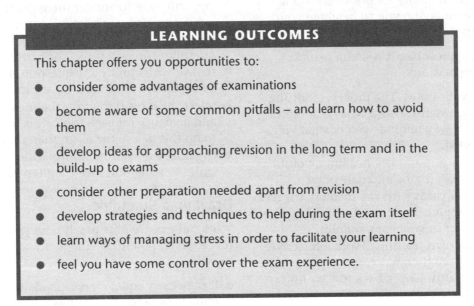

What does revision involve?

The pressure of the exam stimulates you to draw together the strands of your study, and to acknowledge areas that need more work. You can view this pressure negatively, as stress and the likelihood of failure, or positively – as a challenge encouraging you to heighten your own expertise.

As an exam approaches, it is useful to make adequate preparations.

- Organise your notes. The process of sorting out what is essential from what is interesting in a general way reminds you of what you have covered.
- Reduce your notes to key headings, points and references (name and date only).
- Make master cards with key memory triggers for whole topics. These can be in the form of pattern notes or concept pyramids.
- Check your own learning. Work interactively with materials, then write out or tape what you have learnt. Check back to your notes and find the areas you omitted. Write and check three times to build up your memory.

Use past exam papers

Past papers are your best resource. At first, the wording of exam papers can be off-putting: questions may seem vague as they cannot 'give away the answer'. It is important to get used to this style well in advance of the exam.

- Remember that each question links to an area of the course. You need to find that link and consider which issues the question is directing you towards.
- Look for patterns of recurring questions.
- What is the minimum number of topics you can revise to answer the paper?

Select what to revise

The revision process is especially one of selection.

- Select which topics you are going to revise. If you will need to answer three exam questions, revise at least five topics.
- Work out answers to a range of possible exam questions for each topic, so that you feel able to deal with almost any question that might be set on the topics you have chosen.
- Select the most important theories, references and evidence for each topic. It is much easier to do this before the exam than during it.
- Organise the selected information so that it is easier to remember (see Chapter 10).

Draw up a timetable

Work out exactly how much time you have to revise, given potential 'emergencies', and time to relax.

- If they carry equal marks, divide the time equally between each subject, and then each selected topic.
- Set aside time for practising past papers.
- See 'Time management' in Chapter 4.

Build up writing speed

Quality and relevance is more important than quantity. Concise answers can get high marks.

However, if you are used to word-processing most of your work, your handwriting speed may have diminished. Practising timed essays – or writing anything at speed every day – will help build the muscles needed for handwriting at speed.

New reading just before the exam

Opinion varies on whether you should read new material just before exams. It can keep your thinking fresh and bring your work into perspective. If reading new material confuses you, however, just focus on the notes you have already.

Effective revision

Ten common pitfalls in revision ...	... and how to avoid them
1 Leaving revision until the last minute.	Revision is a way of pulling your understanding together in preparation for the exam. You can include and plan for revision from the *beginning* of the course. Here are some examples. ● When planning and reading for a part of the course, write alternative essay titles on separate pages. Jot brief notes, or page references to material, under each title. ● Make your notes readable, attractive and visually compelling as you go through the course – this builds the memory. ● If possible, start to over-learn names, dates and key details from index cards at odd moments early in the term (see page 211). Even if you forget them, they will be easier to learn a second time round. ● Begin intense revision about four weeks before the exam. ● Read the sections on 'Exams' well before the exam.
2 Reading through notes over and over again.	● Use creative and interactive strategies (see Chapters 4 and 10). This keeps your mind alert, and helps to integrate information. ● Instead of just reading, read in order to *find out*. The best way to do this is to look for material related to possible exam answers. Ask in the library for past exam papers for your course, and invent your own questions. ● Discussing past exam questions with friends makes this process more interesting. ● Time yourself writing some essays without looking at your notes. This not only shows you which areas need more work but helps to increase your handwriting speed and your ability to think and write under pressure.
3 Writing notes out over and over again.	● This can be a good strategy if you learn through 'motor memory'. Working to *different* essay plans keeps the information fresh and develops your thinking about the subject. ● Some people find that rewriting notes interferes with visual recall of their original set of notes. For them, it is preferable to develop one good complete set of notes, plus a series of index cards. ● Reduce information to a series of memory triggers. Reduce a set of triggers to one key word or image.
4 Writing out essays and learning them off by heart.	This is time-consuming and counter-productive – it is unlikely that the identical question will come up in your exam. It is better to spend time reflecting on, and practising, a range of answers, so that you over-learn the material (see Chapter 10). You will then be able to work with it flexibly during the exam, selecting exactly what you need for the exact title given.

Ten common pitfalls in revision …	… and how to avoid them
5 Finding ways of putting off revision (such as 'urgent' things that need to be done, watching TV, or chatting with friends or family).	● Make a revision timetable which leaves empty spaces to cater for real emergencies. Do a spell of revision before each 'urgent task'. ● Use watching television or other distractions as a reward – put them in your timetable. ● See 'Tricks for getting started' (page 137). ● You may be missing company. Try revising with other students, or involve others in your revision. Explain a subject to them: can they understand your explanation? Could they test you on your memory triggers, or ask you questions from your notes?
6 'I can't force myself back to study.'	● Go back over Chapter 4. Check your motivation. ● Rather than 'forcing' yourself, *encourage* and *entice* yourself to study through short-term goals, challenges, creativity, and company. ● Check that your timetable has sufficient breaks for rest.
7 'I start to panic. I feel I'm never going to get through it all or remember it.'	● Work with positive-minded people. ● Read about 'Stress' (pages 227–9) and 'Memory' (Chapter 10). ● Work steadily to small goals (page 66). ● Speak to a professional counsellor at the university.
8 'I can't cope with the boredom of it. I start to daydream or wonder why I am bothering.'	● Work in a lot of shorter spells. ● Boredom suggests that you are not using a variety of interactive learning techniques, nor your creativity (Chapters 4 and 10). ● Look for ways of introducing variety into your study sessions. ● Look for unusual angles on the material you have, or images that sum up the material. Think of ways in which seemingly unrelated material could be linked. Invent an essay or a test for yourself.
9 'I have too many responsibilities to make revision practicable.'	● Make use of short spells of time, on buses, tea breaks, and the like. ● Break the work into small pieces. Always carry some work with you. ● Carry an exam question in your head and scribble down ideas in odd moments.
10 Stopping revision before the process of over-learning is complete.	● It is important to keep checking back what you have learnt, and to reduce your material to shorter, key memory triggers. ● Keep asking yourself: 'How can I use what I have learnt to answer other questions that might come up?' ● Over-learning takes time – use spare moments well.

Revision strategies

A good revision mentality requires creativity, interactive study techniques, a high degree of motivation, time management, working well with others, writing skills and being able to use your powers of selectivity, critical thinking and memory.

As you can see, if you have used the strategies suggested in earlier chapters, you have already advanced towards doing well in your exams. Tick the boxes beside specific revision activities listed below if you consider they would help you. Work these into an ***Action plan*** (page 221).

Have a revision mentality for the whole term or year

- ☐ Make your notes clear, visual, colourful, dynamic, and memorable. Leave lots of space to add new information later in the term.
- ☐ Make up index cards of key information as you go along.
- ☐ Go over your work at regular intervals so that you have less to do at the last minute.
- ☐ See 'Revision pitfalls' (1) on page 217.

Use time carefully

- ☐ Start as early in the year as possible.
- ☐ Draw up a revision timetable.
- ☐ Draw up a ***Priority organiser*** (page 72).
- ☐ Make a ***Time circle*** for revision (page 70).
- ☐ Use stray moments for revision.

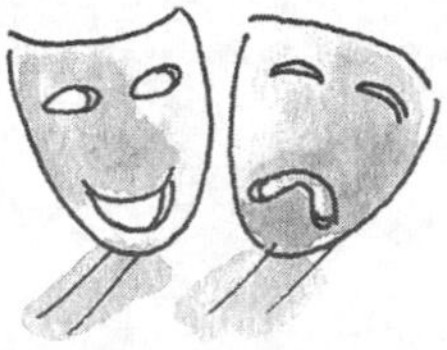

Keep a positive mindset

- ☐ Work on your motivation (Chapter 4) and your attitude towards exams. See difficulties as challenges for which you can devise new strategies.

Work with others

- ☐ Arrange revision sessions with friends.

Ask for help

- ☐ Find out from tutors how exam answers differ from course essays.

Use memory triggers

- ☐ Devise memory triggers (Chapter 10).
- ☐ Distil your notes to key points, key words, and memory triggers.
- ☐ Learn by heart essential information only, such as dates, names and formulae.

Revise by ear

- ☐ Record yourself answering questions – listening to your own voice may help memory.

Stay healthy

- ☐ Sleep, relax and take plenty of breaks.

Use exam papers from former years

- ☐ Check which questions come up regularly.
- ☐ Brainstorm answers to past questions.
- ☐ Make outline plans for as many questions as you can.
- ☐ Time yourself writing *some* of these, to build writing speed and for general practice.
- ☐ Discuss questions with others. Work out plans together.
- ☐ Consider in advance what detail needs to be *left out* of exam answers.

© Stella Cottrell 1999, *The Study Skills Handbook*, Macmillan Press Ltd

SELF EVALUATION

Revision and exam preparation

- ☐ I can find something positive for me in taking these exams
- ☐ I know exactly when the exams are
- ☐ I am aware how many questions are required for each exam
- ☐ I can work out how many topics I need to revise for each exam
- ☐ I am aware of the range of questions that can come up for each topic
- ☐ I have made a realistic revision timetable, with clear priorities
- ☐ I know how to work on exam answers using past papers
- ☐ I have started to practise writing out answers at speed
- ☐ I am aware of the memory strategies I need to revise for the exam
- ☐ I am aware of how to use time most effectively in the exam
- ☐ I am aware of how to avoid common pitfalls in exams
- ☐ I am aware of the differences between exam answers and coursework
- ☐ I know how to manage stress and use it effectively

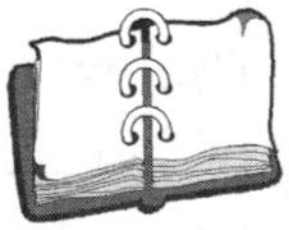

In what ways have your past revision strategies and your approach to exams helped or hindered your exam success? What can you change or improve for your next set of exams?

© Stella Cottrell 1999, *The Study Skills Handbook*, Macmillan Press Ltd

Revision: seven-point action plan

1 Positive state of mind e.g. checking my motivation; listening for negative voices in my head; working on stress; accepting the challenge. *Things I will do to stay positive:*

2 Time e.g. going over my work from early in the year in different ways; organising a timetable, ***Priority organiser*** (page 72) or ***Time circle for revision*** (page 70); dealing with my excuses for not revising; using spare moments. *I will:*

3 Variety e.g. working in many short spells; using varied and interesting ways of going over my material. *I will:*

4 Over-learning e.g. rewriting notes, index cards, new essay plans, memory triggers. *I will:*

5 Practice e.g. doing past questions; working under exam conditions; over-learning basic facts. *I will:*

6 People e.g. sharing revision with other people where possible. *I will:*

7 Selection What topics will I revise? What level of detail can I really use under exam conditions? *I will:*

© Stella Cottrell 1999, *The Study Skills Handbook*, Macmillan Press Ltd

Advance preparation for the exam

Find out basic information

- How many exams will you have?
- When are the exams?
- What are these exams?
- How will you be assessed?
- Are any mock exams provided?
- Where you can get past papers?

Keep a record of this information – see the exam checklist on page 223.

Find out the 'exam instructions'

Familiarise yourself with the instructions written on exam papers: these can be difficult to understand if you read them for the first time under the stress of the exam itself. They usually tell you about where to write your name and exam number, and how many questions you have to answer. (The invigilator may read the instructions aloud at the start of the exam.)

Plan out your exam time in advance

For each paper, work out the time that you will start and finish each question – this is one less thing to do in the exam room. When you get into the exam room, write your timings on a piece of paper and keep sight of them.

Practise

Like most things, exam performance improves with practice. Attend any mock exams provided, even if you feel you are not at all ready – the experience is important. If no mocks are provided, arrange your own with friends or by yourself.

- Pick out an old exam paper or make up your own questions.
- Arrange the seating so that you cannot see each other's papers.
- Write the answers within a set time limit – work alone, in silence.
- Afterwards, discuss your answers with each other.

The week before

- Drink plenty of water in the week before the exam so that you are not dehydrated.
- Build in movement and exercise so that you work off excess adrenalin.
- Work daily on relaxation, so that your thinking remains clear and focused. You will still feel some nervous energy, which is useful for exams.
- Move towards learning master sheets and checking your learning. Find ways of keeping up interest and motivation.
- Organise cover for any domestic or employment responsibilities. Plan for emergencies. If possible, arrange for childcare or other support from the day *before* the exam, so that you are free for final revision.
- Avoid people who may make you feel unsure of yourself – those who are super-confident, and those who panic!
- Visit the exam room and get the feel of it.

The night before

- Check over any exam details you have.
- Prepare what you will need – pens, ruler, water, a snack, the exam room number, your identity card, a jumper, and so on.
- Avoid people who panic.
- Have a snack and a hot, relaxing bath before bed. Leave plenty of time to sleep.

The day of the exam

- Eat well before the exam, to keep up your stamina. Slow-releasing carbohydrates, such as bread and cereals, are best.
- Leave plenty of time for the journey in case of delays.
- Plan to arrive at the exam room as it opens: it may take time to find your seat.

CHECKLIST

Exams

Subject area: **Exam title:**

Date: **Day:** **Time:**

Campus: **Building:** **Room:**

Length of exam:

Number of questions I have to answer (in each section, where applicable):

Preparation: reading through questions; choosing questions; planning answers.

Finishing: checking through – for sense, for errors, that questions are correctly numbered, neatening the script, and so on.

Total preparation and finishing-off time needed:

Time left for writing answers (total time *minus* preparation and finishing-off time):

Total marks available for each question	Length of time to spend on each question	Time to start each new answer
1		
2		
3		
4		
5		

Any unusual features of the paper or exam conditions?

Which aids – dictionaries, calculators, etc. – are permissible for this paper?

What must I take to the exam room? Identity card? Pens? Coloured pencils? Any special equipment? A jumper? Water? Snacks, to be eaten quietly? Glucose tablets?

© Stella Cottrell 1999, *The Study Skills Handbook*, Macmillan Press Ltd

In the exam

First things

- Orientate yourself.
- Find a positive, calm, focused state of mind.
- Check that you have been given the right exam paper. (Mistakes *have* happened!)
- Read the instructions slowly, at least twice.
- Fill out personal details as required.
- Read the whole paper. Always check both sides, even if you think one side is blank.
- Divide your time equally among questions that carry the same marks. Jot down the times you will begin each question.

Selecting exam questions

- Read each question through at least twice.
- Work out what is expected, in general, for each question. Which part of the course does it refer to? Towards which issues is the question directing you?
- If a question sounds like one you have done before, check the wording very carefully before you select it. A slight difference in wording might require a very different answer.
- Tick all questions you could attempt. Tick twice the ones you could answer best. Don't rush this – it's vital that you choose the questions that will do you justice.
- For the questions you select, highlight key words in the title. Notice how many parts there are to the question. Read questions through again very slowly to make sure you have not misread any key words. At this stage you may realise that a question is not what you thought, and may need to select a different one.
- At any time, jot down ideas you have about any of your selected questions on a separate sheet. Note the relevant question number beside each idea.

Writing exam essays

Follow a similar procedure to that used when writing any other essay. Show structure, organisation, evidence and a clear line of reasoning – without these, you will get very few marks for content.

Exam essays can be *easier* to write because:

- you need less evidence and fewer examples than for coursework
- you can write less about each point
- you can miss out some background detail
- you don't need to give a bibliography or supply detailed references
- minor grammatical and spelling errors, and rushed handwriting (provided it's readable), are generally less important.

'What if I go blank?'

- Don't try too hard to remember a point in the back of your mind. Leave a space – it may come back later.
- You may be too tense – use a relaxation exercise you have used before (page 229).
- Use a 'getting started' trick: see page 137.
- Keep writing. On spare paper, jot down any words that have anything to do with the question. These should eventually start to prompt your memory into action.
- Ask yourself questions, starting with the most basic – who? when? what? how? – until you become more focused.

Use pyramid questions to guide you

Learn the pyramid questions (page 155) as a song, a list or a chant. Use them to guide your essay plan in the exam room. This is especially useful if you experience great difficulty in organising and structuring information at speed, or if you go blank in exams.

Doing well in examinations

Common pitfalls in examinations ...	... and how to avoid them
1 Doing silly things Silly things can fail exam candidates or lose marks or the examiner's goodwill.	Make sure you turn up at the right exam centre on the right day. Check that you have been given the right exam paper. Be sure to write your name or exam number on their answer paper and on additional sheets. Answer the right number of questions. Read the questions. Check the back of the exam paper. Well before the exam, find out what is required. In the exam itself, schedule time to check such details carefully.
2 Mystifying the exam The examiner won't pore over your script for hours, nor see through your answer to what you don't know. There is no 'magical ingredient' you have to deliver.	Examiners have a large pile of scripts. They want to get through these as quickly as they can, with just a few minutes for each. They may check your introduction and conclusion for the gist of your argument, skim the answer to evaluate your line of reasoning, check that you are using material from the course to support your answers, and evaluate roughly what grade the work is worth. They are unlikely to mark it as closely as tutors mark for coursework. Often a second marker goes through the same process: if she disagrees, the external examiner's opinion will be asked. Only excessively bad grammar, spelling errors or handwriting is likely to stand out.
3 Using exam time poorly and answering too few questions	Give equal time to questions that carry equal marks – and more time to any that carry extra marks. The law of diminishing returns applies to the amount of time spent on any one question: if you spend twice as long on one question, you are very unlikely to get twice as many marks. You are more likely to pass if you give reasonable answers to the set number of questions than if you spend all your time writing some brilliant essays but miss out one question completely. If you run out of the time you have allocated to one answer, leave a space – there may be time to come back to it at the end.
4 Writing everything you know about a topic There is no value in simply writing down all you know to prove you've learnt it.	The examiner is not interested in how much you know – indeed, you may get no marks at all for simply listing a lot of information. Just as for coursework, marks are given for showing you can make sense of the question, relate it to course issues, develop a line of reasoning, evaluate opposing viewpoints, and offer supporting evidence.
5 Abandoning structure and the usual essay-writing techniques	Because of the speed at which exam markers work, they appreciate answers with clear, well-organised structures, good introductions and conclusions, correctly numbered questions, and clearly labelled scripts which are easy to read. You lose goodwill if your script is messy, illegible or confusing to read.

SELF-EVALUATION

Exam strategy

Do I ...	Yes	No	Things to do, or to watch out for
read the whole exam paper carefully?	☐	☐	
follow all instructions?	☐	☐	
answer the correct number of questions in full?	☐	☐	
plan time, so that I can check my answer?	☐	☐	
know exactly how long I have for each question?	☐	☐	
share out time according to the marks available?	☐	☐	
use all of the available time?	☐	☐	
read each question at least twice?	☐	☐	
spend time working out what all the questions mean?	☐	☐	
ask myself what the examiner is looking for?	☐	☐	
spend enough time considering the best questions for me?	☐	☐	
feel confident about what I am expected to do?	☐	☐	
find questions that are similar to ones I have practised?	☐	☐	
find I have revised enough topics?	☐	☐	
know what a 'good' answer looks like?	☐	☐	
know which style is appropriate?	☐	☐	
know the correct format or layout?	☐	☐	
plan my answers (on paper or in my head)?	☐	☐	
develop a clear argument (where appropriate)?	☐	☐	
use examples from the course materials?	☐	☐	
keep strictly to answering the question set?	☐	☐	
avoid irrelevant detail and going off at tangents?	☐	☐	
get to the point quickly?	☐	☐	
avoid flowery language and vague introductions?	☐	☐	
include an introduction and a conclusion?	☐	☐	
keep focused on the exam during the exam?	☐	☐	
check my answers for mistakes?	☐	☐	
check my answers to see if they make sense?	☐	☐	

If you answered 'yes' to most of these questions, then your chance of exam success is high.

If not, look again through the relevant sections of this *Handbook* and work out what you need to practise. If you are still uncertain about any aspects, consult with your tutor.

© Stella Cottrell 1999, *The Study Skills Handbook*, Macmillan Press Ltd

Dealing with stress

A *mild* degree of stress can be helpful, providing a challenge with stimulation, excitement, and focus. Some people deliberately search out stress to make life more exciting.

Studying towards deadlines and exams involves different amounts of stress for each student. Added life pressures, such as shortage of money, difficult relationships, bereavement, or changes in your work, family or housing situation, can all add to your stress level. Excess stress can severely affect physical and emotional health, concentration and memory.

If you suffer from excess stress, you need to take steps to reduce it. The signs can be extremely varied.

Spot the signs

Do you …

- ☐ lie awake worrying?
- ☐ feel guilty when you aren't working?
- ☐ get frustrated easily?
- ☐ get a dry mouth, heavy pounding or a 'butterfly' feeling in the heart, sweaty hands, nausea, or twitching muscles?
- ☐ grit or grind your teeth?
- ☐ flare up easily at other people?
- ☐ regularly eat in a hurry, or go on binges?
- ☐ smoke or drink 'to unwind'?
- ☐ drop or break things frequently?
- ☐ notice signs of increased irritability, tearfulness or moodiness?

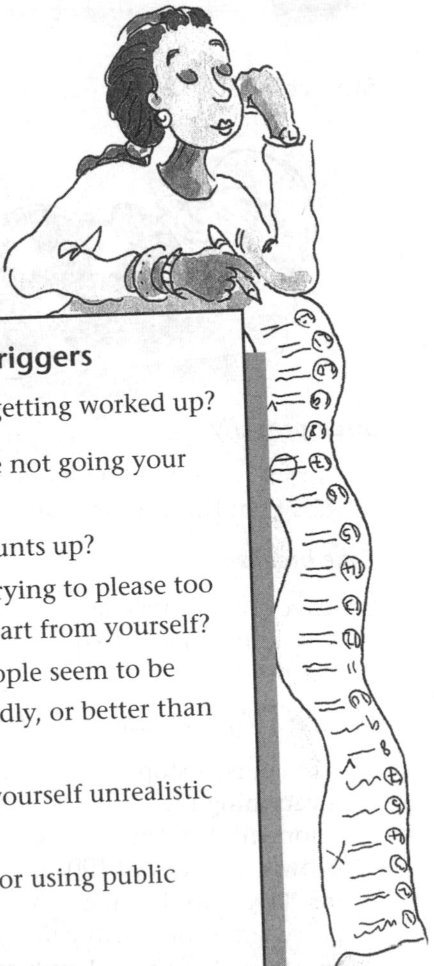

Know your own triggers

When do you start getting worked up?

- ☐ When things are not going your way?
- ☐ When work mounts up?
- ☐ When you are trying to please too many people apart from yourself?
- ☐ When other people seem to be doing things badly, or better than you?
- ☐ When you set yourself unrealistic goals?
- ☐ In traffic jams, or using public transport?
- ☐ Other triggers?

In your journal, list the times when you get most stressed – or what makes you feel tense. Describe what happens. What do you do to handle the situation? What else *could* you do?

Look at the suggestions on the following page. Tick things you could try out. Which *one* will you try first, or next?

Managing stress

Stay relaxed

Sleep properly

- ☐ Aim to sleep for 8 hours each day. More or less than this can tire you.

Take breaks

- ☐ Give yourself regular breaks in whatever you are doing.

Use the STOP! exercise

- ☐ Let yourself stop everything for a moment. Breathe slowly or count to 100.
  - Let yourself smile – even if this is difficult.
  - Spread out your hands and relax your fingers. Let your hands and feet be still.
  - Repeat 'Stop' to yourself until you feel calm.

Monitor your state of mind

One aspect of stress is the attitude we take towards challenges. The situation and feelings that panic one person may excite and interest another.

Listen to the voice in your head

- ☐ If you tend to think, 'I can't …', 'Other people can …' or 'I'm useless at …', you need to change the record!
  - Turn the message round: 'I can …', 'I have already …', 'I am able to …', 'I am going to …'

Question your way of thinking

Ask yourself questions such as:

- ☐ Is there another way of thinking about this?
- ☐ Am I being a perfectionist?
- ☐ Am I expecting too much of myself (or others) in the current circumstances?
- ☐ Am I getting things out of proportion?
- ☐ What is the effect on me of having this attitude?
- ☐ Am I blaming myself for things that can't be helped?
- ☐ What can I do to improve matters?

Manage your time

Be organised

- ☐ Organise yourself to avoid stress. Make timetables and action plans to avoid predictable crises and panics. Take control of your time.

Set priorities

- ☐ Work out your priorities and when you will do each of the tasks. Work out which things can wait – and let them (see page 72).

Take care of your body

Get exercise

- ☐ Do something energetic – walk, swim, run, play a game, clean the room, do some gardening. Get rid of pent-up energy and excess adrenalin (see pages 205–6).

© Stella Cottrell 1999, *The Study Skills Handbook*, Macmillan Press Ltd

Have a healthy diet

☐ Check what you are putting into your body. Could you fill it with less coffee, less smoke, less alcohol and fewer chemicals? Does your body need bigger helpings of substances that help it renew itself – such as food and water?

Relax

Treat yourself

☐ Take a relaxing bath. Don't rush it. Light a candle, or treat yourself to aromatherapy oils.

☐ Put some time aside every day just to enjoy yourself or to do nothing. Try to get at least 20 minutes on your own in quiet.

Celebrate success

☐ Reflect on your achievements over the day or week – and reward yourself.

Daydream

☐ Imagine that the floor is a cloud or a big ball of cotton wool, and that you are sinking down into it and floating away.

☐ Imagine that you are on a magic carpet. Look down at the landscape moving beneath you. Where would you like to visit?

☐ Imagine that you are on a mountain top, enjoying the view.

Use a relaxation exercise

☐ Take time to relax, consciously.

1. Lie on the floor or sit in a comfortable chair.
2. Close your eyes and breathe out slowly several times. Don't force the breathing.
3. If your mind is racing, do the 'Stop!' exercise (page 228).
4. Notice where your body feels tense.

Then do each of the following several times.

5. Clench your toes tightly, count to three, then 'let go'. Repeat this several times.
6. Repeat this with all the muscles you can, working from your toes up to your neck.
7. Pull your shoulders right up to your ears – and let them drop. Repeat several times.
8. Screw up all the face muscles. Then relax. Open your mouth into a big yawn.
9. Imagine yourself in a peaceful, beautiful, safe place. Listen for sounds and look at the colours there. It can be any place, real or imaginary. This can be a safe 'retreat' in the mind for you to go when stressed.

Breathe calmly

☐ After relaxation, sit or lie comfortably. Close your eyes. Put on relaxing music if you wish.

1. Imagine that you are breathing in calm and tranquillity with each in-breath, and letting go of stress with each out-breath.
2. Think of one word you find soothing, and repeat this in your mind.
3. Do this for about ten minutes – or longer if you like.

☐ If you find that difficult, just stay still and be quiet. Listen to the sounds around you.

☐ Meditation classes may also be helpful.

Further reading

- Wilkinson, G. 1997. *Understanding Stress.* London: British Medical Association ('Family Doctor' series).
- Wilson, P. 1997. *Calm at Work*. London: Penguin.

Review

Examinations are a culmination of your term's or your year's learning – not just of the course content but also of strategies you have developed over the year. Many of the strategies that help you to do well at exams are similar to those needed for any assignment: organisation, selection, developing your point of view and line of reasoning, and structured writing skills.

This means that revision and exam preparation are not separate events, completely divorced from the other learning activities you undertake in the year. If you have worked steadily all year, the exam period will be more manageable.

Don't build the exam out of proportion. If you don't pass, you are usually offered a second chance. If you *still* don't pass it, it's not the end of the world – there's life beyond exams and success without a degree. Your health, family and friends are not worth sacrificing for the sake of a degree.

Regard heightened nervous energy and some stress as a useful friend. However, take care to relax and keep stress to a manageable level. Remember that the examiners – often your tutors – generally *want* you to do well. They will be looking for ways to give you marks and help you pass.

Exams can be an exciting time. By the time the exam is over you will probably feel that you really know your subject! Immediately after the exam you may feel a little deflated – be prepared for that. Arrange something enjoyable and relaxing as a reward.

Celebrate your achievements.

Endnotes: what next?

Although this is the end of the book, it is not the end of your development as a student. Below are some ideas about what you might do next.

Using the *Handbook* after a first reading

As you develop as a student, you may find that you discover things in the pages of this *Handbook* which were not evident to you the first time round. Browse through it from time to time – you may be surprised at what catches your eye. You may like to go into some of the ideas in the book in more depth.

Monitoring your progress

As the *Handbook* has emphasised, one difference about being an adult student is that you are ultimately responsible for monitoring your own progress. If you keep a study journal, read back over it and note changes in your ideas. Return to the self-evaluation questionnaires and try them again. Compare your current answers with your earlier ones. What changes do you note? What do you still need to work on to improve your performance?

Additional reading

See the follow-up reading suggestions below. Select only what you feel you *need* to read.

Also, browse through bookshop sections on personal development, education, psychology and study skills.

Seeking help at the university

If you are not making progress, work on the problem area as far as you can before you seek help. But if you *need* help, don't be afraid to ask for it. Make an appointment to see a study adviser, student counsellor, or your personal tutor or year tutor.

When you go to the appointment, take with you evidence of the difficulties as well as your attempts to solve them. Tutors can help you best if they can see how far you have managed on your own, and how you have approached the problem. If you turn up empty-handed, there may be very little they can do.

Preparing for a career

Update your skills profile or portfolio (Chapter 2) every few months, so that it is up to date when you start to seek employment. Take it with you when you see the careers staff at your university.

Meet the careers staff early in your studies. Many students leave it until the last year and then find that their options have been limited. You may find that your current choice of subjects is not the best for what you want to do. You may even be inspired to take up a career other than the one you had planned!

Thinking about the skills you will need for employment will encourage you in developing your study skills, as study skills link closely with professional skills.

Good luck!

Enjoy your learning and experience success with your studies.

Suggested further reading

General

Baddeley, A. (1993). *Your Memory: a user's guide.* London: Prion.

Bourner, T. and Race, P. (1990). *How to Win as a Part-Time Student.* London: Kogan Page.

Buzan, T. (1993). *The Mind Map Book.* London: BBC. (Or any other book by Buzan.)

Creme, P. and Lea, M. R. (1997). *Writing at University: a guide for students.* Milton Keynes: The Open University.

Flanagan, K. (1997). *Maximum Points, Minimum Panic: the essential guide to surviving exams*, 2nd edn. Dublin: Marino.

Northedge, A. (1990). *The Good Study Guide.* Milton Keynes: Open University Press.

Rose, C. and Goll, L. (1992). *Accelerate Your Learning: the action handbook.* Aylesbury: Accelerated Learning Systems Ltd.

Thompson, A. (1996). *Critical Reasoning: a practical introduction.* London: Routledge.

Williams, K. (1989). *Study Skills.* Basingstoke: Macmillan.

Mature students

Buzan, T. and Keene, R. (1996). *The Age Heresy: you can achieve more, not less, as you get older.* London: Ebury Press.

Rickards, T. (1992). *How to Win as a Mature Student.* London: Kogan Page.

Dyslexic students

Miles, T. R. and Gilroy, D. E. (1995). *Dyslexia at College*, 2nd edn. London: Routledge.

Developing English

Jordan, R. B. (1990). *Academic Writing Course.* London: Collins. (Especially useful if you are still developing English as an additional language.)

Murphy, R. (1991). *English Grammar in Use.* Cambridge: Cambridge University Press. (A self-study reference and practice book, with answers.)

Strunk, W. and White, E. B. (1979). *The Elements of Style*, 3rd edn. Basingstoke: Macmillan. (Brief basic guidance for more accurate and elegant writing.)

Personal development/relaxation

O'Connor, J. and McDermott, I. (1996). *Principles of NLP.* London: Thorsons.

Van Oech, R. (1990). *A Whack on the Side of the Head: how to be more creative.* London: Thorsons.

Wilkinson, G. (1997). *Understanding Stress.* London: British Medical Association ('Family Doctor' Series).

Wilson, P. (1997). *Calm at Work.* London: Penguin.

Technology

Honeycutt, J. (1996). *Using the Internet*, 2nd edn. Indianapolis: Que Corporation.

Inspiration V5. Inspiration Software Inc. (A visual tool for organising written information. Details at: http://www.inspiration.com)

Kinkoph, S. and Grimes, G. A. (1997). *10 Minute Guide to Netscape Communicator 4.* Indianapolis: Que Corporation.

Lojkine, M. (1998). *Internet Explorer 4 in Easy steps.* Southam: Computer Step.

References

Bower, G. H., Clark, M., Lesgold, A. and Winzenz, D. (1969). 'Hierarchical retrieval schemes in recall of categorised word lists', *Journal of Verbal Learning and Verbal Behaviour* **8**, 323–43.

Bowlby, J. (1951). *Maternal Care and Mental Health.* Report to the World Health Organisation. New York: Shocken Books.

Bowlby, J. (1969). *Attachment and Loss: Attachment.* New York: Basic Books.

Butterfield, G. (1992). 'Context and cognition in models of cognitive growth'. In Light, P. and Butterworth, G. (eds). *Context and Cognition.* London: Harvester.

Buzan, T. (1993). *The Mind Map Book.* London: BBC.

Buzan, T. and Keene, R. (1996). *The Age Heresy: you can achieve more, not less, as you get older.* London: Ebury Press.

Clarke, A. M. and Clarke, A. D. B. (1976). *Early Experience: myth and evidence.* London: Open Books.

Clarke-Stewart, A. (1988). 'The "effects" of infant day care reconsidered: risks for parents, children and researchers', *Early Childhood Research Quarterly* **3**, 292–318.

Colon, J. (1982). *A Puerto Rican in New York and Other Sketches*, 2nd edn. New York: International Publishers.

Donaldson, M. (1978). *Children's Minds.* Glasgow: Fontana.

Flanagan, K. (1997). *Maximum Points, Minimum Panic: the essential guide to surviving exams*, 2nd edn. Dublin: Marino.

Freeman, R. and Mead, J. (1991). *How to Study Effectively.* Cambridge: National Extension College.

Gardner, H. (1993). *Frames of Mind: the theory of multiple intelligences*, 2nd edn. London: Fontana.

Glaser, E. (1941). *An Experiment in the Development of Critical Thinking.* New York: Teachers' College, Columbia University.

Harris, J.E. and Sunderland, A. (1981). 'Effects of age and instructions on an everyday memory questionnaire'. Paper presented at the British Psychological Society Cognitive Psychology Section Conference on Memory, Plymouth, 1981.

Karmiloff-Smith, A. (1992). *Beyond Modularity: a developmental perpective on cognitive science.* Cambridge, Mass.: MIT Press.

Keane, M., Kahney, H. and Brayshaw, M. (1989). 'Simulating analogical mapping difficulties in recursion problems'. In Cohn, A. G. (ed.) (1989). *Proceedings of the Seventh Conference of the Society for the Study of Artificial Intelligence and Simulation of Behaviour.* Morgan Lauffman. (Cited in Kahney, H. (1993). *Problem Solving: current issues*, 2nd edn. Buckingham: The Open University.)

Mackintosh, N. J. and Mascie-Taylor, C. G. N. (1985). 'The IQ question'. In *Report of the Committee of Inquiry into Education of Children from Ethnic Minority Groups.* London: HMSO, pp. 126–63.

O'Connor, J. and McDermott, I. (1996). *Principles of NLP.* London: Thorsons.

Reed, S. K., Dempster, A. and Ettinger, M. (1985). 'Usefulness of analogous solutions for solving algebra word problems', *Journal of Experimental Psychology; Learning, Memory and Cognition* **11**(1), pp. 106–25.

Resnick, L., Levine, J. and Teasley, S. D. (eds) (1991). *Perspectives on Socially Shared Cognition.* Washington, D.C.: American Psychological Association.

Rose, C. (1985). *Accelerated Learning.* Aylesbury: Accelerated Learning Systems Ltd.

Simon, H. (1974). 'How big is a chunk?' *Science* **183**, 482–8.

Spearman, C. (1927). *The Abilities of Man.* London: Macmillan.

Sternberg, R. J. (1984). 'Facets of intelligence'. In Anderson, J. R. and Kosslyn, S. M. (eds). *Tutorials in Learning and Memory: essays in honor of Gordon Bower.* San Francisco: W. H. Freeman.

Sternberg, R. J. (1985). *Beyond IQ: a Triarchic Theory of Human Intelligence.* Cambridge: Cambridge University Press.

Terman, L. M. (1975, first published 1916). *The Measurement of Intelligence.* New York: L. L. Arno Press.

Thompson, A. (1996). *Critical Reasoning: a practical introduction.* London: Routledge.

Thurstone, L. L. (1960). *The Nature of Intelligence.* Littlefield: Adams.
Tizard, B. (1991). 'Working mothers and the care of young children'. In Woodhead, M., Light, P. and Carr, R. (eds). *Growing Up in a Changing Society.* London: Routledge.
TMP Worldwide Research (1998). *Soft Skills: employers' desirability and actual incidences*. London: TMP Worldwide Research.
Vygotsky, L. (1978). *Mind in Society.* Cambridge, Mass.: Harvard University Press.
Wilkinson, G. (1997). *Understanding Stress.* London: British Medical Association ('Family Doctor' Series).
Wilson, P. (1997). *Calm at Work.* London: Penguin.

Index